access to history

context

An Introduction to

TUDOR ENGLAND

1485–1603

Angela Anderson and Tony Imperato

Hodder & Stoughton

A MEMBER OF THE HODDER HEADLINE GROUP

ACKNOWLEDGEMENTS

The front cover illustration shows A Fête at Bermondsey by Hoefnagel, Hatfield House, Hertfordshire/Bridgeman Art Library.

The publishers would like to thank the following individuals, institutions and companies for permission to reproduce copyright illustrations in this book: AKG Photo page 78; AKG/Erich Lessing page 218; © Bettmann/Corbis page 182; © Corbis page 156; The Duke of Rutland, Belvoir Castle page 52; © The Fotomas Index (U.K.) pages 11, 15, 21, 27, 73, 107, 109, 125, 145, 159, 173, 214, 215, 223; The Frick Collection, New York page 123; © Hulton-Deutsch pages 47, 174; © Hulton Archive page 216; Musée Calvet, Avignon, photographer: Andre Guerrand page 38; © National Maritime Museum, Greenwich page 160; Francis Drake's 'Revenge' off Gravelines Armada c.1588 © National Maritime Museum, London page 222; © National Portrait Gallery, London pages 83, 87, 105 left, 105 right, 111, 141, 149, 176, 179, 193, 197; Queen Elizabeth I dancing with Robert Dudley, Earl of Leicester, Penshurst Place page 180; © Clay Perry/Corbis page 13; The Royal Collection © 2001 HM Queen Elizabeth II page 116; © Staatl. Museen Kassel page 175.

The publishers would also like to thank the following for permission to reproduce material in this book: Blackwell Publishers for the extracts from *The English* by Geoffrey Elton, Blackwell, 1992 and *They Saw It Happen 1485–1688* by C.R.N. Routh, Blackwell, 1956; Cambridge University Press for the extracts from *Elizabeth I* by Geoffrey Regan, Cambridge University Press, 1988 and *Authority and Disorder in Tudor Times* by Paul Thomas, Cambridge University Press, 1999; Routledge for the extracts from *England Under the Tudors* by Geoffrey Elton, Methuen, 1985 and *Henry VII* by Alexander Grant, Methuen, 1985; Thames & Hudson for the extract from *The English Reformation* by A.G. Dickens, Thames & Hudson, 1964.

Every effort has been made to trace and acknowledge ownership of copyright. The publishers will be glad to make suitable arrangements with any copyright holders whom it has not been possible to contact.

Orders: please contact Bookpoint Ltd, 78 Milton Park, Abingdon, Oxon OX14 4SB. Telephone: (44) 01235 827720. Fax: (44) 01235 400454. Lines are open 9.00–6.00, Monday to Saturday, with a 24 hour message answering service. Email address: orders@bookpoint.co.uk

2001000 076

British Library Cataloguing in Publication Data
A catalogue record for this title is available from The British Library

ISBN 0 340 68388 0

First published 2001
Impression number   10 9 8 7 6 5 4 3 2 1
Year   2007 2006 2005 2004 2003 2002 2001

Copyright © 2001 Angela Anderson and Tony Imperato

Cover photo from Hatfield House, Hertfordshire/Bridgeman Art Library.
Typeset, illustrated and edited by Hardlines Ltd, Charlbury, Oxford
Printed in Great Britain for Hodder & Stoughton Educational, a division of Hodder Headline Plc, 338 Euston Road, London NW1 3BH by Martins The Printers, Berwick upon Tweed

CONTENTS

List of Figures

List of Profiles

List of Tables

PREFACE

Access to History Context

Structure

In some ways *Access to History Context* volumes are similar to most text-books. They are divided into chapters, each of which is focused on a specific topic. In turn, chapters are divided into sections which have self-explanatory headings. As is the case with most textbooks, *Context* authors have organised the chapters in a logical sequence so that, if you start at the beginning of the book and work your way through to the end, everything will make sense. However, because many readers 'dip' into textbooks rather than reading them from beginning to end, care has been taken to make sure that whichever chapter you start with you should not find yourself feeling lost.

Special Features in the Main Text

Points to consider – at the start of each chapter this shaded box provides you with vital information about how the chapter is organised and how the various issues covered relate to each other.

Issues boxes are a standard feature of each chapter and, like points to consider boxes, are designed to help you extract the maximum benefit from the work you do. They appear in the margin immediately following most numbered section headings. The question(s) contained in each issues box will tell you which historical issue(s) the section is primarily going to cover. If the section you intend to start with has no issues box, turn back page by page until you find one. This will contain the questions the author is considering from that point onwards, including the section you are about to read.

Boxed sections appear in both the margin and the main column of text. In each of the boxes you will find a self-explanatory heading which will make it clear what the contents of the box are about. Very often, the contents of boxes are explanations of words or phrases, or descriptions of events or situations. When you are reading a chapter for the first time you might make a conscious decision to pay little attention to boxed entries so that you can concentrate your attention on the author's main message.

Q-boxes appear in the margin and contain one or more questions about the item they appear alongside. These questions are intended to stimulate you to think about some aspect of the material the box is linked to. The most useful answers to these questions will often emerge during discussions with other students.

Activities boxes – as a general rule, the contents of activities boxes are more complex than the questions in Q-boxes, and often require you to undertake a significant amount of work, either on your own or with others. One reason for completing the task(s) is to consolidate what you have already learnt or to extend the range or depth of your understanding.

Profiles – most of these are about named individuals who are central to an understanding of the topic under consideration; some are about events of particular importance. Each profile contains a similar range of material. The two aspects you are likely to find most useful are:

▼ the dated timeline down the side of the page; and
▼ the source extracts, which provide you with ideas on what made the subject of the Profile especially notable or highly controversial.

Profiles also provide useful points of focus during the revision process.

End-of-chapter Sections

The final pages of each chapter contain different sections. It is always worthwhile looking at the **Summary Chart** or **Summary Diagram** first. As their names suggest, these are designed to provide you with a brief and carefully structured overview of the topic covered by the chapter. The important thing for you to do is to check that you understand the way it is structured and how the topics covered inter-relate with one another.

The **Working on …** section should be studied in detail once you have finished your first reading of the main text of the chapter. Assuming that you read the Points to Consider section when you began work on the chapter, and that you followed any advice given in it when you read the chapter for the first time, the Working on … section is designed to suggest what form any further work you do on the chapter should take.

The **Answering extended writing and essay questions on …** sections, taken as a whole throughout the book, form a coherent body of guidance on how to tackle these types of examination questions successfully.

The same is true of the **Answering source-based questions on …** sections which have been carefully planned bearing in mind the ways you need to build on the skills you have already developed in this area. You may find these sections particularly helpful during the time you are preparing for an exam.

The last part of each chapter contains a **Further Reading** section. These are of vital importance to you in chapters covering topics you are expected to know about in some detail. To do well in any History course it is essential to read more than one book. However, it is possible to find individual books which can act as your guide and companion throughout your studies, and this is one of them. One of the major ways in which it fulfils this function is by providing you with detailed guidance on the way you can make the most effective use of your limited time in reading more widely.

This book is an integral part of the *Access to History* series. One of its functions is to act as a link between the various topic books in the series on the period it covers, by drawing explicit attention in the Further Reading sections to where, within the series, other material exists which can be used to broaden and deepen your knowledge and understanding. Attention is also drawn to the non-*Access to History* publications which you are likely to find most useful. By using material which has been written based on the same aims and objectives, you are likely to find yourself consistently building up the key skills and abilities needed for success on your course.

Revision

Context books have been planned to be directly helpful to you during the revision period. One of the first things many students do when starting to revise a topic for an examination is to make a list of the 'facts' they need to know about. A safer way of doing this (because it covers the possibility that you missed something important when you originally worked on the topic) is to compile your lists from a book you can rely on. *Context* volumes aim to be reliable in this sense. If you work through the chapter which covers the topic you are about to revise and list the events contained in marginal 'events lists' and in boxed lists of events, you can be confident that you have identified every fact of real significance that you need to know about on the topic. However, you also need to make a list of the historical issues you might be asked to write about. You can do this most conveniently by working through the relevant chapter and noting down the contents of the 'Issues boxes'.

For almost everybody, important parts of the revision process are the planning of answers to all the main types of structured and essay questions, and the answering of typical questions (both those requiring extended writing and those based on source material) under exam conditions. The best way to make full use of what this book has to offer in these respects is to work through the two relevant sets of end-of-chapter sections ('Answering extended writing and essay questions on …' and 'Answering source-based questions on …') in a methodical manner.

Keith Randell

SOCIETY AND THE ECONOMY

1 A Changing Population

a) Population Growth

When historians make claims about population change in Tudor times, they do so with caution. No national population surveys were conducted by the government and even when Thomas Cromwell ordered in 1538 that each parish should keep records of births, marriages and deaths, the accuracy of data collected by church officials varied from place to place. Reconstructing with any certainty changes in the size, composition and distribution of the population in the sixteenth century is a massive undertaking. Patterns have been built up by looking at a variety of local sources, including wills (which give clues about the size of families from the number of people to whom possessions were bequeathed), tax records, and family bibles (which often had a record of ownership over the generations carefully inscribed inside the cover). Obviously, local evidence is very fragmentary and tends to centre on richer families. Yet from these sorts of sources, a generally agreed picture has emerged.

ISSUE:
How did the population level change between 1450 and 1600?

Population gradually expanded for much of the medieval period. By 1300, there may have been up to 6 million people living in England and Wales. During the fourteenth century, however, the number of deaths began to exceed births and so the population level began to decline. Disease was a major cause. A series of outbreaks of plague, of which the most famous was the 'Black Death' of 1348–51, reduced the population by between a third and a half. Other diseases, such as the 'sweating sickness', and bad harvests kept the population vulnerable throughout the fifteenth century. However, the population did begin to increase again from the end of the fifteenth century and continued to grow throughout the sixteenth.

Figure 1 Population change 1100–1750 and developments in the sixteenth century.

1a. English population 1100–1750

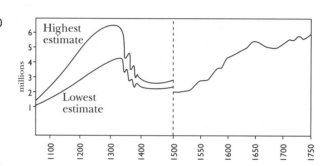

1b. Population change 1541–1601

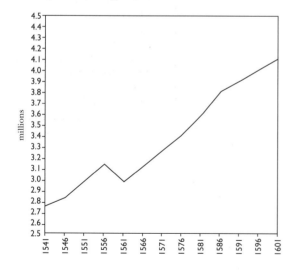

1c. Population figures 1541–1601

Year	Millions
1541	2.774
1546	2.854
1551	3.011
1556	3.159
1561	2.985
1566	3.128
1571	3.271
1576	3.413
1581	3.598
1586	3.806
1591	3.899
1596	4.012
1601	4.11

ACTIVITY

As the information in Figure I reveals, by 1601 the population stood at approximately 4.1 million, twice the level at the start of the Tudor period. Although there had obviously been significant growth, it was not steady across the whole period. Study the graphs and statistics and use them to construct your own description of population change in Tudor England by identifying periods of dramatic growth and times of slower change, or even decline. Summarise your findings by writing a short paragraph which sets out this complex pattern of development.

Underneath this description, you could then create a table of factors to show what made growth possible, and what continued to threaten it. The information you will need to complete the table begins on this page, although you will find ideas throughout the chapter.

Explaining why, in a little over a century, there was such a dramatic increase in the population after a long period of stagnation is no easy task. Contemporaries such as William Lambarde thought that a variety of reasons were at work:

> That the number of our people has multiplied is both demonstrable to the eye and evident in reason. On the one side, nowadays not only young folks of all sorts but churchmen do marry and multiply at liberty (which did not used to be). On the other side, we have not, God be thanked, been touched with any extreme mortality, either by sword or sickness, that might abate the overgrown number of us.
>
> *Source A* From *William Lambarde and Local Government*, published in 1594.

Q What reasons does Lambarde give for population increase? What is the background to his comment about churchmen? Why do his comments about mortality seem strange given that he is writing in the 1590s?

In addition to the causes identified by contemporaries, historians have also pointed to the greater number of years where there were good harvests and to the encouragement that a greater sense of security and prosperity gave to people to marry younger. The combined effect of these factors reduced the risk of an early death because people were better nourished and so were able to withstand illnesses more effectively.

People were still vulnerable to sudden and unpredictable changes, however. Plague did not disappear; it simply became less frequent and less intensive. The most destructive illness of the Tudor period seems to have been influenza. Between 1557 and 1559, an epidemic spread across much of England, reducing the population by about 6 per cent. Towns were especially affected by disease. Crowded and insanitary living conditions allowed the rapid spread of viruses which Tudor medicine could not cure. In London, as much as a quarter of

Q Why did the population level change between 1450 and 1600?

the population died in one such plague in 1563. Bad harvests remained common, and their effect was worsened by the growing number of mouths to feed. During the 1550s, six of the annual harvests are judged by historians to have been bad – and the harvest of 1556 to be the worst of the century. A similar pattern occurred in the 1590s when England was at war with Spain. Once again a series of failed harvests between 1594 and 1598 left the population vulnerable to disease.

b) Population Distribution

ISSUE:
Where did people live?

Throughout the Tudor period, England was an overwhelmingly rural country. Over 90 per cent of the population lived in communities of fewer than 3,000 people. The most densely populated areas lay in the south, in a belt from Devon and Cornwall across to Kent and London. The least populated areas were in the north and west, especially in the marginal lands on the borders with Wales and Scotland. Within this generalisation, however, we must be careful to note that there were exceptions. Northern towns, such as Newcastle, York and Hull, were important population centres and towns such as Manchester and Leeds grew rapidly in the sixteenth century, whilst in the south, by far the majority of people still lived in small villages.

Recent research into the development of urban life has shown two contrasting stories. On the one hand, more people moved into towns and cities during the sixteenth and seventeenth centuries. Whereas in 1500 the urban population has been calculated at 6 per cent of the total, it had risen to 15 per cent by 1700. The biggest increase was in London, which dwarfed all other towns.

On the other hand, historians have spoken of an 'urban crisis' affecting some towns in this period. In Lincoln, Salisbury, and other centres, the population declined. The reasons differ from place to place, but some generalisations are possible. Lincoln was a market town and an important religious centre because of its cathedral. Plague struck particularly hard because of the numbers of visitors passing through the town for business or religious reasons. By the mid-sixteenth century, it had lost two-thirds of its population to disease. The town was also involved in the cloth trade, but was remote from the specialised centres of fine wool production that had developed in Wiltshire, Gloucestershire and elsewhere in the south and west of England. The net result of these factors was a substantial decline, which made the town even less attractive to newcomers. Houses were tumble-down, whole streets deserted, others badly kept.

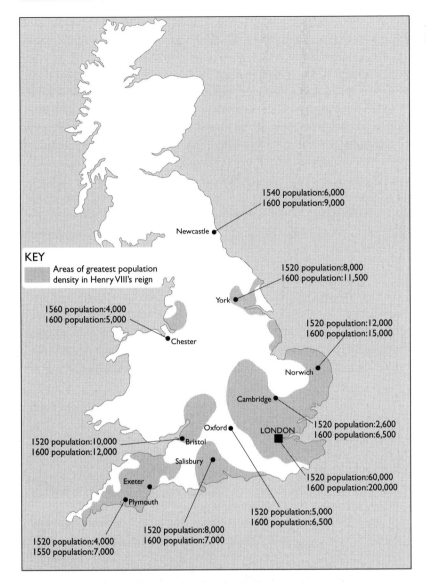

Figure 2 Population distribution in the sixteenth century.

Within the map:

1540 population:6,000
1600 population:9,000
Newcastle

KEY
Areas of greatest population density in Henry VIII's reign

1520 population:8,000
1600 population:11,500
York

1560 population:4,000
1600 population:5,000
Chester

1520 population:12,000
1600 population:15,000
Norwich

Cambridge

Oxford
LONDON
1520 population:2,600
1600 population:6,500

1520 population:10,000
1600 population:12,000
Bristol

Salisbury

1520 population:60,000
1600 population:200,000

Exeter

Plymouth

1520 population:5,000
1600 population:6,500

1520 population:4,000
1550 population:7,000

1520 population:8,000
1600 population:7,000

ACTIVITY

Choose one of the towns, other than London, which is closest to where you live. Try to research what features of its location and industry might have encouraged its growth in this period.

c) Social Structure and Distribution

During the sixteenth century population growth meant that English society became younger. By Elizabeth I's reign, about 40 per cent of people were under 16 years old. People also lived slightly longer –

ISSUES:
What were the different social ranks in Tudor England? What changes were taking place in the relative status of these ranks?

AVERAGE AGE

Figures based on average population age are frequently given in textbooks, but you must treat them cautiously. An average life expectancy of 38 does not mean that there were almost no elderly people; it means that the high probability of death from childhood diseases during the first couple of years of life reduces the overall average. In fact, if someone survived beyond childhood it was quite possible that they would live to a good old age of at least 50 or 60 because they had built up some immunity to the dirt and disease around them.

PRIMOGENITURE

Literally means 'first-born', and in the context of land holding meant that estates should be passed down to the eldest son or nearest male relative rather than be divided among all male heirs. This was good for eldest sons, but had significant effects on social development.

the **average age** had been 36 but rose to 38 by 1600. The increased number of children affected rich and poor alike. Poorer families had extra mouths to feed, putting pressure on their income and pushing some into poverty. Landowning families faced a different problem. Rules of inheritance were governed by the principle of **primogeniture**. More children meant more younger sons without an inheritance. These men were often forced to move and to find property through the growing **land market**. So, people were more mobile in the sixteenth century than ever before.

In theory, Tudor England was a structured society. Although people did not speak in terms of 'social classes', they recognised an elaborate hierarchy of ranks which could be distinguished by title,

The Land Market

Before the sixteenth century little land came up for sale on the open market. Most land was simply passed from one generation to the next, given away as part of marriage agreements or granted by the crown. People without land, such as those whose fortunes came from trade rather than inherited wealth, had few opportunities to move into land ownership. However, the land market opened up after the 1530s. Various factors can explain this development:

▼ the dissolution of monasteries and lesser church houses put some of the associated land onto the open market (although the crown took the lion's share)

▼ the crown began to sell (or 'alienate') its own lands to raise additional money for the royal treasury

▼ legal changes in 1540 allowed family estates to be divided between male heirs rather than just passed to the eldest son. With more people inheriting land because of this, sales of smaller plots increased.

Historians have debated the consequences of these changes. Lawyers and financiers certainly benefited and relevant trades (such as map-making and surveying) also developed. Less clear is the effect on social structure. On the one hand, the gentry's share of total land increased slightly at the expense of traditional nobles, helping to support the 'rise of the gentry' argument (see page 14). On the other hand, there is also evidence that the aim of many sales was to build larger estates in one place by selling off parcels of land that had been bought over a wide area in the past. In these cases, it was not the 'new money' of the gentry coming in, but the traditional nobility making additional purchases.

income, occupation, lifestyle, or manners. This hierarchy was maintained by generally accepted social theories, such as the '**Great Chain of Being**' and customs of deference such as taking off a cap or kneeling in the presence of someone with a higher social rank. During the sixteenth century concerns at the narrowing of ranks produced legislative efforts such as **sumptuary laws** to distinguish between people.

Figure 3 A contemporary representation of the Great Chain of Being, showing God and the angels at the top, descending through princes and people down to animals and plants.

SUMPTUARY LAWS

The main purpose of sumptuary laws was to make clear distinctions between social ranks. By regulating the colour and fabric of clothing that different groups of people could wear, it was possible to tell at a glance what status someone held at a time when income and possessions were no longer a reliable guide. In legislation passed during Henry VIII's reign, only the most senior noblemen could wear cloth of gold or silver thread, silks and satin. Velvet was used to indicate someone of lesser nobility. Sumptuary laws could also be applied to what people ate as a further indicator of status. In the 1530s Parliament restricted meals to two courses (except on holidays) and set out an elaborate series of exceptions to this depending on the status of the dinner guest. Cardinals, for example, were allowed nine courses, but bishops only seven. As well as revealing concerns about the narrowing of social status, sumptuary laws also reflected religious fears about over-indulgence and economic pressures to discourage imports of luxury items at the expense of domestic production.

The Great Chain of Being

The theory of the 'Great Chain of Being' was a commonly accepted belief that society had been ordered by God into a strict hierarchy of ranks. This chain began with God at the top and descended through the king and the different social ranks of nobility, gentry and commoners down to animals, plants and rocks. Everyone was expected to accept their place within the Great Chain and to follow the conventions of dress and behaviour that went with it.

It was useful for the monarch and local landowners to maintain this theory because it both justified their place in society and required those lower down the social scale to accept inequality. It also gave particular importance to the church as part of government, since these ideas were mainly taught through the church.

> Almighty God hath created and appointed all things to heaven, earth and waters in a most excellent and perfect order. In heaven he hath appointed distinct orders of archangels and angels. In earth he hath appointed kings, princes and other governors under them, all in good and necessary order. Every degree of people, in their vocation, calling and office, hath appointed to them their duty and order. Some are in high degree, some in low; some kings and princes, some inferiors and subjects; priests and laymen; masters and servants; fathers and children; husbands and wives; rich and poor; and every one hath need of the other so that in all things is to be lauded and praised the goodly order of God, without which no house, no city, no commonwealth can continue to endure.'
>
> **Source B** Part of the sermon *Concerning Good Order and Obedience for Rulers and Magistrates* which was read out annually in every church in England during Elizabeth I's reign.

Q Why do you think people accepted inequality?
What can the homily tell us about family life?

As society grew, differences between one class and another narrowed. Men who had acquired wealth through trade or farming built houses and bought lands that were every bit as impressive as those of the traditional aristocracy. 'Emparking' – the consolidation and enclosure of fields to create parkland for country estates – was another sign of new-found wealth. The clergyman William Harrison commented on the pride in building that he observed during the 1570s:

> Houses that are recently built are commonly either of brick or hard stone or both [a change from the timber construction of medieval

Figure 4 Little Moreton Hall in Cheshire. The black and white half-timbered design is typical of the architecture of the sixteenth century.

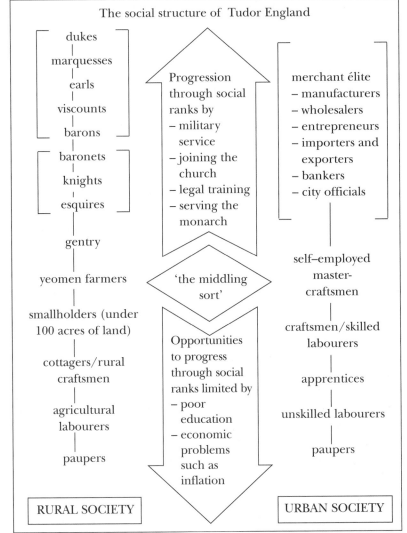

The social structure of Tudor England

dukes
|
marquesses
|
earls
|
viscounts
|
barons

baronets
|
knights
|
esquires
|
gentry
|
yeomen farmers
|
smallholders (under 100 acres of land)
|
cottagers/rural craftsmen
|
agricultural labourers
|
paupers

Progression through social ranks by
– military service
– joining the church
– legal training
– serving the monarch

'the middling sort'

Opportunities to progress through social ranks limited by
– poor education
– economic problems such as inflation

merchant élite
– manufacturers
– wholesalers
– entrepreneurs
– importers and exporters
– bankers
– city officials

self–employed master-craftsmen
|
craftsmen/skilled labourers
|
apprentices
|
unskilled labourers
|
paupers

RURAL SOCIETY

URBAN SOCIETY

Figure 5 A model of the social structure of Tudor England, based on M. A. R. Graves and R. H. Silcock, *Revolution, Reaction and the Triumph of Conservatism* (1984). The diagram shows that there were four main ways of rising through the ranks of the gentry, and that a slightly differ-ent structure operated in rural and urban areas.

Source C From William Harrison, *The Description of England (1577).*

houses]. Their rooms are large and comely, and places of work are becoming more distant from lodgings. Houses of the nobility are likewise built of brick and stone, but so magnificent and stately that the house of the poorest baron matches that of princes in the old time. There are old men dwelling in the village where I live who have noted the multitude of chimneys lately erected, compared to in their young days when there were not above two or three, if so many, even in the most wealthy towns of the realm.

Historians have suggested that the sixteenth century saw the rise of the gentry class. This was a large, ill-defined group below the titled nobility, but above tenant farmers and small landowners. They were defined more by their personal wealth than by titles. They could be prosperous farmers, wealthy merchants, or men from long-standing families of knights, esquires or gentlemen, but all were able to live comfortably from their income without having to resort to working for a living. The expansion of this group helped to cause an obsession with the symbols of rank as those with traditional status tried to protect their élite position.

2 A Changing Economy

a) The Rural Economy

Farming was the main occupation of Tudor England. As we saw above, nine out of ten people lived in village or small town communities where land ownership was a sign of social status. Poorer families rented a house and the land that went with it from a landlord and farmed to support themselves and to pay rent. Except in years of poor harvests, enough food was produced to feed the family and community. Towns were supplied by nearby farms which were organised to produce the necessary surplus.

Across the country, there was no uniform style of farming. Local traditions, geography and the climate determined whether a region tended to produce crops, livestock (cattle, sheep and pigs), or a combination of the two. In the higher lands of the Peak District and the Pennines for example, livestock farming was more common, whilst in the lower-lying Midlands and Lincolnshire more crops were produced. Similarly, there was no typical approach to crop production (or arable farming). Often, land would be cultivated on the 'open field system' which divided fields around a village into small strips for farming by tenants of the local landowner. To ensure that land was not over-cultivated, one-third of the strips would be left unplanted each year. Most villages

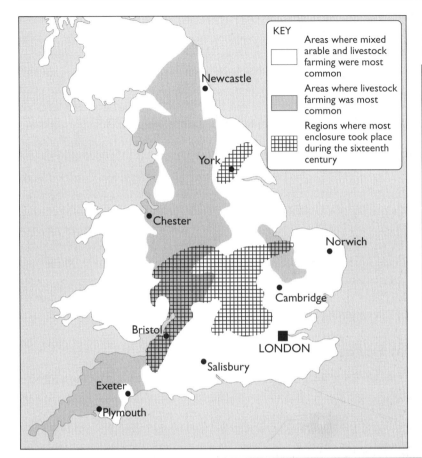

KEY

Areas where mixed arable and livestock farming were most common

Areas where livestock farming was most common

Regions where most enclosure took place during the sixteenth century

Figure 6 The distribution of different types of farming practices in sixteenth-century England.

ACTIVITY

Look closely at Figure 7 – it contains a lot of information about rural life that you might miss on a casual glance. In particular, can you explain or comment on:

1. who the man standing to the left might be (and give evidence for your answer)?

2. the significance of the basket and pitcher in the foreground on the right?

3. whether there is any noticeable difference in what men and women are doing?

4. anything of significance in the background?

Figure 7 A rural scene at harvest time.

also had areas that were never cultivated, perhaps because they were woodland, or contained a pond or stream. On this so-called common land, all villagers had rights of access to graze their animals. However, there were variations on this basic system from place to place and in some regions the idea of having larger fields to produce just one crop or to enclose livestock was not new. Woodland farming was also an important activity in particular areas. In the forests of Nottinghamshire, Suffolk and Essex, for example, timber was cut and woodland used to graze pigs and cattle.

During the Tudor period there were few innovations in agricultural techniques. Work was labour intensive, with tools that had changed little during the Middle Ages. Heavy work such as ploughing and cutting crops was done by men. Women sowed seeds and helped to tie sheaves of cut corn together. Most work was seasonal, so secondary occupations developed which could be conducted at home or near to it. These jobs were often associated with the woollen industry, such as spinning, weaving and dyeing, but other trades derived from agriculture such as leather tanning and cheese making developed in particular areas.

b) Enclosures

ISSUES:
What were enclosures?
Why were they
controversial?

The greatest and most controversial change to Tudor agriculture came with the spread of enclosure into the rich arable farmlands of the Midlands. At its simplest, enclosure meant putting a boundary around a field so that livestock (especially sheep) could be kept together, or so that one type of crop could be produced. For the farmer, this was a more efficient way of managing production than the open field system, but for tenants it could mean the disruption of their traditional ways of farming and even eviction from their land. A point worth remembering is that enclosure could take different forms:

▼ the *enclosure of common land* – this was likely to provoke the fiercest opposition. Villagers claimed customary rights of access to common (or uncultivated) land for pasturing their animals, cutting timber or peat, or for fishing and hunting. Fencing off these areas therefore deprived people of a variety of resources:

Source D From Edward Hall's *The Triumphant Reign of King Henry the VIII,* describing an enclosure riot of 1514.

> The towns about London had so enclosed the common fields with hedges and ditches that neither the young men of the city might shoot, nor the ancient persons walk for their pleasure in the fields. This sore grieved the Londoners, and suddenly this year a great number of the city assembled themselves in a morning, and a craftsman in a fool's coat came crying through the city 'Shovels and Spades!', and so many people followed him that it was a wonder, and within a space all the hedges about the towns had been cast down and the ditches filled.

▼ the *enclosure of cultivated land* – which meant consolidating strips of land into a larger field either for pasture or crops:

> Your sheep, that seem so meek and tame, have become such great devourers and so wild that they eat up and swallow men. They consume, destroy, and devour whole fields, houses and cities. Look in those parts of the realm where the finest and dearest wool grows; there, noblemen and gentlemen leave no ground for tillage, but enclose all into pastures.

Source E From *Utopia*, by Sir Thomas More, 1516.

▼ *engrossing* – which meant amalgamating the lands of two or more farms to make a single large unit. In extreme circumstances, this meant evicting tenant farmers, or simply shutting down a whole village because it lay in the area to be engrossed:

> Your heart would mourn to see the towns, villages, hamlets, manor places, in ruin and decay, the people gone, the ploughs laid down, the living of many honest men in one man's hand, the commons in many places taken away from the poor people, so that they are compelled to give up their houses and know not where to live.

Source F From a letter by the Bishop of Lincoln to Cardinal Wolsey, 30 September 1528.

ACTIVITY

Read Sources D, E and F, all of which provide evidence about contemporary views of enclosure, then answer the following examination-style questions.

1. Read Source E.
Explain what the author means when he says that sheep 'swallow men'.
[4 marks]
2. Read Sources E and F.
How do the authors of these sources agree about the effects of enclosure? **[6 marks]**
3. Read Sources D, E and F.
Which of these sources do you think is the most useful in explaining the effect of enclosures? Explain your answer. **[10 marks]**

Reactions to enclosure were often violent. Mobs tore down the fences and hedges which separated them from their traditional farmland. Larger groups of protesters collected petitions and marched to make the government aware of their grievances. Tudor governments were concerned at the reaction to enclosure, but did little about the

EXAMPLES OF TUDOR ANTI-ENCLOSURE LAWS

1489 Act ordering that land over 20 acres used for agriculture within the previous three years must remain so;

1515 Acts ordering the return of pastureland to arable use in places where crop production was traditional, the rebuilding of decayed houses and the return of people to these areas;

1534 Act forbidding anyone from owning more than 2,000 sheep or having more than two farms except in their own parish;

1551 Act against enclosures appointed a commission to seek out offenders;

1563 Act ordering that all land used for crops for at least four of the previous 35 years must remain arable and forbidding further conversions to pasture;

1598 Act passed after the depression in agriculture during the 1590s. Banned further conversion of arable land into pasture.

ISSUES:

How was cloth produced?

Why was the woollen industry so important to the Tudor economy?

FINISHING

The final stages of woollen production when spun yarn is converted into cloth by weaving, then fulling and dyeing it.

problem. Although efforts were made to limit the extent of enclosure, the government relied upon its agents across the country – Justices of the Peace – to enforce it. Too often, these were precisely the same people who were doing the enclosing so there was little political will to force the issue. Governments also realised that enclosure stimulated the growth of the woollen industry and so indirectly added to national wealth and increased tax revenues from export sales. Curbing enclosure therefore meant not only attacking the men on whose support the stability of Tudor government rested, but also its financial base. What legislation was passed reflected the awkward position of the government. Laws sounded fine on paper but were rarely successful in practice.

ACTIVITY

Test your knowledge of the topic of enclosures with this quick quiz:

1. What is meant by:
   a) the open field system?
   b) common land?
   c) enclosure?
   d) engrossing?
2. Give three explanations why enclosure was unpopular.
3. Give three explanations why Tudor governments were unwilling to take serious action to prevent enclosure.
4. Rewrite these statements so that they are more historically accurate:
   a) Enclosure was an invention of the Tudor period.
   b) Enclosure meant fencing off farmland to graze sheep.
   c) Enclosure was unpopular because it caused unemployment.

c) The Woollen Industry

Although agriculture provided the main livelihood for people in Tudor England, the woollen cloth industry created the most wealth. About 80 per cent of England's exports were of cloth. Different types and sizes of cloths were exported mainly to the Netherlands, but also to Spain, the Holy Roman Empire and Venice. The quality of wool produced by English sheep made both the raw material and cloths woven from it greatly in demand at home and abroad. Tudor governments were keen to encourage this sector of the economy because its success brought in valuable income to the crown from customs duties on exports. In the Middle Ages, raw wool was a primary export, but Tudor governments tried to discourage this as it meant that the **finishing** work to produce a piece of cloth was being done elsewhere, costing the crown export income and hampering the development of a domestic finishing industry. All this, of course, brought the industry into conflict with arable farmers who objected to farmland being converted into sheep-runs, or enclosed. These tensions created a great dilemma for Tudor governments which wanted to reap the quick profits to be made from wool, but which also had to ensure that rural traditions were not so damaged in the process as to cause unrest.

Woollen cloth production was widely scattered, but the best quality cloths came from the west of England – from towns and villages along the Welsh borders and down into Gloucestershire, Wiltshire and Hampshire. Production was specialised but not intensive. Most cloth was made by hand either in a room in a peasant cottage, or in a small workshop within the cloth merchant's house. Few people worked full-time in the woollen industry, although there were 'journeymen' who travelled to make a living from hiring out their skills.

EXAMPLES OF TUDOR LEGISLATION DESIGNED TO PROTECT AND DEVELOP THE CLOTH INDUSTRY

1487 Act forbidding export of unfinished and undyed cloth above £2 in value;

1512 Act to maintain the quality of woollen yarn;

1523 Act forbidding worsted wool woven in Norfolk or Suffolk to be finished anywhere except in Norwich;

1535 Act to maintain standards in making woollen cloth;

1551 Act setting out the standards of 22 types of cloth and establishing enforcement procedures;

1551 Act restricting weaving to those who had served the proper apprenticeship;

1554 Act to encourage the revival of cloth making in towns by relaxing some of the apprenticeship rules;

1557 Act restricting cloth manufacture to places where there had been an industry for at least ten years.

> **Q**
> What concerns about the cloth industry do these laws reveal?
> How did these concerns change during the first half of the sixteenth century?

Figure 8 From the sheep's back to the customer's back: how woollen clothing was made in Tudor England.

Most employees were outworkers – people who worked part-time on a particular aspect of production in their own homes. Cloth merchants were the driving force behind the production process. They bought the raw material, negotiated who was going to refine it, moved the unfinished yarns and cloth from place to place through the production cycle and arranged the sale or export of the finished item.

The process of converting the wool on a sheep's back into a piece of cloth, or tailored item, was lengthy and involved a series of tasks, some more specialised than others. As Figure 8 shows, both men and women were involved, but each sex tended to do different tasks. Women were usually involved in the early stages of production, carding and spinning the wool into yarn. Men (often journeymen) then took over the more skilled tasks of weaving, fulling and dyeing.

Although the tools and techniques of production changed little during the Tudor period, a wider variety of types of cloth came into production as the sixteenth century progressed. This was mainly in response to demand from European markets but was made possible by the arrival of skilled Protestant refugees from the Netherlands and France in the 1560s and 1570s. They produced the 'new draperies' – lighter cloths and knitted cloths – which helped the textile industry to continue expanding after the dramatic slump in woollen exports during the 1550s.

d) Industrial Development

ISSUE:
What industries did Tudor England have?

Although England produced a wide variety of other goods, none came close to the scale of woollen production. Coal was mined, mainly for domestic use, in the north-east around Newcastle and in the south Wales valleys. Iron, copper and tin were also being extracted but not in sufficient quantities for England to be self-sufficient in metals. Recent research has tended to focus more on 'consumer' goods as the growth area in the economy. Some villages and towns began to specialise in one product such as knitted cloth, pins, paper making or brewing, encouraging the slow development of an internal market. Industrial development in general, however, was limited by the low purchasing power of consumers (made worse by the effects of inflation) and by the absence of efficient sources of energy.

e) Commercial Development

ISSUE:
How did trade become more sophisticated in the sixteenth century?

The growth of London in the sixteenth century was spectacular. By the end of Elizabeth's reign, over 200,000 people lived there – over three times as many as a century earlier. This great expansion was

In the background you can see evidence of the agriculture that was essential to supply London's growing population

St Paul's was one of the most imposing features of the London skyline, although churches in general were usually the largest structures

Cheapside ran between St Paul's and the Guildhall. In the sixteenth century it was one of London's busiest shopping streets

The Steelyard was one of the areas occupied by foreign merchants. It became notorious in the sixteenth century as the place where Protestant heretical literature was imported into England

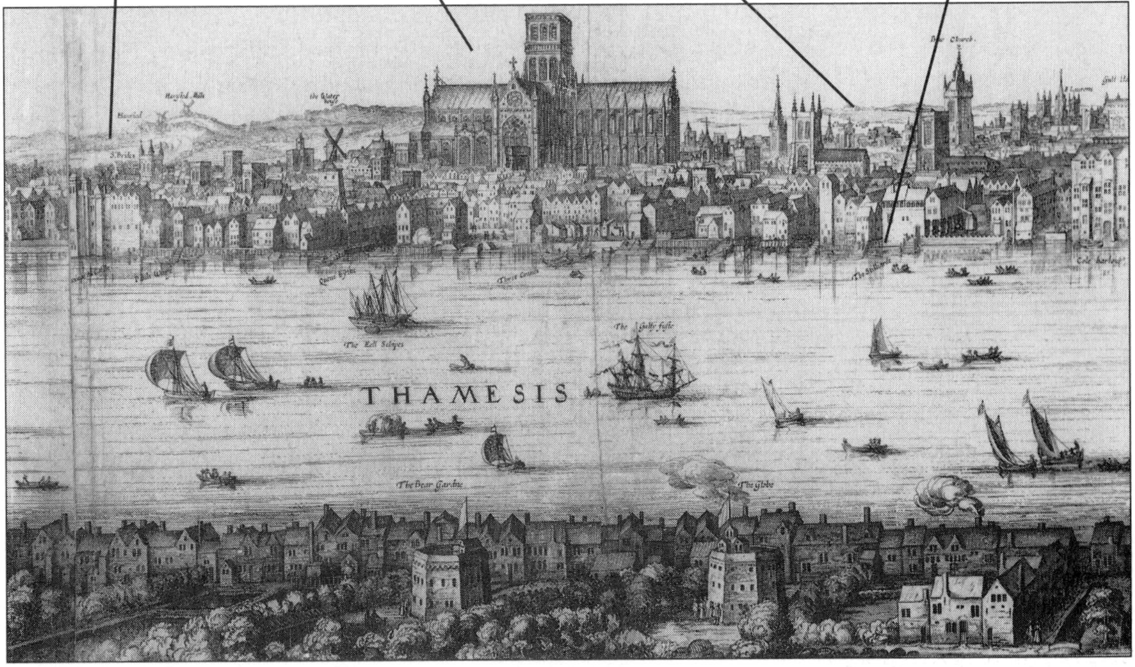

Figure 9 A prospering city: London in the late sixteenth century.

only possible because patterns of trade within England developed to sustain it. Grains, because they were perishable, had to come from close by, but livestock could be brought from further away. Welsh beef could be found on the tables of Elizabethan Londoners. Raw materials could also be transported over long distances. The north-east, around Newcastle, for example, became a principal supplier of London's coal, sending shipments along the North Sea coast and up the River Thames. Such connections began to encourage a national market to develop, stimulating production in outlying areas, but also enabling the further growth of the capital.

During the sixteenth century some merchants also turned their attention to much more distant markets. The conquest of the Americas by Spain in the century after Columbus's discovery and the expansion of Portugal into Africa and Asia opened up new trade opportunities for the English. Although both Spain and Portugal tried to discourage foreign interference in their markets, neither had the resources either to defend their interests or to supply all their colonists' needs. English merchants were attracted by new products from these regions: sugar and tobacco from the Americas and silks and spices from Asia. These were luxury items, well beyond the pockets of ordinary people, but in great demand by the ruling élite in Elizabethan England.

Trade enterprises over such vast distances (the sailing time from England to India could take six months) required careful organisation and much money. The government responded by offering royal charters (essentially documents recognising and approving a company) and trade monopolies to merchants willing to undertake the risks. Trade companies, of which the most famous was the **East India Company**, developed to manage international trade. They pioneered more advanced financial techniques such as share distributions, letters of credit and insurance schemes. In this way, the sixteenth century saw the emergence of the modern **capitalist economic system.**

EAST INDIA COMPANY

Granted a royal charter in 1600 by Elizabeth I to allow it a monopoly of trade in the Indian Ocean region. The company originally had 218 members and raised money for expeditions by selling shares and splitting profits in proportion to the size of each member's investment.

Capitalist Economic System

During the Tudor period more sophisticated ways of organising economic activity began to emerge. In the Middle Ages feudalism – a system based on ownership of land and the rights this conferred – was the dominant economic system. This began to collapse as trade grew and markets expanded. Capitalism is a form of economic organisation based on privately owned companies and competition. To enable goods to be produced, moved and sold, a more advanced financial system geared towards raising money through shares or borrowing was created. To develop wider markets merchants used 'letters of credit' which were issued in one country and could be redeemed for cash somewhere else, avoiding the need to carry large sums of money. Goods could also be insured to protect the value of the merchandise. Companies competed with one another to sell goods and to try to make profits which could be used in part to improve the business and in part to tempt investors. The market place, with its changing patterns of consumer demand, determined the success of companies.

---

3 The Impact of Social and Economic Change

a) Price Inflation

ISSUE:
What were the causes of inflation?

During the Tudor period the price of most goods, but particularly staple items such as grain, rose sharply. The precise starting point of price inflation is difficult to detect. There is little doubt that during Henry VII's reign the cost of living remained at much the same level that it had been at during the later Middle Ages, but that at some point in Henry VIII's reign prices began to rise and did not sink back. The worst affected periods were the years 1540–60 and the 1590s – in the latter decade, for example, the price of corn doubled. Overall, estimates suggest that the cost of grain had risen by something in the order of 600 per cent during the course of the sixteenth century. Other prices rose less steeply, but were still inflated. This imbalance in the degree of inflation and the fluctuations in its severity have allowed historians to narrow down the possible causes.

The growth of population has been regarded as a primary cause of price inflation, although contemporaries were slow to make this connection. More people meant increasing demand for subsistence items (such as bread, cheese, meat and ale), but the supply of these goods was relatively inflexible and could not keep pace. In agriculture, for instance, there were few innovations during the sixteenth century which might have enabled more efficient farming, and the reclamation of land for new cultivation was slow and expensive. As demand outstripped supply, farmers and merchants were able to increase market price. This was not simply profiteering (although people at the time though that this selfishness was an important element in pushing up prices); rather it was a response to other pressures on landowners, such as the higher price of land and increases in their own cost of living.

Other factors also contributed to inflation, but each should be treated with some care, as Table 1 shows.

Debasement

Sixteenth-century coins contained larger amounts of silver and gold than are found in modern currencies, so a *teston* (a silver shilling) in theory contained roughly a shilling's worth of precious metal mixed with baser alloys (hence the phrase 'worth its weight in gold'). This equality between face value and silver or gold content gave merchants and customers confidence when trading. Clearly, if the amount of gold or silver used to make coins was reduced, then the face value would remain the same, but the government could keep the left-over metal. Successive re-minting of coins in the 1540s reduced their silver content and gave the government over £1.3 million of easy income. In the process, this debasement destroyed confidence in the coinage and added to inflationary pressure.

Cause	How this factor explains inflation	Evaluation of this factor
Government spending	Henry VII spent money cautiously, but later Tudors increased spending, especially on foreign wars. This put more money into circulation as the government bought clothing, provisions, weaponry and ships for wars against France and Scotland	Government spending was only a small part of national economic activity
Debasement of the coinage	To generate more money for foreign wars, Wolsey instituted the first debasement of the coinage in 1526–7. Governments between 1544 and 1551 made successive devaluations – the 'Great Debasement'. Reducing the silver content forced people to ask for more money to yield the same metal value	The 'Great Debasement' coincided with the steeper price rises of the 1540s, but the re-minting of coins in the early years of Elizabeth's reign undermines this factor's importance in explaining later periods of inflation – especially the 1590s
Increases in the circulation of bullion within Europe	The discovery of silver in the Spanish Empire led to an influx of bullion into Europe from the mid-sixteenth century. This new quantity of silver did not just remain in Spain – it was used to pay troops in Italy and the Netherlands, to repay debts to bankers in Germany, and by merchants importing items into Spain. The greater quantity of money in circulation meant that prices could rise as there was surplus purchasing power	Although the discovery of the largest deposit of silver in the Americas came in 1545, large-scale importing did not occur immediately, so the timing of this factor does not easily explain why inflation began in England as early as the 1520s. Also, the greater circulation of bullion was more likely to affect merchants importing luxury items, such as European wines or fine cloths, but it was the price of domestically produced grain that rose the most
Bad harvests	Crop failures decreased the amount of available food, forcing prices to increase	Bad harvests caused temporary shortages of foodstuffs, so it is difficult to see why this should explain the continuous price increases of the sixteenth century, or why there was inflation in industry as well as agriculture
Land sales	More land came onto the open market for sale after the 1530s (see page 10). The scramble to buy among the nobility, gentry and wealthy merchants that followed forced up land prices	The timing of the opening up of the Tudor land rush fits the beginnings of inflation and would have had an effect on rents, but land sales only affected the privileged few and cannot easily explain inflation in a wide range of commodity prices.

Table 1 An analysis of the causes of Tudor inflation.

ACTIVITY

As you can see from Table 1, explaining price inflation is not straight-forward. Historians have to struggle not only with incomplete records, but also with the complexities of the explanation itself. It would be easier if all prices rose at an even rate during the century, but unfortunately this is not the case:

▼ the price of some goods, particularly those which were staple food-stuffs or essential for survival, rose more steeply than others
▼ although prices did not tend to reduce, they rose more sharply at some times than at others. The 1540s, 1550s and 1590s were particularly expensive decades.
Bearing these points in mind, try to rearrange the factors in Table 1 to create an analysis that you think is sufficient to explain Tudor inflation.

---

b) Poverty

ISSUE:
What caused poverty?

One consequence of population growth and the inflation it helped to create was an increase in poverty. At various times, localised shortages of jobs became acute, for example when soldiers returned to their homes from war, or when merchant trade was disrupted. In the countryside, a poor harvest meant fewer opportunities for seasonal work at harvest time. Added to these often temporary setbacks were the more permanent structural changes to the economy. Population growth by the late sixteenth century had created a younger society but not the jobs for it. Price inflation meant that those in work were forced to pay more for food, clothing and rents whilst wage rises lagged far behind. The growing profitability of the cloth industry led some landlords to change the use of their land from agriculture to sheep-farming. Not only did this reduce the local food supply and help to inflate prices, but fewer people were needed to work tending sheep. As we saw above, enclosure to create pastureland could also mean amalgamating farmlands, leading to tenant farmers being turned out of their homes or in some cases, whole villages being depopulated.

Government action had also contributed to the problem. Legislation to prevent noblemen keeping large numbers of retainers under arms (see pages 51–2) had reduced the size of households and added thousands more to the job market. The dissolution of the monasteries in the late 1530s might have forced ex-monks to look for work, but the more significant effect lay in the removal of the monastic community from the local economy. Merchants who supplied or bought from monasteries saw their incomes fall, whilst the traditional role of church houses in providing shelter, medical care and food for the needy was removed altogether, pulling away a vital safety net in some villages. For many families the economic shocks of the sixteenth century pushed them from subsistence into poverty.

Source G A description of different sorts of poor people, from *William Lambarde and Local Government*, published in 1594.

The poor are exceedingly much multiplied because for the most part all the children and brood of the poor be poor also, seeing that they are not taken from their wandering parents and brought up to do honest labour for their living. As they be born and brought up, so do they live and die – most shameless and shameful rogues and beggars. And to the increase of these evils we have a sort of poor lately crept in amongst us and not known before to our elders: I mean poor soldiers. We are by many duties bounden to help and relieve them, considering that they fight for the truth of God and defence of their country; yea, they fight in our own war and do serve in our places, enduring cold and hunger when we live at ease and fare well, lying in the open field when we live at ease and are lodged in beds of down, and meeting with broken heads and limbs when we find it good and safe sleeping in a whole skin.

Q

How does Lambarde explain the growth in poverty?
Why does he view poor soldiers differently from others living in poverty?

'IMPOTENT POOR'

People who were unable to work, either because they were too young or too old, or because of disability. There was a generally sympathetic response to these people, who were seen as deserving of charity.

'IDLE POOR'

Until 1572, anyone who was fit to work but could not or would not was regarded as 'idle'. These people were seen as undeserving and in need of correction. They included those who lived off begging and petty crime, and people who had fallen on hard times but who were genuinely seeking work, such as agricultural workers who had seasonal employment, soldiers returning from war, and servants released from work on the death of their master. For them, early Tudor attempts to deal with poverty were unfair and harmful.

At first, Tudor governments did not fully recognise that poverty might be an unavoidable condition or that state intervention was necessary. The authorities were more concerned with the danger that begging and vagrancy caused to the maintenance of social order than they were with establishing a complex solution to the problem. Most Tudor legislation therefore recommended strict punishment for begging and required the return of the vagrant to his or her original parish, so that the problem would not spread. There was a distinction drawn between the '**impotent poor**' and the '**idle poor**', but this was a simplistic analysis of the problem. The initiative to tackle social distress and unemployment came from local authorities, not national government. For those who were deserving of charity, local authorities organised collections of voluntary donations which they distributed to the sick, elderly or other impotent poor. These schemes relied on the consciences of the wealthy and were given added force by the 1572 Poor Relief Act which made donations compulsory. Few authorities had sympathy for the idle poor. They were regarded as a social nuisance and a source of crime and disorderly behaviour. Punishment and eviction were the usual treatments meted out.

However, from 1572 greater recognition was given to those who were genuinely unemployed because of circumstances rather than merely idle. The government tried to support this group especially during the hardship years of the 1590s. These efforts produced variable results, with some communities (such as Norwich) drawing up detailed poor relief schemes. More often, however, local charity did not provide the same level of social support that the church had offered before the Reformation.

Figure 10 The punishment inflicted on those who were caught begging without a licence was to be whipped back to the parish where they were born.

ACTIVITY

Examine the information about Tudor poor laws in Table 2, then answer the following questions:

1. How did the government's response to poverty change as the Tudor period progressed?

2. What were the landmark pieces of legislation which illustrate these changing attitudes?

3. Why does a study of legislation only give an incomplete picture of the response to poverty in Tudor England?

Date	'Impotent Poor'	'Idle Poor'	'Genuine Unemployed'
1495	All beggars punished by placing in stocks, then whipping and return to parish of origin		
1531	Allowed to beg in their parish if they obtained a licence, fined if they begged without a licence	Whipped and returned to parish of origin, fined if they begged without a licence	
1536	Money to be raised through voluntary contributions to assist impotent poor	Whipped and returned to parish of origin, fined if they begged without a licence. Children found begging to be taken from parents and put to work	
1547	Funds collected through churches to support impotent poor, houses to be built to accommodate poor	Anyone unemployed for more than three days classed as vagrant. If convicted of begging, branded and given to informant as a slave for two years. For a second conviction, further branding and lifelong slavery. Death penalty for third offence	
1552	Compulsory census and registration to reduce unauthorised begging, attempts to persuade more people to make contributions	Whipped and returned to parish of origin, fined if they begged without a licence. Children found begging to be taken from parents and put to work	
1563	If people refused to make contributions, they could be taken to court and imprisoned	Whipped and returned to parish of origin, fined if they begged without a licence	
1572	Compulsory contributions to poor relief. Overseers of the poor appointed by the parish to help organise poor relief	Punishments for vagrancy increased: whipping and ear bored for first offence with criminal charges for further offences	Some classes of people excluded from punishment – recognised for first time as 'deserving poor'
1576		'Houses of correction' to be set up to punish those who refused to work	JPs required to buy raw materials to provide work for those who were able
1597	Powers of overseers of poor carefully defined – included finding work for able poor	Whipped and returned to parish of origin. Each county had to have at least one house of correction to which persistent beggars could be sent	Tools and materials to be provided for those able to work. Children to be apprenticed to a trade
1601	Earlier laws brought together and reissued with some amendments		

Table 2 Tudor poor law legislation.

▼ Working on Society and the Economy

The purpose of this chapter is to establish that Tudor England was a dynamic and changing society. The growth and movements in population, the threat to the countryside from enclosure, inflation and the rise of an unemployed 'underclass' presented important challenges for governments to solve if they were to avoid unrest. These developments form the backcloth to the political story, but in every Tudor monarch's reign acted to influence the course of events, either because social rebellion put the brakes on royal plans or because royal income was boosted by the additional taxation some of these changes generated. More important, these changes combined with wider political and religious developments (examined in later chapters) to reshape the ruling class in Tudor society away from its medieval origins in the feuds between great nobles to include a more diverse group of people. At the same time, these changes also widened the gap between rich and poor.

Your notes need to reflect the important social and economic changes of the Tudor period. Look back at the key themes and make sure that you can give the main details of what was *changing* for each:

▼ population
▼ social structure
▼ the enclosure movement
▼ industrial and commercial development
▼ inflation
▼ poverty.

Answering Extended Writing and Essay Questions on Society and the Economy

Extended writing questions come in two main forms – in structured questions such as those suggested here, and in open-ended essays, for which you have to plan your own structure. Therefore, you can use some of the techniques that you develop in practising structured questions to devise your own essay plans and structures.

Look at questions 1 and 2. Although they appear very different, both begin with an instruction for you to describe something. You should treat this with caution, not as an invitation to rush in and tell the examiner everything you know about the topic because more marks will be awarded for *selecting and organising* material to create a structured answer.

Examples of typical questions

1.a) Describe the main features of land enclosure in Tudor England. **[15 marks]**

b) Why did they cause such controversy in the Tudor period? **[15 marks]**

2.a) Briefly describe THREE of the main social and economic changes during the Tudor period. **[30 marks]**

b) Which of these changes do you think had the most effect on sixteenth-century society? Explain your answer. **[60 marks]**

The first step, therefore, is to make sure that you have understood the focus of the question. The key word is not *describe* but the ones that follow – *main features/changes* – which tell you what you have to describe and therefore how to select material. To gain high marks in a question of this kind you also need to do more than simply set out your chosen material – you should show why you have chosen it by drawing out its significance for the question, making explicit statements about the importance of the main features and what they reveal about enclosures, or about the ways in which facts about population, enclosure, price inflation or poverty show change.

Here are some of the things you could write in response to 1(a) or part of 2(a). Reorganise them into a more coherent plan. For example, you could group the statements into different features such as types of enclosure, motives for enclosure, methods, and effects. In each case, provide examples and explain how they illustrate the feature that you are describing or how they illustrate the process of change.

▼ Sir Thomas More said that 'sheep devour men'

▼ Enclosing had already been taking place in some parts of the country – not new in the sixteenth century

▼ acts of Parliament tried to control the spread of enclosure without much success

▼ strip farming in open fields was traditional

▼ land was fenced off to create space for sheep to graze

▼ what was new was the scale of enclosure in traditional arable areas

▼ common land (where everyone in the village had customary rights to graze animals, cut wood, fish in ponds, etc.) was enclosed

▼ sheep farming was very profitable – wool was England's major source of exports

▼ two or more small-holdings – even whole villages – might be torn down to enclose the land

▼ manor houses used nearby land to create parkland.

The second part of the questions requires you to analyse what happened in order to explain (rather than describe) the effects of economic change. Although they are very different types of question, you will need to begin both by analysing the evidence in the chapter and listing the effects of enclosure. Question 2(b) requires you to make a judgement about the extent of each effect, and select the one that you consider most important. Question 1 asks you to show why these effects caused controversy. In both cases you will need to select material to show the effects, and make explicit links to show their relative importance, or why they created controversy.

In some cases, you may wish to use the same events or evidence in each part of the question, since they are relevant to both. You will not be rewarded in one part of a question for information mentioned in the other – you have to treat the parts as separate, and each answer must be complete in itself. This is where it is essential to have a clear view of the focus of the question. If you simply repeat information in the same way, you will not gain marks – what makes the information valid is that it is used to support an argument that relates to the focus of the question. Therefore information used in part (a) of a question will only gain marks in part (b) if it is explicitly shown to illustrate the importance of an effect, or to show why it caused controversy. The question to ask yourself is always, 'Why am I including this information, and have I made the reason clear?'

Although, therefore, you will have to deal with different types of question, and different examples will be offered as you work through this book, there are certain simple rules to follow:
▼ Examine the question carefully and clarify its focus
▼ Construct an argument to answer it in your mind
▼ Select evidence and events to support your argument
▼ State how that evidence/event supports your argument and links to the focus of the question.

With those ideas in mind, you should now attempt one or both of questions 1 and 2.

Other questions for you to consider include:
▼ Why was there so much poverty in Tudor England? How successfully did the authorities tackle this problem?
▼ Who benefited and who suffered as a result of social and economic changes in the Tudor period?

Answering Source-Based Questions on Society and the Economy

Since this is an introductory chapter, we will use it to look at some of the types of source-based questions that you might be asked in an examination. Essentially, you can expect five different sorts of questions:

Question type	What the question is looking for
Comprehension	Have you understood the meaning of particular words or phrases in the source?
Interpretation	Can you select suitable information from a source and draw conclusions about it?
Comparison / cross-reference	Can you identify the similarities or differences between two or more sources?
Usefulness	Can you explain how a historian might use a source, and what its limitations as evidence are?
Synthesis	Can you use a range of sources and your own knowledge of the topic to reach a judgement?

Look at the source-based questions below and decide which type or types each is:

Source H From *A Description of England* by William Harrison, 1577.

The poor is commonly divided into three sorts. Some are poor by impotency, such as the fatherless child, the aged, the blind, lame and the diseased person who is judged to be incurable. The second are poor by casualty, such as the wounded soldier. The third consists of thriftless poor, such as the vagabond who will abide nowhere, but who runs about from place to place, and the rogue.

Source I From a summary of the punishments handed out by Nicholas Powtell to beggars brought before him during August 1571.

Isabell Cotton, Anne Draper and John Draper, taken at Normanton as vagrant persons, examined, whipped and punished, and after sent from constable to constable the direct way to Bolton in Lancashire, where they were born and dwell.

Richard Sexten admitted into Christ's Hospital the thirteenth day of June 1579 by Mr. Gooding, one of the governors, and there to have a bed and room until further orders be taken. His age 56. Born in Lancashire.

Richard Sexten was admitted into the foundation the second day of January 1580, there to begin his relief of eight pence each week.

Source J From the records of poor relief granted in Ipswich.

Of these sorts of wandering idle people there are three or four hundred in a shire, and although they go about two or three in a company, they all or most of them meet either at a fair or a market, or in some alehouse, once a week. And they grow more dangerous because they find they have bred such fear into the Justices and other inferior officers that no man dares to call them into question.

Source K From a letter by the Somerset Justice of the Peace, Edward Hext, to Elizabeth's chief minister, Lord Burghley, in 1594.

▼ QUESTIONS ON SOURCES

1. Read Source H.
   What does this source reveal about the causes of poverty in the Tudor period? **[2 marks]**
2. Read Sources H, I and J.
   Based on William Harrison's classification in Source H, what sorts of poor people were Isabell Cotton and Richard Sexten? Explain your answer. **[4 marks]**
3. Read Sources I and J.
   How does the treatment of the poor in these sources differ?
   [4 marks]
4. Read Source K.
   How valuable is this source as evidence of the problem of poverty during Elizabeth's reign? **[6 marks]**
5. Read all the sources, and use your own knowledge.
   Would you agree that the Tudor authorities understood, and sympathised with, the problems facing the poor? **[9 marks]**

What do you think an examiner would be expecting in an answer to Question 4? Here are some pointers:

▼ the question asks 'how valuable ...', suggesting that the source has both strengths that make it useful and possible flaws which limit how it can be used. To score high marks, you would need to identify examples of both.

▼ some of the clues about its usefulness will be contained in what the source says, but you should also pay close attention to the 'attribution' – the part at the end of the source which tells you who wrote it, when, etc. This can also help you to judge whether the source is helpful.

Based on this advice, judge the quality of the answer below:

4. A historian would find source K useful in a number of ways. It gives information about the scale of poverty in a rural county like Somerset (over 300 idle poor) and tells us something about the activities of vagabonds. There is a strong suggestion that the idle poor turn to crime, or at least to harassment. It also shows that the local authorities felt powerless to tackle the problem. The source is made useful by the fact that it is written by one of the men (a Justice of the Peace) whose responsibility it was to deal with the problem. Because the letter is written to Lord Burghley, we can also use the source to show that the government was aware of the growing problem of poverty in the 1590s. However, we only have a single source to show all of this. We cannot be sure that what was happening in Somerset was typical of elsewhere in the country, or whether Edward Hext was exaggerating the scale of the problem to draw attention to it.

Further Reading

Books in the Access to History series

You will find references to social and economic developments in each of the Access books that deal with a Tudor monarch: *Henry VII* by Caroline Rogers, *Henry VIII and the Government of England* by Keith Randell, *Edward and Mary: A Mid Tudor Crisis?* by Nigel Heard and *Elizabeth I and the Government of England* by Keith Randell.

Other books

There are short chapters on social and economic changes under the Tudors in A. G. R. Smith's *The Emergence of a Nation State: The Commonwealth of England 1529–1660* (Longman, 1984) and in *The Tudor Years* edited by John Lotherington (Hodder and Stoughton, 1994). To follow up the problem of the poor, try *Poverty and Vagrancy in Tudor England* by John Pound (Longman, 1971) or *The Problem of the Poor in Tudor and Early Stuart England* by A. Beier (Methuen, 1983). The causes and effects of price rises are dealt with by R. B. Outhwaite in *Inflation in Tudor and Early Stuart England* (Macmillan, 1968). To find out more about particular industries, consult *England's Agricultural Regions and Agrarian History 1500–1750* by Joan Thirsk (Macmillan, 1987) and *The English Woollen Industry 1500–1700* by G.D. Ramsay (Macmillan, 1982).

2 THE ESTABLISHMENT OF THE TUDOR MONARCHY

POINTS TO CONSIDER

The Tudor period began with a battle. In 1485 Richard III was defeated and killed by Henry, Earl of Richmond, at Bosworth Field. It was an unlikely victory for a young man who had not been raised to rule and who had spent half his life in exile. Yet it was a permanent victory. Henry was king for 24 years, during which time he used cunning and, at times, ruthlessness, to ensure his family's survival and the strengthening of the monarchy. His achievement can be seen by the fact that he was the first king in nearly a century to pass the crown peacefully to his son. In this chapter we will look at how Henry became king, and why his prospects did not seem good. Then, we will examine three key issues: how Henry managed to stay king during the first uncertain years of his reign; how he defeated rivals for his throne; and how he went on to rebuild the image and power of the English monarchy at home and abroad.

ISSUE:

How did Henry VII become king in 1485?

1 Introduction: The Battle of Bosworth Field

On the morning of 22 August 1485 the 5,000-strong army collected together by Henry Tudor, Earl of Richmond, met the royal army commanded by King Richard III in battle at Bosworth Field, near Leicester. Henry had only recently arrived back in England after a long exile in France. He had spent three weeks marching through his native Wales trying urgently to muster support against the unpopular rule of Richard. His chances of success seemed slim: he had not attracted much public support because few people knew who he was; he had never led troops into battle before; and he was facing a well-equipped royal army that was probably twice the size of his own.

The battle was fought in the area on and around a hill near the village of Bosworth. Richard III's forces had arrived first and had gained the better position. The king had put most of his archers, protected by foot soldiers, on the hillside from where they could fire down on Henry's advancing men. Richard himself led the cavalry. However, he had not been able to count on the loyalty of all of his

MAGNATE

The term magnate describes a member of the greater nobility – the barons – who owned large estates. Although William the Conqueror had originally scattered baronial lands through several counties, the greater families had consolidated their holdings through marriage and family links, building up a significant territorial base where they effectively governed in the king's name. Many had built castles and acquired private armies, especially in the borderlands of the north and the Welsh marches, where the crown depended on their power to defend the kingdom. Their power was therefore necessary for effective government, but could prove a serious threat if not carefully managed.

commanders. Crucially, Lord Thomas Stanley and his brother Sir William Stanley were positioned at the north of the battle site with 4,000 men. Both men were reluctant to support Richard, who had taken Thomas Stanley's son hostage to ensure their loyalty, but they were also afraid to support Henry openly in case he lost the battle and they were ruined along with him. For the time being, they stood off to one side, weighing up what was happening. The Earl of Northumberland was also at the battle, but he too had refused to take part until the outcome was clearer.

When the battle began, Henry's foot soldiers ran towards the hill whilst the royal forces fired arrows at them and Richard's cavalry cut into them from the sides. Henry's forces grouped together to defend themselves and in the midst of the confusion the Duke of Norfolk, one of Richard's commanders, was killed. At this point the two sides disengaged and Henry assessed the situation. He knew that it was only a matter of time before Richard's superior forces wore his men down, so he decided to approach the Stanleys to ask them to join him.

Richard saw what was happening and led his personal guard to attack Henry as he rode out to the Stanleys. Richard came very close to success: his men killed Henry's standard bearer and nearly reached Henry himself. However, at that moment Sir William Stanley decided to take action. He ordered his cavalry to attack Richard, who was caught completely by surprise. The king was thrown from his horse, but he ordered that another should be brought to him. Meanwhile, the Earl of Northumberland still remained off to the side

What Do We Really Know about the Battle of Bosworth Field?

Although it is one of the most famous battles fought on English soil, few accounts survive to tell historians for certain what happened. All are second-hand, written after the battle from stories heard at court or by foreign observers who collected information for other rulers. Unsurprisingly, then, the details of the battle vary significantly from account to account. The number of troops at Richard's disposal, for example, was put as high as 120,000 and as low as 10,000. Writers disagree about which **magnates** were present at the battle and about what they did. They even disagree about exactly where the battle was fought – at Bosworth, or closer to the market town of Dadlington, a mile and a half away. If you are interested in looking more closely at the evidence about the battle, the Richard III Society (a group dedicated to preserving his memory and setting the misleading Tudor propaganda about him to rights) has posted the documentary evidence on its website: www.richardiii.net

of the battlefield, choosing not to join in to protect his king. Richard rejoined the fight, but was cut down and killed, the last English king to die in battle. Once their leader was dead, the royal forces broke up in confusion and fled.

According to the legend surrounding the battle, a soldier found Richard III's golden crown in a thorn bush near where the king had fallen. He brought it to Thomas Stanley who placed it on Henry's head, crowning him 'Henry VII, king of England' amid the fallen bodies and blood. Now that the 28-year-old Earl of Richmond had seized the crown, the Tudor family replaced the House of York as the ruling dynasty in England and Wales.

2 The First Tudor King

Henry reigned 23 years and 7 months. He lived 52 years. By his wife Elizabeth he had 8 children. He was distinguished, wise and prudent in character; and his spirit was so brave and resolute that never, even in moments of greatest danger, did it desert him. In government, he was shrewd and far-seeing, so that none dared to get the better of him by deceit or sharp practice. To those of his subjects who did not do him due honour, he was hard and harsh. He knew well how to maintain his royal dignity and everything belonging to it. He was successful in war, although by nature he preferred peace to war. Above all else, he cherished justice.

Source A From the *Books of English History (Anglicae Historicae Libri)* by Polydore Vergil (1534). Vergil was an Italian diplomat who came to England in 1502 and was commissioned by Henry to write a history of England. His account of Henry's character is believed to be among the most reliable because Vergil knew Henry personally; quoted in *Henry VII* by R. Lockyer (1983).

He was of a high mind and loved his own way. Had he been a private man he would have been termed 'proud'; but in a wise prince it was but keeping of distance, which he did towards all, not admitting any near or full approach, neither to his power nor to his secrets. For he was governed by none.

Source B Francis Bacon, *History of the reign of King Henry VII*, written in 1622.

Q What are the points of agreement between these two accounts of Henry's style of kingship?

In Bacon's character sketch of Henry VII, written well over a century after his death, the writer creates the impression of a strong king who projected an aura of majesty. According to Bacon, Henry seems to set himself apart from other men and to keep power jealously to himself. Like most writers of the time, Bacon was presenting Henry according to the 'Tudor myth', a rewriting of history by Tudor monarchs to strengthen their authority and undermine challengers. In fact, Bacon had just been dismissed from King James I's service on allegations of

Figure 11 Henry VII as a young man. This picture was probably painted around the time that Henry became king. (Musée Calvet, Avignon, photographer: André Guerrand)

fraud and wrote his history of the reign of Henry VII in the hope of currying favour with his royal master. The reality of Henry VII's reign was less glamorous. He came to the throne, as we have seen, by killing his rival and snatching the crown from his head, and he went on to rule efficiently, but with a constant fear that the same thing might one day happen to him:

> Henry, after he had subdued the final conspiracy against him might now, after many anxieties and dangers relax his mind in peace, but he began to treat his people with more harshness and severity than had been his custom, in order (as he himself claimed) to ensure that they remained more completely in obedience to him. Thus, the good prince lost, by degrees, all sense of moderation and was led into avarice.

Q

How does Source C help to show that Vergil's view of Henry VII's character can be taken as reliable evidence?

Source C From Polydore Vergil's *Books of English History*, 1534; quoted in *Henry VII* by R. Lockyer (1983).

a) Henry's Early Life

Henry Tudor was born in 1457, the son of Edmund Tudor, Earl of Richmond (who had died a few months before his son's birth), and Lady Margaret Beaufort. His claim to the throne came through his mother and could be traced back to the third son of Edward III (reigned 1327–77). However, because his claim was through the female side of his family, it was far weaker than others who could claim descent through their fathers and grandfathers.

> **ISSUE:**
> **Why was Henry Tudor's early life so disrupted?**

Figure 12 Henry Tudor's family tree, showing his line of descent from John of Gaunt.

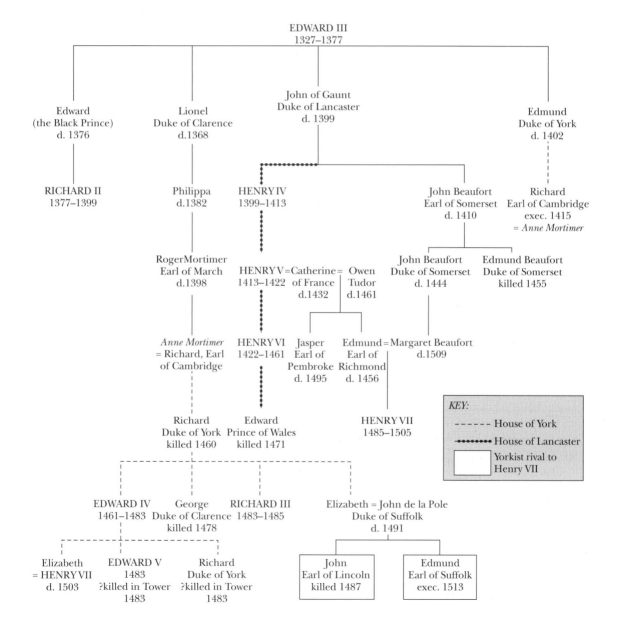

THE WARS OF THE ROSES

A series of short wars fought between the supporters of the House of Lancaster, which had ruled England since 1399, and the supporters of the House of York. The wars came about in 1455 because of the Lancastrian King Henry VI's failures both in war against France and in distributing royal favours evenly among the nobility. These concerns, combined with fears about Henry's personal stability (he suffered at least one breakdown and possibly suffered from schizophrenia), pushed the Duke of York to challenge him for the crown. Henry VI was deposed in 1461 and the Yorkist Edward IV became king. He was then deposed in 1470 and Henry was restored, only to be killed a year later; Edward then reigned until his own death in 1483. The conflict was known as the Wars of the Roses because the House of Lancaster used a red rose as a symbol whilst the House of York used a white rose.

REGENT

If an heir to the throne succeeded under the age of 18, a close relative or supporter was chosen to govern on his behalf as regent. During the Tudor period there was a very short regency for Henry VIII who was 17 when his father died, and a longer ral in future. In effe

Henry's early life was filled with instability, caused by the fact that he was related to the Lancastrian kings at a time when their deadly rival, the House of York, was fighting them for the throne in the **Wars of the Roses**. Henry was brought up at Pembroke Castle in Wales, well away from the centre of political activity, but the seizure of power by the Yorkists under their young king Edward IV in 1461 affected his upbringing and future. The castle was placed under the control of a Yorkist nobleman, Lord Herbert, who was also made responsible for raising Henry. Henry's lands were removed from him and placed under the control of the Duke of Gloucester, later to become Richard III.

In 1470 the political situation shifted and the Yorkists lost power after a rebellion by Lancastrian nobles. Lord Herbert was executed and the future of the 13-year-old Henry seemed brighter now that his relatives were back in control. However, the Yorkists had only suffered a setback, not a defeat, and Edward IV recovered the crown in 1471, killing the Lancastrian king Henry VI and his son in a decisive battle at Tewkesbury. These two deaths radically altered the position of Henry Tudor, because he was now the main surviving Lancastrian claimant to the throne. His uncle, Jasper Tudor, realised that Henry's life might be in danger. He therefore took his 14-year-old nephew to Brittany, where he was protected from English attempts to bring about his return by Duke Francis, ruler of the semi-independent French province.

While Edward IV lived, these efforts were not pursued vigorously, but in 1483 he died and the throne passed to his son Edward V. At 12 years old, Edward V was too young to rule alone, so his uncle Richard of Gloucester acted as **regent**. From this position of power the ambitious Richard soon had his nephew removed and kept in the Tower of London together with Edward's younger brother. Both princes died shortly afterwards in mysterious circumstances; they were probably murdered on the orders of Richard. However, the fate of the princes was never revealed – something that was to cause significant problems for Henry in the future. Noblemen who were alarmed at Richard III's brutal seizure of power and his promotion of northerners to important positions of power began to make contact with the exiled Henry Tudor. They planned to bring peace to the country by encouraging a marriage between Henry and Edward IV's daughter Elizabeth of York, uniting the warring houses of Lancaster and York.

Although these plans fell through for the time being, they certainly interested Henry and placed him in great danger from Richard. The threat was revealed when he was warned of a plot to force the Duke of Brittany to hand him over to Richard's agents. Henry fled to the French king's court in Paris, where he gathered a growing number of English supporters. With help from King Charles

VIII of France he was able to gather an invasion force and set sail for England in 1485. Within a month of landing, he had taken the crown from Richard's corpse.

b) The English Monarchy in 1485

ISSUES:
What problems faced Henry when he became king in 1485? What factors helped him to hold on to the crown?

Taking the crown from Richard did not end the difficulties facing Henry VII. Keeping it on his own head was likely to prove extremely challenging, and the omens were not good. As the story of Henry's early life shows, English politics in the later fifteenth century had been dominated by the struggle between the rival families of Lancaster and York for the throne. In the midst of their battles, which had raged on and off since 1455, the status and authority of the monarchy had suffered.

Henry's seizure of the crown in 1485 could be seen by contemporaries as just another example of the instability of the times, similar to the actions of Edward IV in 1461 or Richard III in 1483, and not necessarily the point at which the monarchy became more stable. Henry's own claim to the throne was weak. Although he had won the crown by right of conquest this was not sufficient to guarantee him loyalty across the kingdom unless he could enforce it further. Although Richard and his nephews in the Tower were dead, the House of York lived on through the de la Pole brothers, who had a claim to the crown at least as valid as Henry's own, and Edward IV's sister, Margaret, who was married to the Duke of Burgundy. She quickly showed her willingness to use the resources of her husband's duchy for the Yorkist cause.

None the less, Henry possessed some advantages. Although the disputes between the Lancastrians and Yorkists had encouraged lawlessness and crime, their wars also meant that members of the greater nobility were engaged in mutual destruction. The death of many noble heirs had allowed their lands to be returned to the crown, whilst the misfortune of being on the losing side had allowed others to be punished and disinherited as traitors. Those beneath the warring great houses – the gentry, merchants and landowning farmers – were tired of the disruption that a generation of sudden changes in political power had brought, and were ready to support the recovery of royal power as the best means of restoring order and prosperity.

Henry also had some personal advantages. He was an adult and had recently proven himself both as a leader and as a soldier. These were admirable qualities and were likely to lessen opposition to his claim to the crown. He was an only child, with no fear of the family rivalry that had shaped events when Edward IV had died. His obscure Welsh origins and years of exile in France also helped because they meant that he had few personal enemies in high places. Whilst none of these factors was sufficient on its own to guarantee success, they provided Henry with the opportunity to build on the power that he had won, if he had the political skill to take it. His objectives were therefore clear:

▼ to establish his claim to the throne and to secure his immediate future;
▼ to eliminate possible rivals by force or by agreement;
▼ to strengthen the monarchy and the kingdom for the future.

In the following sections we will examine each of these aims in turn.

CORONATION

The coronation of a monarch was more than simply a public ceremony to confirm his or her power; it signified the approval of the church and, through this, of God himself. In feudal law the coronation required the nobility to swear an oath of loyalty which could not be broken, and since Anglo-Saxon times the ceremony had conferred a divine status that transformed rebellion into a sin against God as well as a crime against the state. The speed of Henry's coronation was therefore a safety measure as well as a symbol that he claimed the crown as legitimate heir, not just through battle.

How did Henry treat his friends and enemies?

3 Securing the Throne

After the Battle of Bosworth Field, Henry moved quickly to legitimise his claims by being officially crowned as king and by marrying Elizabeth of York. He was careful to ensure that his **coronation** in October 1485 came before his marriage in January 1486, so that no one could say that he had gained the throne through his wife. The marriage, however, was an essential part of his strategy to win support. Elizabeth was the daughter of Edward IV so the union symbolised the reconciliation between the families of Lancaster and York. Elizabeth soon gave birth to a son, Prince Arthur, in September 1486. This helped to establish a future for the new Tudor dynasty, creating a greater sense of permanence about the change that had taken place in 1485. To cement his power further, Henry summoned Parliament (the traditional act of a new king) in November 1485 and embarked on a royal progress to the north in April 1486. The progress was essentially a tour of the kingdom by the monarch and his court. During the progress it was traditional for the king to hear petitions and cases and to grant justice and favours. In this way, he could demonstrate his royal power and presence to his subjects.

Henry displayed the same kind of tactical and political awareness in his handling of the nobility after his victory. His supporters were well rewarded. John de Vere, who had joined him in France, became Earl of Oxford. Lord Stanley was honoured for deserting Richard at Bosworth with the title Earl of Derby and the hand of Henry's mother in marriage. This gave Henry two loyal supporters in the east Midlands and the north-west. His uncle, Jasper Tudor (now Duke of Bedford) represented royal authority in Wales. Other supporters were rewarded with high office. Sir William Stanley became Lord Chamberlain. John Morton (see Profile) became Lord Chancellor from 1486 to 1500 and later Archbishop of Canterbury and a cardinal. Henry's ability to attract and maintain the loyalty of talented men such as these, and his willingness to reward them with recognition and power, were key elements in the stability of his government.

JOHN MORTON
(1420–1500)

Morton was born in 1420 and supported the Lancastrians until disaster befell Henry VI at the Battle of Tewkesbury in 1471. He then shrewdly switched sides and became a strong ally of Edward IV. He joined the Royal Council in 1473 and was appointed Bishop of Ely in 1479. However, when Richard III seized the throne Morton was one of the men who resisted him. His activities during Richard's reign marked him out as a true friend of Henry Tudor's. He warned Henry of Richard's attempt to arrest and remove him from Brittany in 1485, giving the future king time to escape to the French court. He also voiced his criticism of Richard's government and solicited support for Henry from discontented Yorkist nobles.

Morton was 65 when Henry took the throne – nearly 40 years older than the king. Despite the age difference, Henry regarded him as a close friend and ally. He appointed Morton as lord chancellor (the closest post to being chief minister at the time) and in 1486 he became Archbishop of Canterbury, the most senior religious office in England and Wales. In 1493 the Pope made him a **cardinal**.

Morton was an effective servant of the crown, showing his strengths particularly in financial matters. He was active in encouraging the nobility to offer 'loans' to the crown and gained a reputation for not taking 'no' for an answer. One story about him concerns the tactic he used to force everyone to hand over money – nicknamed 'Morton's Fork'. The 'fork' was a dilemma that he exploited – if a nobleman appeared rich because he was dressed expensively, Morton argued that he was well-off enough to make a loan to his master. If he appeared to be poorer and struggling, Morton argued that this was because he was hoarding his money like a miser, so he could still afford to make a loan. Either way, the nobleman could not escape.

-Profile-

1420	born;
1471	switched support to Yorkists after death of Henry VI;
1473	joined Edwards IV's Royal Council;
1479	appointed Bishop of Ely;
1485	warned Henry of Richard III's plot to arrest him;
1486	became Archbishop of Canterbury;
1493	appointed cardinal;
1500	died, aged 80.

CARDINAL

A cardinal is one of the senior officials of the Roman Catholic Church, having the right to vote in the election of a Pope. Cardinals were appointed by the Pope, but the approval of the monarch was also required. In return for wealth, status and the protection of its privileges, the church provided monarchs with an educated force of trained administrators and a cheap way of rewarding those who served them well.

Henry's handling of his opponents was also carefully balanced. He dated his reign from 21 August, the day before the battle at Bosworth, which allowed him to treat Richard's supporters as traitors. He imprisoned Yorkists with a better claim to the throne than his own, such as William de la Pole and the young Earl of Warwick, in the Tower of London and left them there. Nobles whose loyalty was suspect were stripped of their lands and titles, but Henry was shrewd enough to realise that by showing leniency he would win at least the gratitude, and possibly the loyalty, of key families.

The fate of the Percy family, whose head was the Earl of Northumberland, is a good example of this approach. Northumberland had been present at Bosworth, but he had not taken part. His family held significant lands in the north, an unruly region where royal authority had been traditionally weak. More importantly, Northumberland's lands were close to the Scottish border, and Scotland was an independent kingdom which might harbour Henry's enemies. The earl was imprisoned shortly after Henry was crowned king, but he was released in December 1485 and restored to his lands and titles. However, Henry insisted that the earl's son should be brought up at court, where a close royal eye could be kept on his progress. When the earl died (defending Henry's interests in a tax rebellion in 1489), the king did not release his son, but sent an outsider – the Earl of Surrey – into the north to govern for him. He finally allowed the heir to the earldom to return to his family lands in 1499, when the threat from rivals to the throne had subsided.

ACTIVITY

Based on what you have read in this section about Henry's methods of securing his crown, write a brief character sketch of the king, as he might have seemed to his subjects at the time. Would Henry have appeared ruthless? merciful? powerful? indecisive? moderate?

ISSUE:

What threats to his right to rule did Henry face between 1485 and 1500?

4 Defeating Rivals

It is very easy to believe that, because Henry survived as king, the threats to him were more imaginary than real. However, he had grown up in uncertain times and had been isolated from the people he now depended on to help him govern the country. He was king only by virtue of conquest; others lived with a better right to be monarch than he did. There was no doubt that he had enemies and that they were waiting to strike.

Although Henry worked hard during his first years as king to establish his claim to rule, he still faced opposition from the remnants of the House of York and its supporters. Between 1486 and 1499 his political enemies at home (the Yorkist de la Pole family) and abroad (Edward IV's sister, Margaret of Burgundy) remained a serious danger to Henry. There was also discontent within some regions of the country at the financial demands the king was making, provoking rebellions at inconvenient times. Figure 13 summarises the different threats to Henry's crown before 1500.

The main threat that his enemies posed came from their support for 'pretenders' to the crown – boys who were set up either as one of Edward IV's sons (who had been murdered in 1483, but whose bodies had never been revealed to the public) or as the imprisoned Earl of Warwick. These pretenders challenged Henry's claim to the throne and attracted dissatisfied nobles and foreign rulers wanting to undermine or be rid of him altogether.

REBELLIONS AGAINST HENRY VII

1486 Lovell rebellion, by supporters of the House of York;

1487 Simnel rebellion and the Battle of Stoke;

1489 Yorkshire rebellion against tax rises;

1491 first appearance of Perkin Warbeck;

1495 Warbeck landed at Deal in Kent;

1496 –7 Warbeck raided northern England from Scotland;

1497 Cornish rebellion against high taxes;

1498 Warbeck imprisoned in the Tower;

1499 Warbeck and the Earl of Warwick executed;

1502 Edmund de la Pole (Earl of Suffolk) fled to the Netherlands, but was returned;

1513 Suffolk executed by Henry VIII.

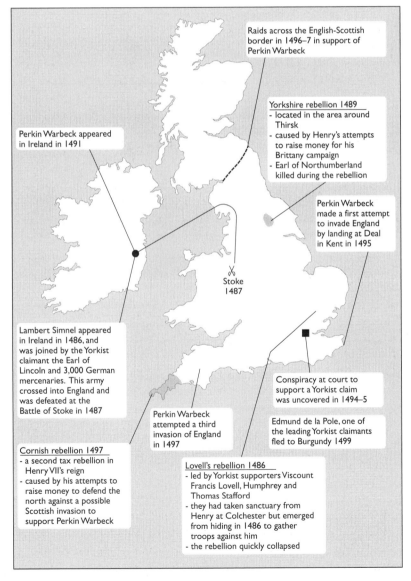

Raids across the English-Scottish border in 1496–7 in support of Perkin Warbeck

Yorkshire rebellion 1489
- located in the area around Thirsk
- caused by Henry's attempts to raise money for his Brittany campaign
- Earl of Northumberland killed during the rebellion

Perkin Warbeck appeared in Ireland in 1491

Perkin Warbeck made a first attempt to invade England by landing at Deal in Kent in 1495

Stoke 1487

Lambert Simnel appeared in Ireland in 1486, and was joined by the Yorkist claimant the Earl of Lincoln and 3,000 German mercenaries. This army crossed into England and was defeated at the Battle of Stoke in 1487

Conspiracy at court to support a Yorkist claim was uncovered in 1494–5

Perkin Warbeck attempted a third invasion of England in 1497

Edmund de la Pole, one of the leading Yorkist claimants fled to Burgundy 1499

Cornish rebellion 1497
- a second tax rebellion in Henry VII's reign
- caused by his attempts to raise money to defend the north against a possible Scottish invasion to support Perkin Warbeck

Lovell's rebellion 1486
- led by Yorkist supporters Viscount Francis Lovell, Humphrey and Thomas Stafford
- they had taken sanctuary from Henry at Colchester but emerged from hiding in 1486 to gather troops against him
- the rebellion quickly collapsed

Figure 13 England and Ireland, showing the location and events of the rebellions of 1486–99.

-Profile-

LAMBERT SIMNEL
(1475?–1525)

1475? born, son of Thomas Simnel of Oxford;

1486 Richard Symonds began to use him in Yorkist plot against Henry VII;

1487 crowned 'King Edward VI' in Dublin; landed in England with an army, but defeated at Battle of Stoke; pardoned by Henry;

1525 last recorded mention of Simnel (by now a royal falconer).

Lambert Simnel was born in Oxford, where at the age of ten or eleven his marked resemblance to the younger son of Edward IV was spotted by his teacher, a priest named Richard Symonds. Symonds taught Simnel to claim that he was Richard, Duke of York, and took him to Ireland, which had become a centre of Yorkist support. There, Symonds seems to have decided that it would be more effective to pass Simnel off as the young Earl of Warwick (who was in the Tower of London at the time), and with the help of Yorkist lords like the Earl of Kildare, Simnel was proclaimed King Edward VI.

This plot was amateurish at best, because Henry immediately produced the real Earl of Warwick to demonstrate the falseness of Simnel's claims. What made it more dangerous was the support offered by Margaret of Burgundy in the form of 2000 German mercenaries, and the flight of John de la Pole, the Earl of Lincoln, to join the rebels. Lincoln must have known that Simnel was an impostor, and may have intended to use him to further his own claims.

Simnel's arrival in Ireland in the company of the German mercenaries was the signal for the start of an invasion of England in May 1487. They landed at Furness in Lancashire and marched across the Pennines before turning south, but raised little support in the north, which had only recently seen the fighting of the Wars of the Roses. Henry met them with his army at East Stoke, just outside Newark, and the rebels were defeated in what historians have termed the last battle of the Wars of the Roses. Lincoln and several Yorkist leaders were killed, and Henry showed his ability to judge the nature of his enemies by sparing Simnel and offering him work in the royal kitchens. Symonds was also arrested, but escaped death because of his status as a priest. Henry's real enemies – Kildare, Margaret and the other Yorkists – lived to fight another day.

PERKIN WARBECK
(1474?–1499)

Perkin Warbeck first appeared as a threat to Henry in Ireland in 1491. Aged 17 at the time, he was employed as a servant but claimed that he was Richard of York, the youngest son of Edward IV. Warbeck later admitted that his real name was John Osbeck, and that he was born in Tournai and educated in Antwerp. His Burgundian origins and his appearance in Ireland suggest that the instigators of Simnel's rebellion, particularly Margaret of Burgundy and the Earl of Kildare, were involved at an early stage, but it was Charles VIII of France who first recognised his claims and welcomed him at Court in Paris. Charles was probably using Warbeck to embarrass Henry and to divert him whilst he attempted to annex Brittany (see pages 59–60).

In 1492, Charles made peace with Henry so Warbeck was forced to move on to Burgundy, where he was welcomed by Margaret and her son-in-law, the Holy Roman Emperor Maximilian I. However, Maximilian was too busy with affairs in Italy to offer much immediate support. This gave Henry a breathing space to deal with the English end of the conspiracy. A number of leading figures, including Sir William Stanley were accused and executed for treason in 1495. So, when Warbeck landed in Kent in July 1495, he failed to rouse support and had to sail north to Scotland. There, he was befriended by King James IV, who may have been convinced that Warbeck was genuine, since he granted him an income of £1,200 per year and his own cousin in marriage.

However, James's attempt to invade England on Warbeck's behalf in 1497 was a disaster. Warbeck was horrified by the brutish behaviour of the Scottish troops in raiding the northern borderlands of England and refused to travel further south with them. When Henry offered James a truce, Warbeck fled to Ireland. By now he was running out of support, and gave himself up in August 1497, making a full confession of who he really was. Since this achieved what Henry wanted, the King exercised calculated mercy and allowed Warbeck to remain at Court, but in 1498 Warbeck ran away and was imprisoned in the Tower upon recapture. There, he was involved in plotting to escape with the young Earl of Warwick, and both were executed in 1499. Whether this plot was genuine, or encouraged by the King's agents, it allowed Henry finally to dispose of two troublesome individuals.

1474?	born, son of a Burgundian customs officer;
1491	appeared at French court, claiming to be Richard IV;
1492	sent to Burgundy, where his claim was recognised by Margaret of Burgundy;
1495	first attempt at invasion failed; travelled to Scotland;
1497	second attempted invasion of England; fled to Ireland but gave himself up;
1498	fled court but recaptured and imprisoned in Tower;
1499	executed on charges of treason.

ACTIVITY

The threat of the 'pretenders' is an important element in the reign of Henry VII and one that you should research carefully. Rather than take each threat separately in the examination, you might want to save time by *generalising* about them – that is, making points which are relevant to both. To do this, you will need to compare the stories of Simnel and Warbeck first. Re-read the Profiles and list similarities and differences between the information presented about each. To help, look for the following points:

▼ who they claimed to be
▼ who supported their claim
▼ what international help was offered
▼ how each tried to undermine Henry
▼ Henry's treatment of the pretender.

Once you have compiled your notes, think about whether they give you clues about the seriousness of the threat posed by the pretenders, and compare your ideas to those below.

Q

How serious a threat did the pretenders pose to Henry VII's crown?

Although neither Lambert Simnel nor Perkin Warbeck was a genuine contender for the throne, they posed a real threat because they were used by the Yorkists to question Henry's right to rule and to draw loyalty away from him at a time when he was still new to kingship. The weakness of his claim to the throne and the recent history of sudden changes of monarch made him vulnerable to attack; a victorious rival would soon have been able to justify seizing the throne from someone who had, himself, come to it through battle. Henry's marriage to Elizabeth of York and the birth of an heir had divided Yorkist loyalties, but widows could be remarried and baby princes controlled by their guardians.

On balance, the only effective obstacles to Yorkist success in the early years of Henry's reign were a certain war-weariness that favoured the occupant of the throne, and the skills and abilities exercised by Henry himself. Fortunately for Henry, his skills were up to the task. He placed key Yorkists under arrest and used spies and informers to keep track of what his more distant enemies like the Earl of Kildare were doing. Once the Simnel rebellion had been defeated at Stoke in June 1487 he made an important gesture towards the Yorkists by having Elizabeth crowned queen in November. It is noticeable that when Warbeck appeared, his support was principally from outside England and his two attempts to invade both failed miserably. By isolating Warbeck through agreements with his fellow European rulers, Henry gradually cut off the support he was receiving. At the same time, he was prepared to be generous to Warbeck himself until the young man betrayed his trust. A more cynical view is that Henry was in sufficient control of the situation to use the Warbeck crisis both to root out potential enemies at court in the purge of 1495 and to provide the excuse finally to get rid of the Earl of Warwick in 1499.

ACTIVITY

The comments in the paragraph above are important if you are to analyse the importance of the threat to Henry posed by the pretenders. In your notes, you need to adopt a balanced approach, showing that, on the one hand, there was a real danger but that, on the other, neither pretender ever came close to victory.

Perhaps the best way to organise this sort of analysis would be to draw a table like the one started for you here. If you organise the points carefully, you will be able to match an argument on one side with a counter-argument on the other, as the first point in the table shows.

Simnel and Warbeck: a real threat	Simnel and Warbeck: only a nuisance
1. Simnel's threat arose within two years of Henry becoming king, so was at a point when Henry was still trying to establish his right to rule in his subjects' minds.	1. By the time of Simnel's challenge, Henry already done much to establish himself as the rightful king. Members of the nobility and landowning class who might have supported Simnel were either controlled by Henry's policy of 'calculated mercy' or tired of war and instability.
2. Warbeck was given protection by the rulers of other European countries – France, Burgundy, Scotland.	2.
3.	3. Henry was prepared to show leniency to both Simnel and Warbeck. He recognised that it was restless nobles, not the pretenders themselves, who were the problem.

ISSUE:
What problems did Henry need to solve to ensure his effective government over England?

5 Strengthening Royal Government

If Henry and his family were to achieve genuine security it was not enough to defeat rivals and pretenders. It was also essential to strengthen the power and effectiveness of the monarchy as an institution so that he could build the support and resources needed to ward off any further shocks. Once again, this would not be an easy task. Government by 1485 was well organised, but had come perilously close to collapse on a number of occasions during the fifteenth century. Because of this, the actual authority that it had over the people of England – and, more importantly, the nobility – was questionable. The particular problems facing Henry were:

▼ nobles whose wealth and territorial power made them potential rivals to the crown

▼ the poor finances of the crown, which had been depleted by wars at home and abroad

▼ the uneven control that the crown had over the kingdom, stronger in the more populated areas of the south and east, but looser in the borderlands

▼ how foreign rulers would react to his seizure of power.

Henry had no master-plan to tackle these problems. His solutions, which we will examine below, were often reactions to situations as they arose. However, Henry was determined to manage government by himself (look back at Francis Bacon's comment about his style of kingship on page 37) rather than to delegate too much power to advisers. His natural suspicion and anxieties about rivals forced him to act firmly, and, on occasion, to take harsh measures. This gave Henry a poor reputation. A visitor to England from Florence summed this up well when he said that Henry was 'more feared than loved'.

a) The Nobility

ISSUES:
How did Henry control the actions of his nobles?
Was he 'anti-nobility'?

Q

Why do you think Henry generally regarded his nobles as a threat to be controlled rather than as allies to be rewarded?

Henry's biggest challenge was to win the support of the nobility whilst at the same time making sure that their power and arrogance were controlled. There were two obvious lines that he could take with them: either to buy their support by rewarding them with lands and titles, or to force them to support him by showing them the unwelcome consequences of opposition. Although Henry used the first approach on occasion, he was more inclined to the second.

Henry's relationship with his leading nobles was critical to his survival as king. He depended on them to maintain law and order in the areas where they held land and estates. However, the nobility had grown powerful during the fifteenth century, gaining more lands at the expense of the crown. Their large estates generated income from rents and leases which some had used to build impressive strongholds and to recruit and retain private armies. Henry was fortunate in 1485 that his victory had been so decisive and that a series of deaths in the 1480s meant that key families, such as the houses of Warwick, Northumberland and Buckingham, were now headed by children.

Henry VII used a number of different policies to reduce his dependence on the nobility and to limit their power. The nobility depended upon three factors – land, wealth and support – to maintain their independence from the king. Henry stripped away all three during his reign, whilst being careful not to push them into open rebellion.

i) Attainders

From the start of his reign Henry used attainders to seize the titles and possessions of nobles he suspected of disloyalty. Attainders were special laws passed by Parliament which allowed someone to be declared guilty of treason without going through the process of a trial. Henry asked his first Parliament to issue attainders against men who had opposed him at the Battle of Bosworth, and resorted to using them periodically during his reign. As with other policies, Henry was often prepared to reverse an attainder and restore lands and titles if he thought that would secure the gratitude and future loyalty of the victim.

ii) Patronage

Henry largely abandoned Edward IV's policy of distributing lands to loyal followers. There were some grants at the beginning of the reign (see page 37), but Henry was concerned not to create a new group of nobles who could rise to become a potential threat. The result of his caution was that the number of people who could be described as nobles fell by about one-quarter during his reign through deaths and attainders. Vacant lands were absorbed into Henry's personal domains, making him by far the largest landowner in the country. Often, when Henry needed royal agents in local communities, he looked to men lower down the social scale who did not have extensive lands in the area. These men were therefore dependent on him for the position and status they held and were not distracted by competing loyalties.

iii) Attacks on Retaining

Retaining was the practice by which a nobleman kept a large number of men as his personal staff, to be used in theory as household servants, but in practice as gangs of enforcers. Retainers could be used to put pressure on tenants who were slow in paying their rent, or on juries to return the verdict their master wanted. Henry, like Edward IV before him, rightly regarded them as a lawless element. New laws were passed in 1487 and 1504 against illegal retaining. The 1504 Act required nobles to obtain a special licence from the king before they could retain

Figure 14 Henry VII conferring with Dudley and Empson of the Council Learned in Law.

large numbers of men, and imposed severe fines if they did not. The ideas behind the law were sound, but the problem had gone on for too long to be settled so easily. Nobles found ways to avoid getting a licence, for example by covering up records of the wages they paid to servants so that no one knew exactly how many men were being retained.

iv) Financial Controls

Another of Henry's devices was to demand a financial bond from individual nobles or their families. This would place the noble in debt to the crown so that he would remain loyal in future. In effect, Henry forced nobles to agree to behave themselves or face a ruinous fine. It was a widely used policy – in Henry's last decade as king about two-thirds of the nobility were held under bonds.

The most extreme example was Lord Burgavenny. He was convicted in 1507 of illegally retaining 471 men and fined £70,000. Henry knew that paying this amount would bankrupt the lord, so he generously agreed to place him under a bond to repay £5,000 over ten years. The conditions attached to this included an instruction that Burgavenny should not set foot on his family lands in the southeast until the debt was settled. In this way, Henry both raised money from someone he did not trust and obliged him to keep in the king's favour or risk ruin. To enforce these rights, Henry established the **Council Learned in Law** to act as a royal debt collector.

THE COUNCIL LEARNED IN LAW

An offshoot from the main Royal Council which dealt initially with managing and pursuing the king's feudal rights but soon assumed control of all financial matters relating to crown lands. All the members of the council had legal training (hence the name) and acted both as investigators and judges in cases where there was suspicion that a nobleman was not paying his proper dues to the king. As a result, the council and its leading figures – Sir Reginald Bray to 1503, then Edmund Dudley and Richard Empson – were universally hated and feared.

b) Local and Regional Government

Effective government depended on having a reliable network of officials throughout the country to carry out the king's laws. Particular parts of the country, especially those most distant from London, were notoriously difficult to control except by relying on the presence of the local nobility. Elsewhere, in the more settled regions, earlier kings had built up the numbers and powers of Justices of the Peace. Since royal control over the kingdom was so uneven from place to place, Henry did not attempt to create one system of local government but relied instead on the most appropriate solution for each region, as Figure 15 illustrates.

c) National Government

Fifteenth-century government was, in effect, personal government by the king and his advisers at court. Parliament existed, but had a minor role in political life – mainly to pass laws that the king wanted and to vote him additional taxes. Parliament met infrequently and usually not for more than a few weeks or months at a time. For most of the time, the king ruled directly through decrees and proclamations. Henry kept things this way. He used Parliament sparingly, often during his first decade as king to support him in controversial policies such as limitations on the traditional privileges of the nobility or new financial demands on his subjects, but he usually ignored it.

Of more importance to Henry were the committees and law courts within his government. Chief among these was the Royal Council. It was the place where Henry gathered together his most trusted supporters to give him advice and to take on some of the tasks of day-to-day management of the kingdom. Although records from Henry's reign list 227 men as members of the council, in practice regular membership was much smaller and included John Morton and Reginald Bray.

ISSUE:
How did Henry try to extend his royal authority into the English and Welsh regions?

ISSUE:
How did Henry take decisions?

Figure 15 Local and regional government in England and Wales under Henry VII.

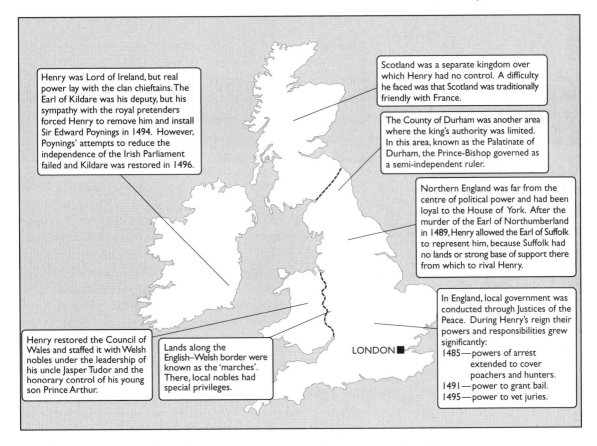

Henry was Lord of Ireland, but real power lay with the clan chieftains. The Earl of Kildare was his deputy, but his sympathy with the royal pretenders forced Henry to remove him and install Sir Edward Poynings in 1494. However, Poynings' attempts to reduce the independence of the Irish Parliament failed and Kildare was restored in 1496.

Scotland was a separate kingdom over which Henry had no control. A difficulty he faced was that Scotland was traditionally friendly with France.

The County of Durham was another area where the king's authority was limited. In this area, known as the Palatinate of Durham, the Prince-Bishop governed as a semi-independent ruler.

Northern England was far from the centre of political power and had been loyal to the House of York. After the murder of the Earl of Northumberland in 1489, Henry allowed the Earl of Suffolk to represent him, because Suffolk had no lands or strong base of support there from which to rival Henry.

In England, local government was conducted through Justices of the Peace. During Henry's reign their powers and responsibilities grew significantly:
1485—powers of arrest extended to cover poachers and hunters.
1491—power to grant bail.
1495—power to vet juries.

LONDON

Henry restored the Council of Wales and staffed it with Welsh nobles under the leadership of his uncle Jasper Tudor and the honorary control of his young son Prince Arthur.

Lands along the English–Welsh border were known as the 'marches'. There, local nobles had special privileges.

Star Chamber

Historians have debated the importance of this court of law in Henry's methods of controlling his leading subjects. It was created by the Star Chamber Act in 1487 and was responsible for prosecuting anyone who behaved in a rebellious or lawless manner. Members of the Royal Council – the king's most favoured advisers – sat on the court to make these judgments, so it was possible to haul even the greatest nobleman before it. However, some writers argue that Henry made little use of Star Chamber during his reign, preferring instead to control unruly subjects by financial and other means.

> A decree made to confirm an order taken by the Mayor and commons of Plymouth for the expulsion of Nicholas Lowe and Alice his wife, out of Plymouth for their misdemeanours and evil living in the keeping of brothels, night watching beyond reasonable hours, maintaining and keeping dicers, carders, gamblers and other misgoverned and evilly disposed persons. And Sir John Croke, knight, and his sons and servants, by the same decree, ordered not to maintain or uphold the said case against the Mayor and commons. And for having done so up to the present, they are ordered to keep the peace upon pain of a fine of £200.
>
> **Source D** A judgment made by the council in Star Chamber, 6 May 1494.

The council met when the king needed it and there were no written rules governing its procedure. During Henry's reign the key development was the emergence of committees of the council to deal with specific matters of policy. As we have already seen, the Council Learned in Law and the **Star Chamber** were two such committees.

ISSUES:

How did the crown raise money?

How did Henry improve the administration of his finances?

d) Financial Management

Henry VII has gained a reputation for having a keen financial mind, so historians have tended to look at his policies in this area with special interest. By the end of his reign he had ensured that the crown had built up enough annual income to meet its commitments, and that money was carefully accounted for. In part, Henry achieved this by taking a more direct personal interest in the state of national finances. Finding that departments of state such as the Treasury and the Exchequer were clumsy and inefficient, he followed Edward IV's example by dealing with the administration of finance from his private rooms in the palace – the Chamber and Privy Chamber. He also established a new post of Surveyor of the King's Wards to investigate cases of money owed to him from wardships (see Table 3 for more information), and a Court of Audit to monitor government spending. As well as these institutional reforms, Henry also improved and developed the sources of his income.

Table 3 The sources of royal income under Henry VII.

Source of income	Organisation / administration	Improvements / developments under Henry VII
Ordinary revenue		
Crown lands Henry inherited all the lands held by the Houses of York and Lancaster, the Earldoms of Richmond and Warwick, the Duchy of Lancaster and the Principality of Wales. These were further increased by attainders (51 in one Parliament alone) and *escheats* – the reversion of land to the king if a tenant died without an heir.	Edward IV had improved the administration of crown lands by introducing techniques of estate management. Sir Reginald Bray developed these further in the Duchy of Lancaster then applied them to other lands. Henry was less inclined to grant lands to friends and family than Edward. He preferred to hold on to them to maximise both his influence and his income from leases and rents.	In 1486 Henry used the Act of Resumption to reclaim all crown lands that had been granted away since the start of the Wars of the Roses, but he did not always act on these claims. The potential threat to a noble family could be more useful to control them than actually pressing the demand for return of land to him.
Feudal dues Traditional rights held by the crown to demand money, deriving from the principle that the king was the sole owner of all the kingdom's land and that others held it as his tenants.	The main types of payments that the king could demand from the nobility were: *Relief* – paid by an heir when he received his inheritance *Marriage* – the king's right to arrange marriages for the daughters of tenants at a profit *Wardship* – control of the estates of heirs under adult age allowed the king to manage these lands for his own profit *Livery* – payment made by a ward on reaching adulthood and taking control of his lands.	Henry exploited feudal payments for both financial and political purposes. He used them to ensure good behaviour, but also benefited from wardships in certain powerful families, for example when the Earl of Northumberland was killed in 1489 leaving a ten-year-old son. Henry also improved the management of these revenues. For example, he appointed a Master of the King's Wards (Sir John Hussey) in 1503 to administer wardships. In 1487 his income from wardship and marriages was £350; by 1507 it had risen to £6,000 per year.
Customs duties Paid on goods entering or leaving the country. By the fifteenth century it was traditional practice for Parliament to grant these revenues to a monarch for life.	Money came mainly from tunnage (taxes on exports) and poundage (taxes on imports), particularly on the sale of wool, wine and leather. Both Edward and Henry tried to promote trade to maximise this type of income, and to close loopholes.	Henry largely continued the work and methods of Edward. He introduced certificates for coastal trade, and twice updated the Book of Rates, which set out the charges on imports and exports of a wide range of items. Customs duties rose from about £33,000 per year at the beginning of the reign to about £40,000 at the end.
Legal dues Money from fines and other payments made by people appearing before the king's courts.	Payments came from both common law courts and the special courts operated by the Royal Council.	Henry increased the use of fines and attainders. These could be very lucrative sources of income – the attainder of Sir William Stanley in 1495 brought an immediate payment of £9,000 and £1,000 per year thereafter.

Table 3 (continued)

Source of income	Organisation / administration	Improvements / developments under Henry VII
Extraordinary revenue		
Bonds and recognisances Payments made as a guarantee of good behaviour (see page 52).	Demanded from those whose loyalty was suspect, such as Yorkist supporters. Also applied to merchants who owed customs duties.	Used by Henry for both political and financial purposes. Payments could be substantial – the Earl of Westmorland had to pay £10,000 after the Battle of Bosworth – but it was also an effective way of maintaining control. Henry used a special government court – the Council Learned in Law – to enforce payment of these debts.
Loans and benevolences The king's right to ask for financial help in particular emergencies.	Organised by the Royal Council, loans could be requested from both individuals and institutions, such as town corporations.	The Council Learned in Law was also used to enforce these payments. This was an irregular source of income, raised as and when the king needed funds. In 1491, £48,000 was raised for war in Brittany, of which £9,000 was contributed by the City of London.
Feudal dues Based on the same claims as in ordinary revenue, but related to single, extraordinary occasions.	The king was entitled to gifts for special occasions, such as when one of his sons was knighted, or when a daughter married. Gifts were paid by leading nobles, but Parliament was also expected to make a grant on behalf of the people it represented.	Henry exploited this source of income fully – for example, he received £30,000 from Parliament in 1504 for the knighthood of Prince Arthur (who had died in 1502). He also increased his demands for payments from nobles who had tried to save money by being 'in distraint of knighthood', i.e. who had chosen not to take on the expense of becoming a knight.
Clerical taxes Special taxes which the king could levy on the church.	The clergy were exempt from paying taxes to Parliament, so this form of taxation was the only way of securing money from the church. It usually came in the form of a voluntary 'gift'.	Gifts from the church were similar in amount to those received by earlier rulers. Henry used his right to appoint leading churchmen to raise money by selling offices – he raised £300 for the post of Archdeacon of Buckingham for example. This practice, called 'simony', was forbidden by the church but widely practised.
Parliamentary taxes Special grants of taxes by Parliament to finance royal policies such as military action in Europe or Scotland.	Usually voted in the form of 'tenths' or 'fifteenths', taxes on the value of moveable property. Henry also tried a form of direct taxation, not unlike income tax, but it was widely resented and soon abandoned.	Parliamentary taxes were available when needed, but they were often unpopular, and triggered two rebellions (in Yorkshire in 1489 and Cornwall in 1497) in Henry's reign. He avoided parliamentary taxes as much as possible.

Henry's financial policies were cautious and realistic. He realised that foreign wars had been the single biggest reason for the poverty of earlier kings, so he largely avoided conducting an aggressive foreign policy. He exploited his legal rights to claim special payments from his nobles both to swell his treasury and to remind them of his control over them, but he was also prepared to overlook or to reverse his claims when it was necessary to win support.

To some writers, Henry was a miser, obsessed with hoarding more and more money from every source he could find. There is some truth in this, especially in the final decade of his reign. However, Henry always spent money extravagantly when it was necessary to enhance the image of his kingship. For instance, he maintained a lavish court and entertained foreign guests with good food and entertainments. Henry also used royal funds to patronise philosophers, writers and explorers.

ACTIVITY

The strengthening of royal finances is an important aspect of Henry's reign, and is often a subject for examination questions. To prepare your notes on this topic, research answers to the following questions:

1. What is meant by 'ordinary' and 'extraordinary' revenue? Which was most important to the day-to-day financing of government and which to funding special projects such as wars?
2. Why were royal finances in such poor shape at the beginning of Henry's reign?
3. Which sources of income did Henry increase most during his reign?
4. What opposition did Henry's policies encounter?
5. How did Henry strengthen the collection and administration of his revenues?
6. How wealthy was the crown by 1509?

---

6 Relations with Other Countries

ISSUE:
What considerations shaped Henry's relations with foreign powers?

Henry VII's foreign policy was dictated by two things: the circumstances surrounding his succession, and his lack of money. He had become king by killing Richard III, but his legal status was insecure. There were other claimants to the throne and England's recent history had been punctuated by struggles for the crown. In the first years of his reign, Henry's priority was to gain acceptance of his right to rule from other monarchs. This was important not only because rivals for his crown might seek shelter or assistance from other countries (as Henry had done in Brittany), but also because favourable words from a foreign ruler might give him more credibility at home.

KEY DATES IN FOREIGN RELATIONS, 1485–1502

1486 truces signed with Scotland and France; commercial treaty with Brittany; treaty of friendship with Emperor Maximilian;

1487 French truce extended;

1488 succession of 15-year-old James IV as King of Scotland; French attack on Brittany;

1489 Henry intervened to help Brittany remain independent; Treaty of Medina del Campo with Spain;

1491 Perkin Warbeck appeared in Ireland;

1492 resolution of the Breton Crisis in the Treaty of Etaples;

1493 trade embargo against Burgundy;

1496 'Magnus Intercursus' restored trade relations with Burgundy;

1497 Scottish invasion of northern England; Truce of Ayton;

1501 marriage of Prince Arthur to Catherine of Aragon.

Between 1485 and 1492 Henry built a series of truces with potentially dangerous neighbours: France in 1485, Scotland in 1486 and the Habsburg Empire (which included the Netherlands) in 1487. Henry also saw advantages in building a longer term alliance with Spain as an insurance policy against any future problems with France. In 1489, as part of the Treaty of Medina del Campo, both sides decided to work together to defend their lands and promised not to make agreements with France without consulting each other first. To deepen the alliance, arrangements were made for the marriage of Prince Arthur to the daughter of the Spanish monarchs. This treaty cemented an Anglo-Spanish friendship that was to last, despite some rocky moments, until the era of the Elizabethan Reformation.

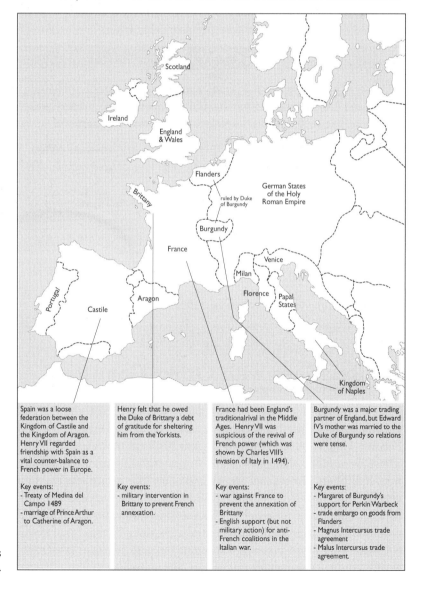

Figure 16 England's interests abroad, 1485–1509.

Spain was a loose federation between the Kingdom of Castile and the Kingdom of Aragon. Henry VII regarded friendship with Spain as a vital counter-balance to French power in Europe.

Key events:
- Treaty of Medina del Campo 1489
- marriage of Prince Arthur to Catherine of Aragon.

Henry felt that he owed the Duke of Brittany a debt of gratitude for sheltering him from the Yorkists.

Key events:
- military intervention in Brittany to prevent French annexation.

France had been England's traditional rival in the Middle Ages. Henry VII was suspicious of the revival of French power (which was shown by Charles VIII's invasion of Italy in 1494).

Key events:
- war against France to prevent the annexation of Brittany
- English support (but not military action) for anti-French coalitions in the Italian war.

Burgundy was a major trading partner of England, but Edward IV's mother was married to the Duke of Burgundy so relations were tense.

Key events:
- Margaret of Burgundy's support for Perkin Warbeck
- trade embargo on goods from Flanders
- Magnus Intercursus trade agreement
- Malus Intercursus trade agreement.

Relations with France were initially friendly because Henry's fight for the throne had been encouraged by the French court. However, he had also depended on Brittany for sanctuary during his 14-year exile. These debts put Henry in a difficult position when France moved to absorb Brittany between 1488 and 1492. He faced a serious problem because an accepted view of national security included the belief that the coastline across the Channel should not be held by just one power. If France gained control of Brittany the south coast of England would be in a militarily weaker position; Calais (the last surviving outpost of England's medieval empire in France) would be more vulnerable; and trade could be disrupted. These considerations made the 'Breton Crisis' of 1488–92 the major foreign policy problem of Henry's reign, and the only time he committed troops outside the British Isles.

a) The Breton Crisis

The way in which the crisis unfolded tells us much about Henry's aims and methods in foreign policy. He did not rush towards war because it would be dangerous to annoy France when pretenders to the throne were active and also because he lacked funds. Instead, Henry opened negotiations with France whilst at the same time secretly allowing English troops to cross to Brittany to help the Bretons repel the French army. When these manoeuvres failed, he tried to win support at home and abroad for a short campaign. The Treaty of Medina del Campo bought off Spain and Henry also approached the rulers of the Netherlands, some north German states and even the Pope for either assistance or at least their neutrality. Parliament was summoned to make a grant of £100,000 to finance a small force (estimates suggest between 3,000 and 6,000 men).

When this army crossed the Channel in April 1489 Henry made it clear to the French that he was only acting in the defence of Brittany; there was no intention to go further and reopen the longstanding English claims to French lands that had been the issue in the Hundred Years' War. These reassurances did not satisfy the French, who showed their displeasure by receiving the pretender Perkin Warbeck at court and by pouring more of their own troops into Brittany. In the final stages of the war, Henry took a great risk. He led a larger force of 12,000 troops into Brittany, gambling that France did not want a long conflict. He was right: France was beginning to take interest in the divisions within the Italian peninsula and wanted to be free of commitments elsewhere. Under the terms of the Treaty of Etaples (1492), Henry's army left France in return for a payment to cover the costs of the expedition and an agreement by the French king not to support Henry's enemies.

> **ISSUES:**
> What does the Breton Crisis reveal about Henry's approach to foreign policy?
> Was his handling of the problem successful?

At face value, the Breton Crisis had been a successful baptism of fire for Henry VII. Early in his reign, whilst still insecure at home, he had pursued a difficult diplomatic path with skill. England's basic friendship with France had remained intact; military intervention had been brief, and had not damaged England's reputation. Moreover, France had been persuaded to stop supporting pretenders to the throne and had made payments that offset the cost of the conflict. However, it must be remembered that England's armies did not win any of the main engagements in Brittany and at the end of the crisis the fact remained that Brittany was little more than a satellite of France (it was finally absorbed into the French state in 1532).

Henry VII and Scotland

Throughout this book you will find boxed sections dealing with Anglo-Scottish relations.

In the Tudor period Scotland was a distinct country, with its own Parliament and monarch. Relations between Scotland and England were usually strained. To preserve their independence, the Scots had looked to France for support, which created the uncomfortable situation for England of having potential enemies to both the north and the south. Henry VII was concerned that if James III of Scotland refused to accept him as King of England there could be problems in the north, where the Yorkists still had support. He quickly arranged a truce in 1486, but his efforts were ruined by James's death two years later. As you will see in other chapters, Scottish history in this period was to be punctuated by the sudden deaths of monarchs and the instability caused by long regencies. The nobles who governed on behalf of James IV were hostile to England and James himself showed a willingness to upset his southern neighbour by harbouring Perkin Warbeck between 1495 and 1497. Relations were improved by the Truce of Ayton in 1497 which matured into a formal peace treaty in 1502. In a significant move for the future, Henry's eldest daugher Margaret was married to James IV in 1503, apparently settling the ill-feeling between the two monarchs.

ISSUE:
Why did Henry's government become more severe in his final years?

7 The Last Decade: Security and Insecurity

By 1502 Henry seemed to have achieved most of his aims. He had established his dynasty, defeated key rivals, strengthened the institutions of government, put finances back on a sound footing and reduced his dependence on the nobility for support. Overall, England was better governed, more prosperous and more peaceful than at any time in the past 50 years. Nevertheless, when Henry died in 1509 his death was apparently greeted with relief and his son permitted a reaction against some of his father's ministers and policies.

The explanation for this change in Henry's fortunes can be found in two factors: first, a series of deaths that suddenly made his dynasty seem insecure; and, resulting from this, the increasingly harsh application of the financial and political measures that Henry used to maintain control.

a) Renewed Instability

By 1500, Henry had four children, including three sons (Arthur, Henry and Edmund). The prospect of a smooth succession to his eldest child Arthur, who was 14 at the time, seemed certain. However, a series of shocking events changed all that. In 1500 his youngest son, Edmund, died. This was followed in 1502 by the death of Arthur, and in early 1503 by the death of Henry's wife Elizabeth of York shortly after she had given birth to a daughter. This sequence of events clearly devastated Henry personally and politically. The loss of two sons left the future of the Tudor dynasty dependent on the life of Prince Henry, and Elizabeth's death robbed him of some Yorkist loyalty as well as the possibility of more children born from a union of Lancastrians and Yorkists. The renewed danger was highlighted by the departure of Edmund de la Pole, the Earl of Suffolk, to take refuge in Burgundy in 1503.

A further complication was the damage that the death of Arthur might do to relations with Spain. Henry was keen to remain on good terms with the Spanish monarchs, Ferdinand and Isabella, as they shared a common distrust of France. To secure this friendship, he had negotiated the marriage in 1501 of Prince Arthur to Catherine of Aragon, daughter of the Spanish monarchs. Arthur's death threatened to disrupt the close relationship that Henry had worked hard to achieve, but he was able to secure a new **royal marriage between Catherine and Prince Henry**. Because Catherine was marrying her husband's brother, Henry had to get special permission from the Pope but he felt that this was a small price to pay to protect the Anglo-Spanish alliance and to keep the money and gifts that she had brought with her to her first marriage.

> **THE PROBLEM OF THE ROYAL MARRIAGE**
> The issue of Catherine's marriages was to cause enormous problems in English politics during the 1520s and 1530s. The official position of the Catholic Church was that marriage between a man and his brother's widow was forbidden, but if there had been no sexual relations between the couple, then it was not a proper marriage so the restriction did not apply. According to Catherine, their youth (Arthur was 15 and she was 13 when they married), Arthur's poor health and the fact that they had only been married for five months before he died, all meant that she had remained a virgin, so was free to marry Prince Henry.

b) Harsh Policies

The sudden deaths of Henry's wife and two sons had exposed a weakness in the Tudor dynasty that its enemies might exploit. To prevent this, he seems to have spent his final years using the powers at his disposal to make certain that the nobility was not in a position to threaten him or his only surviving son. Earlier in his reign, Henry had exercised his powers flexibly. He had used punishments such as placing nobles under a bond or recognisance sparingly, often showing leniency or reversing a fine after a few years to win gratitude and loyalty. This skill of manipulating the powers at his disposal lay in using them just enough to maintain the threat of penalties for disloyalty or rewards for service, whilst not over-using them to the point where they created resentment and open opposition. In the last years of Henry's reign there is evidence that he got that balance wrong.

The most obvious source of resentment was the activity of the Council Learned in Law. This council was used by Henry, in conjunction with his other special courts such as Star Chamber, to maintain his feudal rights over his leading subjects. In 1493 bonds from the nobility brought in £3,000 in cash, although much more had been demanded and promised. In 1505 the equivalent sum was £35,000. To some extent this might have reflected a change of personnel – the death of Sir Reginald Bray led to the appointment of Sir Richard Empson as the Chancellor of the Duchy of Lancaster in 1504. None the less, there is evidence that royal demands were increased and enforced far more rigorously than in earlier years. Empson's partner Edmund Dudley confessed in 1509 that in at least 84 cases he had extracted money illegally. Since this information was revealed after he had been arrested by Henry VIII, it is difficult to know how accurate it is, because he might have been pressured into exaggerating the scale of his crimes. Allowing for this, it remains the case that the Council Learned in Law was conducting its activities in a way likely to cause resentment, and it is difficult to avoid the conclusion that Henry VII was aware of this.

▼ Working on The Establishment of the Tudor Monarchy

How historians have approached the topic

Traditional views of Henry VII's reign tended to be influenced by the image created by Francis Bacon and other writers of the period. For them, 1485 was the start of a new era of kingship. In the late nineteenth century this view was formalised by historians who described Henry's kingship as a 'new monarchy'. They saw his reign as an era in which Henry exercised a professional control over government, reforming financial and administrative systems to make them more efficient. It was also the moment at which the power of the great

Winning the Throne	1471	Death of Henry VI and his son advanced Henry's claim
	1471–85	Exile in Brittany
	1483	Supporters dissatisfied with Richard III's rule join Henry Support from King of France for an invasion of England
	1485 August	Battle of Bosworth Field – Richard III killed, Henry proclaimed king
Securing the Crown	1485 October November	Coronation First session of Parliament
	1485	Acts of Attainder against possible rivals
	1486 January April September	Marriage to Elizabeth of York Royal progress Birth of Prince Arthur
	1485–7	Truces with Scotland, France and the Holy Roman Empire
Rivalry and Opposition	1485	Imprisonment of Earl of Warwick
	1486–7	Simnel's rebellion
	1489	Yorkshire rebellion
	1491–2	Perkin Warbeck
	1491–2	Breton Crisis
	1492–6	Problems in Ireland
	1493–6	Trade difficulties with Burgundy
	1495	Conspiracy at court
	1497	Cornish rebellion
Strengthening Government	1485–1509	Attainders against the nobility Bonds and recognisances Star Chamber Council Learned in Law Chamber system of finances Strengthened role of JPs Regional solutions to the problem of royal control
The Last Decade	1500	Death of Prince Edmund
	1502	Death of Prince Arthur
	1503	Death of Elizabeth of York
	1504	Law against illegal retaining
	1500s	Increased use of financial penalties to control the nobility Unravelling of foreign diplomacy

Figure 17 Outline of events, 1485–1509.

noblemen was broken and Parliament pushed to one side, creating the conditions necessary to establish the powerful Tudor state. Such views were commonly accepted until the 1970s, when historians such as S. B. Chrimes (1972) pointed out the similarities between Henry's methods and those of the Yorkist king, Edward IV. The debate over whether Henry was a moderniser or simply maintained existing Yorkist practices goes on, but writers such as Alexander Grant (1985) have tried to find a middle way by suggesting that whilst there were similarities between Henry's methods and those of earlier kings, there were sufficient differences to regard his efforts as significant.

Research and Notemaking

The theme of this chapter has been 'new beginnings' – the succession and settling-in of a new king after a long period of uncertainty, and Henry's policies to establish an effective monarchy which was in control of the government and the country.

Within these new beginnings, a number of themes need to be noted:
▼ control over the nobility
▼ the improvement of royal finances
▼ the extension of royal power within government and the law
▼ relations between England her neighbours.

A good way to begin your review of the period 1485–1509 is to focus on these themes. You will find all of them covered by the timeline at the beginning of this section, so you could start either by colour-coding each event on it according to which theme it fits, or by copying the events into a table with a column for each theme (see pages 163–4 for an example of this sort of layout).

Once you have collected the facts together, you must then interpret them. For each theme, try to decide:
▼ in what ways Henry VII was successful
▼ how successes in one area helped in others
▼ whether there were any failures or limitations.

This should help you to reach the point where you can come to a judgement about Henry's overall achievement.

Even if you are studying the reign of Henry VII only for your course, you should not forget to look at events immediately after his death, because these reveal something about his successes and failures.

Answering Extended Writing and Essay Questions on The Establishment of the Tudor Monarchy

Because Henry VII governed, as the historian John Guy puts it, like a man trying to ride a bicycle – making mistakes and wobbling about until he finally got the hang of it – examination questions will often focus on Henry's achievements. The trend is to recognise that Henry did achieve a great deal, but to set those achievements into context. That means looking at the work Edward IV did in reasserting royal power which Henry was able to build on (such as the use of the chamber to direct finances) and looking at the increasing unpopularity of Henry, especially in his final years.

These are examples of the sorts of questions you might be set which include references to his achievements:

1. **a)** What problems faced Henry VII at his accession in 1485?
   b) How successfully had he overcome these problems by 1509?
2. What was Henry VII's legacy to his son?
3. Was Henry VII's only real achievement to pass the crown on to his son?

The common feature of these types of questions is that you are asked to use your knowledge to form a judgement. This is one of the approaches most often used in examination questions, both in essay questions and in the 'synthesis' questions of source-based papers. It will help you greatly if you learn how to plan answers to these, first by carefully 'unpacking' what the question means, and then by organising your answer into clear sections so that you can come to an overall conclusion.

To judge Henry's achievements, you need to decide what his aims were and whether he accomplished them. Historians would generally agree that Henry saw his tasks as:

▼ to defeat rivals to the throne
▼ to restore the prestige of the monarchy
▼ to control the nobility
▼ to revive effective law and government across England
▼ to strengthen royal finances
▼ to maintain good relations with his European neighbours.

For each of these aims, list the evidence you have that Henry achieved it and note down any reservations you have about the extent of that achievement. This will provide you with a solid set of notes which can be adapted to answer each of the questions above.

Make sure you read each question carefully and think about what you are being asked to do. Unpacking the meaning of the question is vital to understanding how to structure your response (see Figure 18).

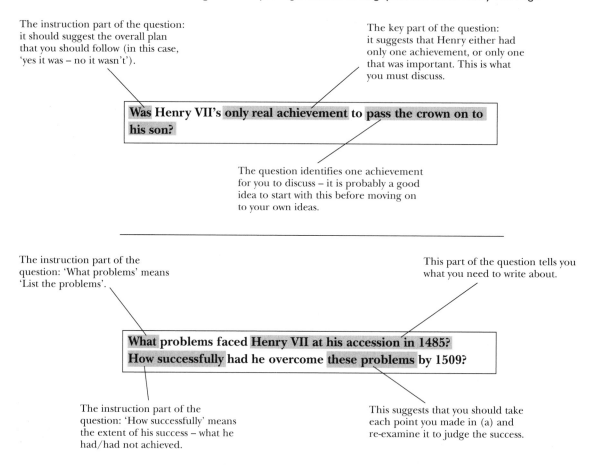

Figure 18 Unpacking extended writing questions about Henry VII's reign.

The instruction part of the question: it should suggest the overall plan that you should follow (in this case, 'yes it was – no it wasn't').

The key part of the question: it suggests that Henry either had only one achievement, or only one that was important. This is what you must discuss.

Was Henry VII's only real achievement to pass the crown on to his son?

The question identifies one achievement for you to discuss – it is probably a good idea to start with this before moving on to your own ideas.

The instruction part of the question: 'What problems' means 'List the problems'.

This part of the question tells you what you need to write about.

What problems faced Henry VII at his accession in 1485?
How successfully had he overcome these problems by 1509?

The instruction part of the question: 'How successfully' means the extent of his success – what he had/had not achieved.

This suggests that you should take each point you made in (a) and re-examine it to judge the success.

Answering Source-Based Questions on The Establishment of the Tudor Monarchy

Henry VII is a popular topic for source-based questions in examinations, partly because it can be divided into a series of themes, such as Henry's style of kingship, rivals to the throne, foreign policies, the succession, financial policies and control of the nobility. In the example that follows, the subject matter is Perkin Warbeck.

On the 6th of this month Perkin landed in Cornwall at a port called Mount St. Michael with three small ships and about three hundred persons of various nationalities, who had followed him for some time before. As he had so few with him, it is thought that the Cornishmen must have invited him. In fact eight thousand peasants soon joined him, although they were ill-disciplined and without any gentlemen, who form the governing class of England. They proclaimed Perkin *as King Richard* and they marched towards His Majesty, who did not hear of them until the 10th.

Source E From a letter by Raimondo de Soncino, a Venetian merchant living in London, to the Duke of Milan, written on 30 September 1497.

With respect to the observations of your Highnesses on Perkin, there is nothing to be said, except that he is kept with the greatest care in the Tower, where he sees neither sun nor moon. The King sent a few days ago for Perkin and asked him, in my presence, why he had deceived the Archduke of the Netherlands and the whole of that country. Perkin answered as he had done before, and solemnly swore to God that *the Duchess, Madame Margaret*, knew as well as himself that he was not the son of King Edward.

Source F From a report by de Puebla, the Spanish ambassador in London, to Ferdinand and Isabella of Spain, 1499.

▼ QUESTIONS ON SOURCES

1. Explain the references to (a) 'King Richard' in Source E and (b) 'the Duchess, Madame Margaret' in Source F. **[3+3 marks]**
2. What does Source F reveal about Henry VII's attitude towards Perkin Warbeck? **[4 marks]**
3. How useful is Source E to a historian studying the history of Perkin Warbeck? **[5 marks]**
4. Using both sources and your own knowledge, would you agree that the threat posed by Perkin Warbeck was greatly exaggerated? **[10 marks]**

The last of these question is typical of the style that you will find on examination papers. Some exam boards call it a 'lead-out' question, others a 'synthesis' question. Either way, they are all asking you to draw together the information from the sources and what you can recall about the topic to develop an argument. You will see that you are asked 'Would you agree …?'. You might decide that, on balance, you do, or you might decide that you do not. What you must do, however, is outline both sides of the argument before reaching your conclusion or you will lose marks.

Here are some ideas for using Sources E and F to argue about the degree of threat posed by Perkin Warbeck. What other points would you add from your general knowledge?

Source	Evidence that Warbeck posed a real threat	Evidence that Warbeck's threat was exaggerated
Source E	• invasion of Cornwall, an area that had proven troublesome for Henry VII (see the tax rebellion of the same year) • collected together 8,000 supporters • claimed to be King Richard – difficult to disprove this claim	• appeared to have little foreign backing at this point • his followers were 'ill-disciplined' and lacking support from the gentry or nobility, so were unlikely to be a serious threat
Source F	• Warbeck claimed to have support from foreign rulers • Henry saw him as enough of a problem to keep him imprisoned.	• Warbeck was in captivity.

Further Reading

Books in the Access to History series

The period 1485–1509 is given excellent and thorough coverage in *Henry VII* by Roger Turvey and Caroline Rogers.

Other books

Henry VII has had a mini-boom in recent years. Introductory surveys can be found in *Henry VII* by Tony Imperato (Stanley Thornes, 1999) and *Henry VII* by Jocelyn Hunt and Carolyn Towle (Longman, 1998). Some of the short works which have helped to define writing about this period are *Henry VII: The Importance of His Reign in English History* by Alexander Grant (Methuen, 1985) and *Henry VII* by Roger Lockyer and Andrew Thrush (Longman, 1997). The most comprehensive biography of Henry is by S. B. Chrimes (a reissued edition was published by Yale University Press in 1999). For another personal analysis of Henry, Bryan Bevan's biography *Henry VII* (Rubicon, 2000) could also be consulted. One book which takes an unusual view of the beginning of the Tudor period is Susan Brigdon's *New Worlds, Lost Worlds* (Penguin, 2000). In it, she uses Henry's arrival in Wales in 1485 and his march towards the Battle of Bosworth to paint a picture of what the country would have seemed like to him. The book contains much fascinating detail and having read the early chapters, you will no doubt enjoy the style of the rest of the book.

THE BEGINNINGS OF THE ENGLISH REFORMATION

CHAPTER 3

POINTS TO CONSIDER

One of the most important contributions made by the Tudors to future generations was the establishment of a national Church of England separate from, and different from, the traditional Catholic Church in Rome. The process of creating a distinctive church organisation and religion in England was very slow and did not always proceed smoothly or in the direction people intended. This chapter looks at the state of the English church at the beginning of the sixteenth century and outlines the early steps by which this reformation came about. However, the story of the English Reformation was, from the start, tangled up with the aims and ambitions of monarchs and their ministers, so you will also find references in this chapter to political events between 1520 and 1547.

1 Introduction: The Strange Shape of the English Reformation

ISSUE:
How was the English Reformation different from those taking place in Europe during the sixteenth century?

The word 'Reformation', when applied to the religious changes of the sixteenth century in England and continental Europe, refers to the collapse of traditional Roman Catholic organisation and teachings and their replacement with more Protestant forms. In essence, this meant substituting what people regarded as a centralised and powerful church with faiths which emphasised the individual's search for God through Bible-reading, debate and a strongly held private faith.

In Europe, the Reformation is associated with religious revolutionaries such as the German monk Martin Luther (see page 77) or the French lawyer **John Calvin**, both of whom challenged fundamental aspects of Catholic teachings. These men, and many others, printed their criticisms and sought to persuade people that reform was needed urgently. They often worked closely with sympathetic rulers of the countries they lived in, to gain protection from the Catholic Church's reaction and slowly to restructure the church according to their vision of a purer form of Christianity. In the German states and Switzerland this process of change began during the 1520s and proceeded at different rates, depending on the particular circumstances, over the next generation.

JOHN CALVIN

Calvin (1509–1564) was a second generation religious reformer (that is he began to challenge the church once the Reformation started by Martin Luther and others had taken root in Europe). His view of religion was more uncompromising than Luther's, and put him towards the radical end of the religious spectrum. In particular, Calvin went further than many reformers in denying God's presence in the bread and wine during communion, and made the theory of predestination central to his church. According to Calvin, God had chosen (or predestined) those who were to be given salvation, so the establishment of an elaborate church built on ceremonies designed to cleanse people of their sins was irrelevant. In England, these sorts of ideas were shared by the Puritans in Elizabeth I's reign.

England was different. No great religious reformer came from outside the political élite to challenge the established order. Religious reform crept through the church because the monarch allowed it, and it was the monarch and his advisers who decided the pace and tone of the changes. On the continent, reform of religious practices tended to begin before a country moved towards a position of independence from the Pope. In England, the opposite occurred; religious reform had not got very far until the break with Rome happened. There were sincere religious reformers in England, including some who shared the Protestant ideas of Luther and others. Until the 1530s they were restricted and persecuted by the king and his advisers (such as Sir Thomas More) but when Henry decided to challenge the authority of the Pope, he sought their help. As allies and servants of the king they were appointed to powerful positions, from which

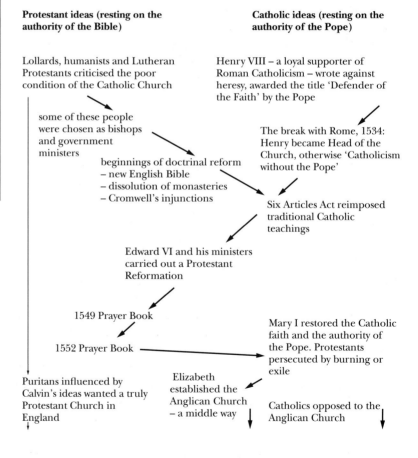

Protestant ideas (resting on the authority of the Bible)

Catholic ideas (resting on the authority of the Pope)

Lollards, humanists and Lutheran Protestants criticised the poor condition of the Catholic Church

Henry VIII – a loyal supporter of Roman Catholicism – wrote against heresy, awarded the title 'Defender of the Faith' by the Pope

some of these people were chosen as bishops and government ministers

The break with Rome, 1534: Henry became Head of the Church, otherwise 'Catholicism without the Pope'

beginnings of doctrinal reform
– new English Bible
– dissolution of monasteries
– Cromwell's injunctions

Six Articles Act reimposed traditional Catholic teachings

Edward VI and his ministers carried out a Protestant Reformation

1549 Prayer Book

1552 Prayer Book

Mary I restored the Catholic faith and the authority of the Pope. Protestants persecuted by burning or exile

Puritans influenced by Calvin's ideas wanted a truly Protestant Church in England

Elizabeth established the Anglican Church – a middle way

Catholics opposed to the Anglican Church

Figure 19 Royal policy towards religion, 1500–1600.

they were able to bring about the radical reforms which they desired. However, there was also no great collapse and reconstruction of the organisation of the English church during the Reformation. The traditional Catholic structure of a church run by bishops remained, in stark contrast to the insistence of European Protestants that every congregation should be its own master. Similarly, there was not the revolutionary redesigning of faith in England that was the hallmark of the European Reformation. In England, some of the milder Catholic teachings continued, stitched to the more radical Protestant ideas about the purpose and essentials of worship which reformers in government had been able to introduce when the opportunity arose.

Finally, although the Reformation in some European countries was slow, it usually proceeded away from Catholicism and towards Protestantism. England, by contrast, wavered between the two religions as different monarchs imposed their religious or political convictions on the church.

In every sense, then, the English Reformation was a compromise. It was a compromise between deeply felt and popular Catholic traditions which stretched back over many centuries and the new ideas of Protestantism. It was a compromise between what religious reformers wanted and what their political masters – the monarch and his advisers – felt was acceptable. Ultimately, it created a compromise church, one which was recognisably Protestant in its teachings, but which drew on a Catholic heritage to satisfy and pacify as many people as possible. This was the strange shape of the English Reformation which historians have tried both to outline and to explain.

> **ACTIVITY**
>
> If you are studying the European Reformation on your course you will be able to draw your own, more detailed, comparisons between the causes and process of religious change in England and elsewhere. For the moment, check your understanding of section I by making a list of points to answer the following question:
>
> What was unusual about the English Reformation?

2 The Traditional Church in the Early Sixteenth Century

At the beginning of the sixteenth century English people, with few exceptions, followed the teachings (or doctrines as they were called) of the Roman Catholic Church. This meant that they accepted that:

▼ the Pope, in Rome, was head of the church and supreme authority over all spiritual matters

▼ there was an elaborately organised hierarchy of churchmen, some of whom were 'secular' because they worked in the community tending to the spiritual needs of ordinary people, and others of whom were 'regular' clergy because they shut themselves off from the community to concentrate on prayer

▼ the clergy held a special and powerful place within the community. Only formally appointed priests could conduct services in church and only priests had access to the Bible, which was written in Latin and interpret-

Figure 20 The structure of the Roman Catholic Church in England at the beginning of the sixteenth century.

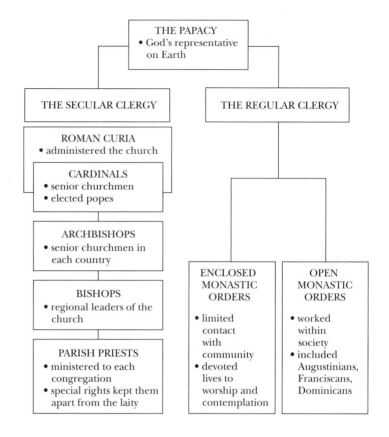

ed by them for the benefit of their parishioners. The unique role of the priesthood was confirmed by their appearance (they wore special clothes – vestments – to conduct services) and by their behaviour (they were not allowed to marry or to have sex)

 people should submit to the authority of the church when it came to important moments in their lives. According to the teachings of the Roman Catholic Church there were seven essential ceremonies – sacraments – which the church performed. These were the eucharist (or mass), baptism, holy orders (the granting of the status of priest to someone who had completed their religious training), confirmation, marriage, penance and extreme unction (the last rites)

 for their souls to be saved, people should attend church regularly, participate in the sacraments and show their faith in God.

The virtue of ye masse.

Figure 21 A sixteenth-century woodcut print showing a priest conducting the mass. In this picture the priest is holding up the bread which is about to transubstantiate (transform the essential elements) into the body of Christ so that the congregation can then take Christ into themselves and receive His mercy.

a) The Role of the Church

As an institution, the Roman Catholic Church had a long history in England, dating back before the Norman Conquest. Over five hundred years of continuity had enabled it to bury deep roots into all aspects of people's lives. Its most obvious role was to provide for the spiritual needs of its parishioners. Through the mass, priests could bring the comforting presence of God into the hearts and souls of worshippers, whilst other sacraments connected the church to important moments in people's lives. Priests also gave spiritual guidance through the sacrament of confession and taught congregations how to live godly lives by interpreting the Bible for them.

ISSUE:
What part did the church play in everyday life at the beginning of the sixteenth century?

The church was also part of the social fabric of the community. It was the most common building to be found across the country, an easily identifiable landmark in nearly every village and town. Great pride was taken by the community in building and maintaining their church as a sign of their devotion to God. In Louth, Lincolnshire, for example, fund-raising had produced £305 to build the parish church and more money had been raised between 1501 and 1515 to construct a magnificent spire. Most people went to church regularly, not just because attendance was required by law, but because the church was a special place. Think for a moment about how the interior of a parish church, with its large open space, ornate windows and decorations, must have seemed to its congregation. It was probably the most impressive building they would ever enter. In church, the village gathered together to worship but also to celebrate Holy Days and other festivals with dancing and drinking. In an age long before summer vacations and Bank Holidays, the church organised the few days in the year when the daily routine was broken. In these ways, it bound villagers together into one community. From constructing and maintaining the building through to the emphasis on communal rather than individual worship, the church helped the village to find a sense of identity and collective purpose.

In these different ways the church had become an accepted and intrinsic part of the lives of ordinary people. However, it was also a force in national and international politics. Since the Norman Conquest the church had operated its own law courts to try crimes involving priests or breaches of doctrine. These were still active in the sixteenth century, although medieval kings had done their best to weaken the church courts' independent power. Bishops and abbots had a political role; they sat in the House of Lords. Churchmen were often the best educated, most literate people in the country, so their skills as administrators were valued. In the early Tudor period it was not uncommon to find that government advisers and ministers were also members of the clergy. The church also offered a different service to monarchs. Its power over people's minds through its teachings created a channel through which obedience to the will of the king could also be taught.

<table>
<tr><td>

ISSUE:

What complaints were made about the English Catholic Church at the beginning of the sixteenth century?

</td><td>

3 The Church in Crisis?

a) The Criticisms

Given the value that people attached to the church it is not surprising that they were willing to voice their complaints when it fell short of their expectations. Criticism of the church was not just a feature of the Tudor period: serious and scathing public attacks had been common

</td></tr>
</table>

throughout the Middle Ages. In Geoffrey Chaucer's fourteenth-century *Canterbury Tales* for instance, there is much satire at the expense of the Pardoner, the Summoner and other church officials.

By the sixteenth century complaints encompassed a variety of themes. The ignorance of some parish priests, the encouragement of superstitious practices in order to make money, the greed and tyranny of the church courts, general moral laxity and the neglect by priests of their duties were among the commonest criticisms:

These are not the shepherds, but ravenous wolves going about in sheep's clothing, devouring their flock. The goodliest lordships, manors, lands and territories are theirs. Besides this, they take a tenth part of everyone's wages, a tenth part of the wool, milk, honey, wax, cheese and butter that is produced, and even every tenth egg from poor widows. And what do these greedy, idle, holy thieves do with all these yearly exactions that they take from the people? Nothing, but suck all rule, power, authority and obedience from you [Henry VIII] to themselves!

Source A From Simon Fish's *A Supplication for the Beggars*, published in 1529. It is written in the style of a plea (a supplication) to Henry VIII from the poor, sick and needy.

It is from stupidity and the darkness of ignorance that there arises a great and deplorable evil throughout the whole Church of God. Everywhere through town and countryside there exists a crop of oafish and boorish priests, some of whom are engaged on ignoble and servile tasks, while others abandon themselves to tavern-haunting, swilling and drunkenness. Some cannot get along without their wenches; others pursue their amusement in dice and gambling all day long. There are some who waste their time in hunting and hawking, and so spend a life which is utterly and wholly idle and irreligious even to advanced old age.

Source B An extract from a sermon (in Latin) preached by William Melton, the Chancellor of York Minster. It was published about 1510.

And here out of our records I shall mention some of the images and relics to which the pilgrimages of those times brought devotion and offerings such as the milk of our Lady (shown in eight places), the bell of St. Guthlac and the belt of St. Thomas of Lancaster (both remedies for the headache), the coals that roasted St. Lawrence, the ear of St. Malchus and the blood of Jesus Christ brought from Jerusalem to Gloucestershire, being kept for many ages. This last has brought many great offerings to it from remote places, but was proved to be the blood of a duck, every week renewed by the priests. Besides which, it is possible to see an image of St. John of Osulston (also called Mr. John Shorne) who was said to have shut up the Devil in a boot.

Source C A description of the various holy relics that could be visited and viewed in England before the Reformation. From Lord Herbert of Cherbury's *Life and Reign of King Henry VIII*, published in 1649.

ACTIVITY

Read the criticisms of the Catholic Church made in Sources A to C and answer the following questions:

1. What aspects of religious life do these writers criticise?
2. On what points do the writers of Sources A and B agree?
3. Are these sources challenging religious practices, religious beliefs, or both?
4. How might a historian check the accuracy of the impression of religious life that these sources create?
5. Why might a historian have reason to doubt the accuracy of some of the information in these sources?

ISSUE:
Who was making these complaints?

LAITY OR LAYMEN
A general term referring to people who had not been trained and accepted as priests.

INDULGENCES
Originally granted to those who had committed venal (minor) sins in return for an action which showed repentance. The indulgence was a document, issued with the Pope's authority, setting out the cancellation of the punishment in Purgatory (see page 77). Over time, however, the church began to sell indulgences to raise money. Protestant reformers objected both to the idea that the Pope had the power to cancel the punishment of sin and to the way in which the church played on fears of Purgatory.

---

b) The Critics

Complaints about the poor state of the church were voiced by different groups and social classes. For the most part, these critics were passionate about their faith. They loved and valued the church, which is why they were determined to shout so loudly when individual priests or religious practices disappointed them. The main critics before the Reformation began were:

▼ humanist scholars
▼ Lollards
▼ Protestants.

i) Humanist Critics

During the fifteenth and early sixteenth centuries the cultural movement known as the Renaissance spread from its home in Italy to England. An important part of Renaissance thinking was the emphasis on the power and potential of mankind. Artists celebrated man's connection to God, most famously in Michelangelo's painting on the ceiling of the Sistine Chapel in the Vatican which shows Adam stretching out to touch God's fingers. Renaissance scholars believed that it was possible to improve human knowledge and behaviour through education. Such ideas led to their being dubbed 'humanists'.

Humanists became involved in the religious debate in England because they were disturbed by the poor quality of the parish clergy and wanted to improve standards of education among both the clergy and the **laity**. They attacked the church's exploitation of superstitious practices such as the worship of saints and the selling of **indulgences** in order to raise money. They were concerned that this exploitation not only misled souls away from God, but also raised money that was spent on luxurious living for the higher clergy, or ostentatious church building, rather than the promotion of education or charitable works.

ii) Lollards

The Lollard movement had existed for over a century before the English Reformation began. It was based on the teachings of John Wycliffe, who attacked the church for its wealth, greed and superstitious practices such as the worship of saints. However, Wycliffe went further than the anti-clericalism of the times and denied that priests had the power to transform the bread and wine during the mass into Christ's body and blood. Although there was some initial sympathy for Lollard ideas, the movement became associated with peasant rebellion against their masters and quickly lost noble and gentry support. Despite the collapse of the movement in the first decades of the fifteenth century, its ideas survived in scattered groups and congregations, emerging to blend in with the new Protestant ideas of the sixteenth century.

iii) Protestants

Chief among the new reforming ideas of the sixteenth century were the teachings of **Martin Luther** (1483–1547). His writings, which filtered into England from the 1520s, added another dimension to the criticisms made of the church at this time. Martin Luther was the first Protestant reformer. He went much further than Wycliffe in condemning the work of the church and the behaviour of its priests; ultimately he moved towards his own definition of faith based on salvation as a gift from God to the faithful, not as something to be earned by following superstitious rituals. This meant that the core of Protestantism lay in an individual's relationship with God, a direct connection established through prayer and biblical study, not through the rituals imposed by priests.

In England, the Protestant attack on the church can be exemplified by the work of Thomas Bilney, Miles Coverdale and William Tyndale. While Bilney spread Protestant ideas through preaching, Coverdale and Tyndale produced translations of the Bible into English, and Tyndale attacked the authority of the Pope.

The doctrine of Purgatory was a particular source of criticism and complaint. According to the church, the souls of those who died did not usually go straight to heaven or hell, but waited in some discomfort in an area called Purgatory for God's final decision. It was possible for the prayers of the living to intercede with God and shorten the time of waiting – hence many people paid priests to pray for them after their deaths, or bought prayers for their dead relatives. There were several reasons for complaints about this:

▼ the church earned a great deal of money from the sale of prayers

▼ it encouraged priests and monks to spend time in prayer rather than useful occupations

▼ it implied that the church had some power to lighten sin

MARTIN LUTHER

A German monk and lecturer in theology whose researches into the original sources of the New Testament led him to the realisation that his church had made mistakes in its interpretation of what people needed to do to be saved by God. In doing so, he made an enemy of the Pope and the Catholic Holy Roman Emperor, Charles V. Although Luther had not intended it, his criticisms of the church found a sympathetic audience among Germans tired of the money-making schemes of Rome and he was encouraged to develop his ideas to the point where it was not possible for him to remain within the Catholic Church.

▼ it suggested that people were not responsible for their own souls

▼ it was open to abuses such as indulgences

▼ there was no evidence for the doctrine in the Bible.

Figure 22 A European woodcut showing what Protestants saw as the corruption of the Catholic Church.

ACTIVITY

Re-read the section above about the doctrine of Purgatory and make a list of:

1. the church's critics who might be particularly offended by the different complaints listed here

2. the abuses mentioned in this section which would arise from or be justified by the doctrine of Purgatory.

Beyond these specific groups was a general air of dissatisfaction within some parishes at the quality and behaviour of their priests. This feeling – known as anti-clericalism – was felt especially among the merchants and lawyers who dominated the upper levels of urban society. It did not have the intellectual foundations of humanism, but was usually generated by real-life examples of abuses and corruption, as the case of Richard Hunne shows. Apart from Hunne, other prominent individuals who voiced their anti-clericalism included Simon Fish, a common lawyer who published the scathing attack on the clergy entitled *A Supplication for the Beggars* in 1529 (see Source A on page 75).

Richard Hunne

The Hunne case involved one of the most infamous scandals of its age, and led to intense anti-clericalism in London, at least for a while. Richard Hunne was a London merchant whose baby son died in 1511. After the funeral his local parish priests demanded heavy payments for mortuary dues, including the child's burial robe, to which Hunne objected. The grieving father responded with a series of lawsuits, and found himself persecuted in return by the church to the point of having his house searched. There, the Bishop of London's men found, or claimed to have found, a large quantity of heretical literature. Hunne was arrested and put into the bishop's prison at St Paul's, where he was found hanged, or more probably strangled, in his cell. The authorities' claim that he had committed suicide was widely disbelieved, and was the subject of debate 15 years later in the Reformation Parliament.

This complex mixture of anti-clericalism, humanism, Lollardy and Protestantism swirled around in the heads of educated, concerned Christians in the early sixteenth century. These people began to explore new ideas and enter into religious debates without any clear sense of where they might lead. The so-called 'White Horse' meetings of the 1520s in Cambridge illustrate this atmosphere well. Young scholars met at the White Horse tavern to discuss and debate the latest religious ideas, under the leadership of Robert Barnes, a scholar and Augustinian prior. He was unwise enough to speak publicly against the arrogance of priests and to call for better preaching. To his astonishment he was accused of being a follower of Martin Luther and was forced to recant (i.e. to deny such ideas) at a book-burning ceremony in London in 1526. Members of the Cambridge group included:

▼ Thomas Bilney, who developed ideas similar to Luther's, and who was eventually burned as a heretic

▼ Stephen Gardiner, who became Bishop of Winchester and a fierce defender of traditional Catholic teachings

▼ Thomas Cranmer (see page 87), who became Henry VIII's Archbishop of Canterbury in 1532 and who gradually worked his way towards a moderate Protestant position before his execution in 1556.

In the 1520s these were young men, concerned about the state of their church and the need to reform it, exploring and debating the best solutions. Their different development and various later careers illustrate that they were not fully formed 'Lollards', 'Protestants' or 'humanists' at this point, but, like so many other people, they were influenced by the different emphases and ideas of these streams of thought.

ISSUE:

Was the church in serious danger of collapse in the early sixteenth century?

c) The Extent of Criticism

Historians who believe that a reformation of some kind was inevitable argue that abuses of the church were widespread, and that the church was in a state of spiritual decay, incapable of finding the energy and discipline to reform itself from within. They regard the debates of groups such as the White Horse scholars and the criticisms voiced by humanists, Lollards and Protestants as contributing to this fragmentation of the church.

There is no doubt that, in some parishes, the concerns of the critics were justified. The humanist John Stokesley was appointed Bishop of London in 1530. He carried out a survey of the churches under his care and, as a result, banned 21 parish priests from taking services and suspended a further 16 because they were unfit for the job. Of 58 curates, some of whom were employed only to cover for the absentee office-holder, 44 were considered inadequate for the work. Stokesley expected high standards from his clergy and it is clear that many were not meeting them.

However, it would be misleading for us to assume that the critics were entirely correct. The church employed thousands of men, and for every example of a failing priest it is possible to find someone else who worked carefully and conscientiously for his parishioners. In a series of investigations conducted by the Bishop of Lincoln between 1515 and 1527, for instance, only 10 per cent of the clergy were accused of immorality, whilst in Winchester only 11 cases of misconduct were found in 230 parishes.

Those who reject the argument that the early sixteenth-century church was in a state of spiritual decay also point to the extent of popular piety (individual acts of faith). These acts were expressed time and again through grants of money or property to the church in wills, fundraising to improve a parish church, or observance of the church's rituals. During the fifteenth and early sixteenth centuries over 60 per cent of the parish churches in England were extensively rebuilt using money donated by their congregations, of which the church and spire in Louth (see page 74) is just one illustration. Pilgrimages were popular, and often undertaken in a genuine search for spiritual knowledge and experience.

The real question is how effective these efforts to respond to criticism could be. It is clear that there were significant problems – corruption, or at least lax standards in some areas, anti-clericalism, greed and superstition, as well as the doctrinal attack of Lollard and Protestant heretics. It is clear that these attitudes and concerns were not limited to one social class or to one area of the country. But it is also clear that the church was generally accepted as an institution and had strong support. It satisfied the daily needs and concerns of many parishioners, leaving only a minority dissatisfied. It was also beginning to address the need for reform and to defend itself against its critics. Those wanting change were not sufficient in number to bring about the reforms they desired. So it is unlikely that England would have experienced a Protestant Reformation in the 1530s and 1540s had it not been for the 'King's Great Matter' and his entirely separate quarrel with the Pope.

4 The 'King's Great Matter'

ISSUE:
Why did Henry VIII want a divorce?

Although the critics of the church were discussing change and opening their minds to the new ideas of the Renaissance and European Protestantism, they were not making much headway in actually bringing about reforms. The official line was that Catholicism was the only acceptable form of worship in England, and the authorities persecuted anyone who openly disagreed with this policy.

Fifteen years into his reign, and into his marriage, Henry VIII did not have a son to succeed him. Catherine of Aragon's failure to produce a son, and the fact that she was reaching an age when she would probably never become pregnant again, began to raise suspicions in the king's mind. Henry was strong and healthy, so it seemed impossible to him that there was a natural cause for this problem. By 1525 he was becoming increasingly convinced that God was refusing to grant him a son, because He disapproved of Henry's marriage to his brother's widow. Henry gradually convinced himself that the marriage was sinful, and that to stay married to Catherine was to place his soul in danger.

Henry also had another reason for seeking to escape his marriage. Although Catherine had borne five children, only one girl, Mary, had lived beyond infancy. England had no recent experience of a female ruler and the only historical example to draw upon was that of the Empress Matilda in the twelfth century. Her reign had seen civil war because a rival male claimant had been able to muster support against her. In 1525 England was only 50 years on from the Wars of the Roses, caused by weak monarchs and over-mighty nobles. With the Yorkist faction still in existence, it was not surprising that Henry feared that his subjects would not stay loyal to a female ruler. He felt that the security of the Tudor dynasty depended on a strong male presence on the throne. A male heir was essential.

However, underlying these moral and political concerns was a more personal reason why Henry wanted to end his marriage. In 1522 he had met **Anne Boleyn**, a niece of the Duke of Norfolk. She was stylish, intelligent, lively, mature enough to flirt with Henry and ambitious enough to refuse to become just another one of the royal mistresses. Henry was infatuated with her. The contrast with Catherine of Aragon could not have been more stark. Catherine was the daughter of Ferdinand and Isabella of Spain, religiously conservative and submissive to her husband in all but the issue of divorce. Anne was much more assertive and personally ambitious. Henry was used to getting his way, so Anne's flirtation and refusal made him frustrated, but all the more determined. Catherine was at first a disappointment to Henry, but increasingly a source of annoyance as she stood in the way of his pursuit of Anne.

Q Why was Henry unable to obtain his divorce during the 1520s?

Source D From a letter by Henry VIII to Anne Boleyn, written in 1528.

I beg you with all my heart to let me know definitely your whole mind concerning the love between us both. For I must of necessity force you to reply, as I have been for more than a year now smitten with love's dart, being uncertain either of failure or of finding a place in your heart and sure affections. If it please you to play the part of a true, loyal mistress and friend, giving yourself body and soul to me, I promise you that I will cast out all others save yourself from my thoughts and affections, to serve you and you alone.

PAPAL LEGATE

A title given to someone who acted with the Pope's confidence and authority, usually to perform a specific task. Wolsey was unusual in that Henry persuaded the Pope to grant him the status of legate in England permanently and for non-specific reasons.

The task of obtaining the divorce fell to Henry's powerful chief minister, Cardinal Thomas Wolsey. When Henry first raised the issue in 1525, Wolsey was at the height of his fame. He not only exercised power as Henry's leading adviser, but also as a cardinal of the Catholic Church and **papal legate** in England. Both men assumed that it would be a relatively easy task to persuade the Pope to allow Wolsey to hear the divorce case in England, so that the preferred verdict could be delivered.

However, political developments in Europe were creating huge obstacles to this plan, as Table 4 shows. Once Charles V, who hap-

Anne Boleyn

Anne was the daughter of Sir George Boleyn, from a junior branch of the Howard Earls of Norfolk, intelligent, assertive and ambitious. Estimates of her character vary widely. Among those who disapproved of the divorce she was a 'goggle-eyed harlot'. Historians have accused her of 'domineering ways' that brought about her downfall, arguing that when Henry had won her sexually he became increasingly disillusioned with her assertive personality as well as her failure to produce a male heir. Her destruction in 1536 was brought about by Thomas Cromwell, who tortured her musician, Mark Smeaton, into a confession of adulteries and in the case of her brother George, incest, allowing her to be convicted of treason and executed by beheading with a sword. Her recent biographer, E. W. Ives, has painted a different portrait, of an intelligent woman with a genuine interest in religious reform, who was betrayed by her husband and family and destroyed by the necessities of court politics and the problems of the succession. She was innocent of the charges of adultery. Arguments as to whether she deserved her fate seem to depend on the preferences and sometimes the prejudices of those who write about her. For the interested student, the best course is to read different interpretations, for example by Ives and Henry's biographer, J. J. Scarisbrick, and decide for yourself.

pened to be Catherine of Aragon's nephew, secured control over much of the Italian peninsula, the Pope had to adopt a cautious line on the matter of Henry VIII's divorce.

Between 1529 and 1532, Henry applied a number of measures designed to pressurise the clergy into supporting his case for a divorce. As we saw above, the church was already vulnerable to attacks from humanists, Lollards, Protestants and the more general feeling of anti-clericalism among parishioners. These critics gave Henry the support he needed to force the church to take his demand for a divorce seriously, but in doing so, they gained positions of power and influence from which they could bring about the religious reforms they desired. This strengthening of the wider religious debate was the unintended effect of the divorce question.

Q How did the Pope manage to satisfy the conflicting demands of both Henry and Charles V at this time?

Date	Events in England and Europe
1525	Henry VIII discussed the possibility of securing a divorce with Cardinal Wolsey
1527	Devastation of Rome by imperial troops. Charles V now the dominant force within the Italian peninsula. Pope's freedom of action severely restricted as a result. Henry tried to undermine Charles's power by making an alliance with France
1528	The Pope agreed to a divorce hearing in England, but said that it should be conducted jointly by Cardinal Wolsey and Cardinal Campeggio. The latter did not arrive in England (deliberately on the Pope's orders) until September
1529	The divorce proceedings opened at Blackfriars in London. Catherine of Aragon appealed to Rome against the proceedings

In Italy, Charles V won a decisive victory over France at the Battle of Landriano, reinforcing his dominance of the peninsula

The Pope announced that Catherine's appeal would be heard in Rome

Henry VIII dismissed Wolsey |

Table 4 Foreign affairs and the divorce question, 1525–9.

Q How did the divorce question become entangled with wider demands for religious change?

The alliance between a king wanting a divorce and reformers wanting radical religious changes was made possible by their common view that the church was the main obstacle to their ambitions. For the reformers, the problems facing the church in the early sixteenth century and the corruption of individual Popes could only be solved by improving religious leadership. They argued that royal power should be strengthened to protect and to develop the Church in England. During the 1520s Henry had opposed this idea and had even written a book, *In Defence of the Seven Sacraments*, which justified the existing system of control from Rome. For this service to the church he had been awarded the title 'Defensor Dei' (Defender of God) by the Pope.

However, as Henry's dispute with the Pope worsened, the ideas of the reformers began to prove more attractive. In 1528 William Tyndale published *The Obedience of the Christian Man*, in which he argued that kings had authority from God which gave them responsibility for the souls as well as the bodies of their subjects, and that royal authority was supreme above any power within or beyond the boundaries of the kingdom. The book was banned in England, but Anne Boleyn had a copy sent to her from France, and brought it to

Henry's attention. In addition, courtiers such as Thomas Cromwell had travelled extensively in Europe, where they would have become familiar with similar ideas. When Henry found himself obstructed by the authority of Rome and the Pope, he was not short of suggestions and ideas as to how he might remove these obstacles once and for all.

Henry's campaign between 1529 and 1534 appears to have had two clear objectives, as Table 5 reveals. To obtain the divorce that he so desperately desired, he put pressure on the English clergy not to oppose him and tried to force the Pope to submit.

> **Q** Did Henry intend to seize control of the church from the Pope?

Control of the English Church

Underlying the methods described in Table 5 was perhaps another policy. By challenging the Pope, Henry was raising the question of who should have final control over the English church. You will see that this issue is visible in the events of 1531 and 1532, for example.

Historians are unclear, however, as to when the idea of taking control over the church changed from being a vague threat in some of Henry's actions to an official policy. According to the historian Conrad Russell, for instance, the idea of divorcing Catherine without the Pope's permission was in Henry's mind as early as 1527, but he had to wait until conditions were right to carry out this plan. In particular, he had to delay until he could appoint to the higher clergy men who were likely to support him. This meant waiting at least until after the Archbishop of Canterbury's death.

Other writers have seen more caution in Henry's policies. They point out that royal policies were applied very hesitantly. In the case of the prohibition of payments of annates, for example, the policy was suspended for a year and then only applied with the king's approval. This suggests that Henry still hoped to use the policy as a bargaining chip in his negotiations to get a divorce. Historians such as Geoffrey Elton and Christopher Haigh both use evidence such as this to suggest that Henry was unsure what to do and feared an open split with the Pope. To challenge the power of the Roman Catholic Church so directly could have been dangerous to him. Whilst there was an anti-clerical element in Parliament, the opposition to the Act against Annates showed that this was not a commonly held view. Moreover, the Pope had the power to excommunicate Henry if things got too far out of hand. For a king, excommunication meant that oaths of loyalty taken by his subjects no longer applied, and that rebellion could be sanctioned, or even regarded as a duty, by the church.

Date	Pressure on the clergy	Pressure on the Pope
1529	Parliament was encouraged to voice anti-clerical feelings – Thomas Cromwell MP began collecting evidence of abuses	
1530	Revival of medieval law of **Praemunire** – 15 of the upper clergy were charged with supporting Wolsey's abuse of power against the king	Scholars from Oxford and Cambridge were sent to European universities to find support for Henry's divorce
1531	Henry 'pardoned' the clergy of crimes against him, but demanded that they should recognise him as 'sole protector and supreme head' of the church. A compromise was reached: he was accepted as supreme head 'as far as the law of Christ allows'	
1532	March: Thomas Cromwell introduced the 'Supplication Against the Ordinaries' into the House of Commons – a petition calling on the king to deal with the abuses and corruption of the clergy. Cromwell held no major office at this time, but was invited to join Henry's inner circle of advisers on the Royal Council May: Henry demanded that the church should agree to the 'Submission of the Clergy' – a document giving him the power to veto church laws and to choose bishops even if not approved by Rome	January: Act of Parliament passed (despite fierce opposition) preventing the payment of **annates** to Rome. Although the amount collected was not great, the banning of the payment was a significant attack on the Pope's rights over the clergy. The Act was suspended for one year
	Resignation of Sir Thomas More accepted	August: Death of Archbishop of Canterbury (William Warham). Henry asked the Pope to appoint **Thomas Cranmer**, a reformer with some Protestant views
1533	January: Henry secretly married Anne Boleyn (now pregnant)	Act in Restraint of Appeals was passed by Parliament, denying Henry's subjects the right to appeal to the Pope against decisions in English church courts. This law effectively prevented Catherine of Aragon from seeking the Pope's arbitration when the divorce case came before the courts.

Table 5 Pressures on the English church and the Pope, 1529–33.

Q How did Henry pursue his demands for a divorce between 1529 and 1534?

PRAEMUNIRE
A Latin term used in medieval laws which made it a crime to use powers derived from the Pope to the disadvantage of the king or his subjects.

ANNATES
A special tax paid by members of the higher clergy to Rome during their first year in office.

-Profile-

ARCHBISHOP THOMAS CRANMER (1489–1556)

Cranmer was one of the young scholars at Cambridge who joined the 'White Horse' group in the 1520s to discuss the exciting new ideas of Lutheranism coming from Europe. He was influenced by these ideas, but stopped short of embracing them to the point of becoming a heretic. Instead, his career took him to the royal court, where he became chaplain to Anne Boleyn's father. He wrote a defence of the king's desire for a divorce, using an erastian argument (which means that he justified divorce on the grounds that monarchs were the highest authority within their lands so could do as they pleased). Henry was impressed by Cranmer's moderate reformist ideas and saw in him a friend of about the same age and an ally against the power of the Pope.

When Archbishop Warham died in 1532, Henry asked the Pope to appoint Cranmer to fill the vacancy, even though he had never held a senior post within the church. Henry was undoubtedly doing this to put further pressure on the Pope to give him his divorce, but he also saw the advantages of having a supporter as the leading English churchman. Cranmer quickly proved to be a loyal friend. He authorised the much-desired royal divorce after the 1533 Act in Restraint of Appeals prohibited Catherine from challenging the matter before the Pope, and he accepted all the measures enacted during the reformation years of 1534–40. However, Cranmer also showed his Protestant sympathies by supporting the publication of the Bible in English and the efforts of Thomas Cromwell to move essential doctrines away from traditional teachings (see pages 92–3).

Ultimately, however, Cranmer was a political servant of the crown first and a churchman second. When Henry attacked the extent of reform by persecuting Lutherans and pushing the Six Articles Act through Parliament in 1539, Cranmer stood by when other Protestant bishops resigned. His loyalty to Henry allowed him to escape the traps set by the conservative faction during the 1540s and to survive as archbishop into Edward VI's reign.

Under the governments of Somerset and Northumberland a more Protestant atmosphere prevailed at court and Cranmer followed this mood in his wording of the 1549 and 1552 Prayer Books. At the same time, he spoke of trying to find a form of religion that would end religious disagreements and establish a permanent basis for faith. He consulted leading Protestant reformers and Catholic theologians from Europe, but never got to the point of setting out what this uniform faith should be. Privately, Cranmer supported moderate Protestant thinking, but respected and saw the value of some Catholic rituals – just as Elizabeth was to do in the settlement of 1559–63.

During Mary's reign, Cranmer's career declined sharply. He had been too deeply involved in the writing of the Protestant Prayer Books to escape the queen's distrust and was arrested on heresy charges. Ever the politician, Cranmer publicly renounced his Protestant 'errors' five times during his trial, but he was executed in 1556.

ISSUE:
What aspects of church organisation were changed between 1533 and 1538?

5 The Henrician Reformation, 1533–8

a) The Establishment of Royal Supremacy

Between 1533 and 1536 a series of Acts of Parliament defined the nature and organisation of the Church in England. These laws systematically stripped away the Pope's control and transferred power in key areas to the king.

Figure 23 How the break with Rome affected Henry VIII's powers as king.

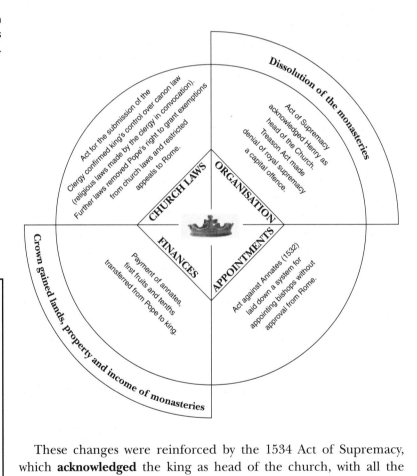

ACKNOWLEDGED
The significance of the term 'acknowledged' is that the Act of Supremacy claimed that the king had always held the right to be head of the church, and was now taking it up. This meant that Parliament was in no sense giving him the right (which it did not have the power to grant), but merely recognising it and setting up the framework to make it legally enforceable.

These changes were reinforced by the 1534 Act of Supremacy, which **acknowledged** the king as head of the church, with all the rights this entailed to decide its organisation, personnel and doctrine. To enforce this, a Treason Act made the denial of royal supremacy a crime punishable by death.

b) The Dissolution of the Monasteries

ISSUE:
Why were the monasteries closed and their assets taken by the king?

i) Causes of the Dissolution

Once Henry was legally acknowledged as head of the church in England, questions about accompanying reform of church institutions needed to be addressed. High on the list of targets were the 800 or so monasteries, convents and other religious houses in England and Wales. In the Middle Ages these had been established as places where men and women could devote their lives to saying prayers on behalf of the souls of the living and the dead. As such, they had enjoyed a powerful reputation within the church and had been treated with awe and respect. Monks, nuns and other members of the regular clergy who lived in these religious houses tended to set themselves apart from the communities close to which they were established, avoiding daily contact if possible. None the less, monasteries played an important part in local life. They were places of shelter and sanctuary for travellers, sources of medicines and food for the needy and centres of education for the wealthy.

Another view of the monasteries, however, is that by the sixteenth century the high regard in which they had been held had almost completely vanished. The number of regular clergy had declined to about 10,000 and some monasteries housed fewer than a dozen monks. Originally, the men and women who had dedicated their lives to prayer had lived simple lives but, over time, they had acquired servants to manage the day-to-day running of their houses and had accumulated luxuries by spending the money they received from renting out some of their land.

This decline gave Henry and Cromwell their first, but not their most important, reason for closing the monasteries. As head of the church, the king could order inspections of any religious establishments. A survey was carried out, on Cromwell's orders, in 1536. It discovered that corruption and abuses were common throughout the smaller monasteries of England and Wales, giving Henry the excuse he needed to close them.

> Sin, vicious, carnal and abominable living is daily seen and committed amongst the little and small abbeys, priories and other such religious houses of monks, canons and nuns. The governors of such houses consume and waste the ornaments of their churches and their goods and chattels to the great displeasure of Almighty God and to the great infamy of the King's Highness and the realm.

Source E From the Act for the Dissolution of the Smaller Monasteries, 1536. This introductory paragraph sets out the official justification for the closure of these establishments.

In reality, the level of corruption was probably not much worse than in the clergy as a whole. However, Cromwell had instructed his commissioners to find the most damaging pieces of evidence about each institution that they visited, even if that meant listening to unfounded gossip and rumours.

Historians have tended to dismiss this official reason for the dissolution and have looked elsewhere for the causes:

▼ monasteries were very wealthy institutions. In 1536 Henry discovered this for himself when he commissioned a survey of the property and value of smaller monasteries, the *Valor Ecclesiasticus*. The survey revealed that these monasteries had the potential to double the crown's annual income. At a time when Henry needed money to further his ambitions abroad, seizing the assets of the monasteries was an extremely tempting prospect

▼ seizure of monastic lands would also give the crown additional property to distribute as a way of buying support from the nobility and gentry at a difficult time

▼ monasteries were permanent reminders of the Roman Catholic Church. Although monks and nuns had been forced to swear an oath recognising Henry as head of the church, they were potential centres of resistance to the royal supremacy

▼ the primary role of monasteries – to pray for the salvation of souls – was not in keeping with the new Protestant theology of individual faith in God. For those critics of the church who wanted genuine reform along Protestant lines, the monasteries were outdated and irrelevant institutions.

The historian John Guy calls the dissolution of the monasteries Cromwell's 'most important assignment'. Why was it such a significant task?

ii) The Process of Dissolution

Cromwell adopted a three-part approach to ridding the country of its monastic traditions (see Table 6). First, he gathered evidence to show that religious houses were unfit to continue. Secondly, he began to dissolve smaller monasteries. Finally, he moved to abolish the rest.

iii) The Effects of the Dissolution

What were the effects of the dissolution of the monasteries?

Within the space of five years Cromwell had ended a tradition of English monasticism stretching back over five centuries. Historians use words such as 'vandalism' and 'plundering' to describe the methods used because religious houses had their valuables confiscated and melted down (whatever their worth as religious artefacts), including the lead from their roofs. Many of the impressive monastic buildings that had been a feature of the medieval landscape fell into disrepair and became crumbling ruins, whilst others were sold off to become houses for the wealthy.

The main beneficiaries of the dissolution were the king and the nobility. Henry's seizure of the lands and assets of the monasteries brought him great wealth. It has been estimated that the total value of the dissolution amounted to about 10 per cent of the entire wealth of the kingdom, and this money came to Henry in one great transfer during the 1530s. For the next half century or so it was used to finance the kind of ambitious foreign policy which Henry had

Date	Cromwell's Actions
1534	• Act of First Fruits and Tenths allowed Henry to tax the church • Act of Supremacy gave Henry the power to supervise and reform all religious establishments in England
1535	• Cromwell sent out commissioners to survey the value of monastic lands and properties, and to produce a report, the *Valor Ecclesiasticus* (meaning 'value of the church') • Cromwell sent out a second set of commissioners to investigate the moral and spiritual standards in the monasteries
1536	• Based on his commissioners's findings, Parliament passed the Act for the Dissolution of the Smaller Monasteries, which closed all religious houses with lands valued at under £200 per year • new commissioners were sent out to supervise the closures (provoking rebellion in Lincolnshire and Yorkshire – see page 96)
1537–8	• closures continued, although some religious houses bribed officials to overlook them temporarily • the opposition of Carthusian monks to the dissolution of their establishments led to their execution on Henry's orders (see page 95)
1539	• Parliament passed the Act for the Dissolution of the Larger Monasteries, extending the closures to all religious houses except chantries (small, private chapels where prayers were said for the souls of the dead)
1540	• The Court of Augmentations was established, with Richard Rich as Chancellor, to handle the property and income from the dissolved monasteries

Table 6 The process of dissolution – how Cromwell destroyed English monasticism, 1534–40.

dreamed about at the start of his reign. In the longer term, it did little to help the monarchy's financial independence. As the cost of wars continued and escalated (because of greater commitments and rising inflation), Henry and his successors sold off monastic lands to raise money. In this way, they lost control of these lands and the possibility of collecting taxes in the future.

Historians are still debating who bought the land from the crown. It is a difficult question to answer because there is no clear national pattern. However, much of the property was bought either by members of the nobility to strengthen their existing regional holdings, or by the lesser gentry as a way of establishing their presence in a local community. For some writers, the growing visibility of the gentry class is the most important effect of the dissolution of the monasteries, because it illustrates an important change in society from the traditional ruling élite to a more widely based ruling class. Another group who benefited from the dissolution were Protestants. For them, the closure of these strongholds of Catholic ritual dealt a great blow to the possibility of a return to Roman Catholicism in England.

The main losers were the inhabitants of the monasteries and, to some extent, the local communities around them. For all their possible failings, monasteries did offer services to people living nearby which were not entirely taken over by other institutions after they closed. Some writers point in particular to the effect of the dissolution on learning. Monasteries were places where great libraries of books had been built up over generations and where the sons of well-off families might go to receive part of their education. Evidence suggests that the great libraries were broken up, as books were taken by private collectors or simply burned. Monks and nuns lost their work and their accommodation, although some received compensation in the form of pensions or one-off payments. Unfortunately, the government was least generous to the friars and nuns who came from the poorest establishments. Despite this, historians have generally refused to link the dissolution to a rise in poverty, because the number affected in each local community was not that great and because there were other opportunities within the church or in the homes of the great Catholic families for these people to take up.

ACTIVITY

Review your understanding of this section by completing the following table. You will need to decide where the following entries should go and to be able to say why:

Henry VIII; Thomas Cromwell; monks and nuns; the nobility; the gentry; Protestant reformers; people living close to monasteries.

Be careful! Some of these entries need to be put on both sides of the table.

Who gained, and who lost, as a result of the dissolution of the monasteries?

Winners	Losers

---

c) Doctrinal Reform

Cromwell also turned his attention to reforming the teachings of the church. In 1536, as Vicar-General of the church, he issued Ten Articles of faith which incorporated distinctly Protestant ideas similar to those proposed by Martin Luther. These were enforced by two sets of Injunctions (or instructions) in 1536 and 1538, which ordered the clergy to follow the articles. A Bishop's Book was published in 1537, offering interpretation and advice. Both the Injunctions and the Bishop's Book attacked the abuses and superstition that had come to be associated with the church, and encouraged Protestant reformers. Also in 1537 the first official translation of the Bible into English was published. In 1538 a royal proclamation ordered that a copy should be placed in every parish church, to be read and examined by the congregation.

These doctrinal changes were swift and significant. Although there was a reaction against them in the final years of Henry's reign, they created a climate for change that could not easily be reversed. In particular, the accessibility of the Bible to a wide range of people, each able to interpret and debate the word of God for themselves, laid the foundations for the variety of religious beliefs that were to appear later in the sixteenth century.

6 Opposition to Change

The main problem facing those who were uneasy about events during the late 1520s and early 1530s was that it was unclear where matters were heading; there was no single great event to take a stand against until the break with Rome was made official by the 1534 Act of Supremacy. Even then, many people (including the Pope) assumed that the break was only temporary, until Henry could sort out his marital problems. So, religious conservatives were unable to mount a successful opposition to Henry's plans because, in the words of Christopher Haigh, 'they did not know that they were in "the Reformation"'. As a result, those opposing religious change mounted only a feeble resistance before 1534 and, although they reacted more vigorously afterwards, they had left the real challenge too late.

a) Resistance at Court

i) Sir Thomas More

Sir Thomas More (see page 123) was the most high-profile opponent of the royal divorce and the changes of 1534. He had replaced Wolsey as chief minister for a brief period after 1529, but had fallen from royal favour when he showed reluctance to support Henry's plans to marry Anne Boleyn. After the passage of the Succession Act, he was required to swear an oath showing his acceptance of Mary's illegitimacy. More refused and was sent to the Tower of London. He refused to explain why he would not take the oath, but it seems likely that he felt that it would go against the Pope's authority, since a judgment had been reached in Rome in 1534 that Henry's first marriage was legal. Although More wisely avoided incriminating himself, a trial rigged by Thomas Cromwell sealed his fate. According to evidence provided by Sir Richard Rich, one of Cromwell's supporters who was to become the head of the Court of Augmentations in 1540, More

ISSUE:
Who opposed the king's divorce?

was alleged to have been overheard in prison saying that he did not accept Henry as head of the church. This was slender proof of treason, but enough for the court, which ordered his execution. More had used passive resistance to signal his opposition to the changes going on around him, but he was too famous as a politician and too widely respected as a humanist to avoid persecution.

Source F An account of the execution of Sir Thomas More, from *The Life of Sir Thomas More,* by William Roper (who was More's son-in-law).

And so the next day, being Tuesday, More's great friend Sir Thomas Pope came to him with a message from the King and his Council that he should suffer death before nine of the clock the same morning. 'Master Pope,' said Sir Thomas More, 'for your good tidings I heartily thank you. I have been always much bounden to the King for the benefits and honours that he has from time to time most bountifully heaped upon me, and I am even more bounden to him for putting me into this place. And, most of all, I am bounden to his Highness that it pleases him so shortly to put me out of the miseries of this wretched world and therefore I will not fail earnestly to pray for him both here and also in the world to come.' 'The King's pleasure is further', said Master Pope, 'that you shall not use so many words.'

And so he was brought out of the Tower, and from there led to the place of execution. Where, going up to the scaffold (which was so weak that it was ready to fall), he said merrily to the lieutenant, 'I pray you, see me safely up, and for my coming down let me shift for myself.' Then desired he that all the people thereabouts pray for him, and to bear witness with him that he should now suffer death in and for the faith of the holy Catholic Church. Which done, he knelt down and turned to the executioner with a cheerful countenance and said, 'Pluck up thy spirits, man, and be not afraid to do your work. My neck is very short, so take heed and do not strike badly, to save your reputation.' So passed Sir Thomas More out of this world and to God.

ACTIVITY

Read this account of the execution of Sir Thomas More.

1. What does it reveal about More's character?
2. How can the account help to show why More was regarded as such a danger by the king?
3. How does the fact that the account was written by More's son-in-law affect the value of this evidence?

ii) The Aragonese Faction

Before 1534, those who opposed the attack on the church generally expressed their concerns by being sympathetic to Catherine of Aragon in the matter of the royal divorce. Within the nobility, and at court, there was a personal following for Catherine among the **'Aragonese' faction**.

ISSUE:
Why was it difficult to oppose the king's plans for a divorce?

b) Resistance Within the Clergy

i) Elizabeth Barton, the Nun of Kent

Elizabeth Barton had been subject to visions since her teens, following an illness in 1525 and an apparently miraculous cure by a vision of the Virgin Mary. She had acquired local fame and been sent to a nunnery under the protection of Dr Edward Bocking, a Canterbury monk. By 1528 her visions had begun to focus on the king's marriage, and she had warned of disastrous consequences if he abandoned his wife. Her threats continued and included telling the king to his face that he would be dead within a month if he divorced Catherine. The likelihood is that Elizabeth herself believed her visions, but those around her were playing a more political game.

By 1530 Bocking had developed Elizabeth's warnings into a wider campaign against changes in the church, the influence of humanism, and the Boleyn marriage, by encouraging pilgrims and publishing books describing her visions and the warnings they contained. Rumours were deliberately circulated about miraculous interventions, including the story that an angel had appeared while the king was at mass and seized the communion bread from his hands. Letters were sent to More and Fisher; links were established with Exeter (Courtenay) and Hussey, and with the Carthusian monks in London who were to prove a centre of resistance to the royal supremacy in 1534. All this suggested that an orchestrated campaign was being prepared.

Faced with this evidence Cromwell acted, and the nun and her mentors were arrested in September 1533. After a public humiliation at St Paul's Cross in London, where Elizabeth confessed that her visions were false, they were executed in April 1534. The judges could find no specific crime committed by Elizabeth, but the group were condemned by an Act of Attainder. While the nun's fate was tragic, her mentors had cynically exploited her fame for several years, and their attempts to co-ordinate a resistance movement represented a genuine threat that no government could afford to ignore.

ii) Monastic Resistance

By far the strongest clerical resistance to Henry came from the monastic orders. While the Cistercians and Benedictines, who owned the great rural monasteries dissolved after 1536, were not widely active, there were many examples of individual monks who preached against the divorce, the supremacy and the new heresies that came with them.

More significant, and certainly more organised, was the reaction of the widely respected London monks of the Carthusian order, who had remained closer to the strict ideals of monasticism. In 1532–3 they refused to accept the divorce and in 1534 resisted government pressure to agree to a declaration against the authority of the Pope. The government could not permit such defiance, and after the passage of the Treason Act, forced the Carthusians to submit, arresting the most reluctant and executing 18 of them.

THE ARAGONESE FACTION

A small group of nobles and courtiers, led by Henry Courtenay, Marquis of Exeter and the northern Lords Darcy and Hussey, who supported Catherine of Aragon in the divorce question. Courtenay was a member of the king's Privy Chamber, while another supporter – Sir Henry Guildford – was the Controller of the King's Household. From 1532, the stronger presence of Anne Boleyn and her supporters at court and the growing influence of Thomas Cromwell within the King's Council had largely silenced the Aragonese faction. However, they remained hopeful after the divorce that Catherine's daughter Mary would be recognised as Henry's heir. Her exclusion from the succession in 1536 helped to push Darcy and Hussey into supporting the rebellion known as the Pilgrimage of Grace (see page 96) and their execution for treason. Courtenay did not become involved in the rebellion, but he did become linked to the activities of Reginald Pole, his distant cousin who was a descendant of the Yorkist kings overthrown by the Tudors. This association was enough to cause Henry to arrest Courtenay and to order his execution in 1539.

c) Resistance Within the Country

The government's success in containing opposition has led some historians to argue that resistance to the Henrician Reformation was both weak and minimal, never a serious threat to the king's position. In 1536, however, riots in Lincolnshire quickly spread across the whole of the north: at the height of the rebellion the king's forces faced 40,000 'pilgrims' in arms. This was the most serious challenge to royal authority so far within the Tudor period.

Figure 24 The course of the Pilgrimage of Grace, 1536–7.

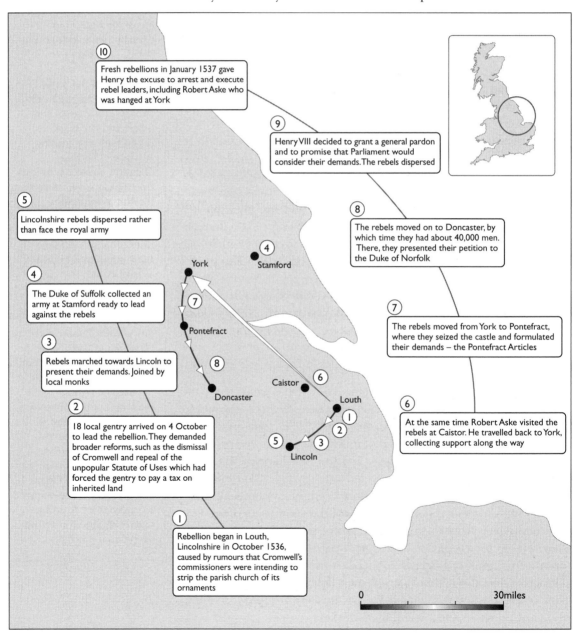

10 Fresh rebellions in January 1537 gave Henry the excuse to arrest and execute rebel leaders, including Robert Aske who was hanged at York

9 Henry VIII decided to grant a general pardon and to promise that Parliament would consider their demands. The rebels dispersed

5 Lincolnshire rebels dispersed rather than face the royal army

8 The rebels moved on to Doncaster, by which time they had about 40,000 men. There, they presented their petition to the Duke of Norfolk

4 The Duke of Suffolk collected an army at Stamford ready to lead against the rebels

7 The rebels moved from York to Pontefract, where they seized the castle and formulated their demands – the Pontefract Articles

3 Rebels marched towards Lincoln to present their demands. Joined by local monks

6 At the same time Robert Aske visited the rebels at Caistor. He travelled back to York, collecting support along the way

2 18 local gentry arrived on 4 October to lead the rebellion. They demanded broader reforms, such as the dismissal of Cromwell and repeal of the unpopular Statute of Uses which had forced the gentry to pay a tax on inherited land

1 Rebellion began in Louth, Lincolnshire in October 1536, caused by rumours that Cromwell's commissioners were intending to strip the parish church of its ornaments

York   Stamford   Pontefract   Doncaster   Caistor   Louth   Lincoln

0   30miles

ACTIVITY

The fact that the Reformation was carried out in a series of stages and steps helps to explain why it was difficult for opponents to organise an effective campaign against it.

To investigate further the failure of resistance:

1. Make a list of all the problems facing those who wished to oppose the changes in the church.
2. Make a list of the weapons which Henry and Cromwell could use to silence opposition.
3. Compare at least two of the people and groups in this section to determine which of the points you have made in your lists seems to appear most often as an explanation for their failure.

---

7 The Spread of Protestant Ideas

From 1529 Henry had encouraged criticism of the Pope and the English clergy. He had allowed those who demanded reform to speak openly because it suited his purpose of pressurising the Pope into granting him a divorce. For the reformers this offered relief from persecution and the opportunity to influence the future of the church in England. The king's divorce, the campaign to win support in the European universities, and the growing influence of sympathetic individuals such as Anne Boleyn and Thomas Cromwell enabled the reformers to develop their ideas, increase support and gain influence within the government and the church itself.

While Cromwell managed the campaign in Parliament, Anne drew Henry's attention to the work of Tyndale, protected heretics like Robert Forman in London, and encouraged the appointment of reformers to positions of power and influence within the church. Her influence led to the appointment of Hugh Latimer and Nicholas Shaxton (who had been accused of heresy in 1531) to vacant bishop's posts, and to the selection of Thomas Cranmer as Archbishop of Canterbury.

By 1536 Protestant individuals were firmly established in government, and able to spread their influence widely. Preachers such as John Bale, Edward Crome and Robert Barnes spread Protestant teachings in London, while Cranmer encouraged similar activities in Suffolk, Essex and Kent. The Injunctions of 1536 further encouraged this sort of preaching, and from 1538 Cromwell's efforts to ensure that parishes had a copy of the Bible in English were beginning to have the effect of opening up interest and debate in the new ideas.

8 The Catholic Backlash, 1540–47

ANABAPTISTS

The term Anabaptist was applied, often inaccurately, to anyone with extreme Protestant ideas. The original Anabaptists had emerged in Germany as a group who denied the right of any authority to set up a compulsory church, and who emphasised the free will of people to accept or reject faith. These ideas were threatening to governments since they challenged compulsion and control and had led, in the case of Münster, to extremes of violence and chaos. Henry, like other European rulers, was sensitive to the possibility of these ideas working their way into England.

By 1540 Protestant converts were probably no more than a tiny minority across the country as a whole, but in some areas they had risen to a sufficient number to alarm the authorities. Although Henry had tolerated their complaints against the Pope, things were different now that he was head of the church. When some Protestants began to adopt more extreme ideas, such as the denial of the mass as anything more than a symbolic service, they offended Henry's Catholic sympathies. Moreover, he was reminded of events that had taken place in the German town of Münster in 1534–5 when **Anabaptists** with similarly extreme ideas had seized control and destroyed the rightful political authorities. The first sign of reaction came in the trial of John Lambert for heresy in November 1538, which was attended by the king himself. Lambert was burned with great cruelty in 1539, and his death was followed by the reimposition of key Catholic doctrines in the **Six Articles Act** in the same year.

Six Articles Act

The Six Articles Act brought to an end the Protestant changes introduced by Cromwell and Cranmer into the Church of England. The Act reintroduced a strongly Catholic interpretation into church services. It enforced the doctrine of transubstantiation, and communion in one kind (bread) only for the laity, and emphasised the seven sacraments as essential for salvation, and the need for priests to remain celibate.

The reaction against Protestant ideas was the first indication that the English Reformation would not progress as smoothly as some on the continent. At court, the fall of Thomas Cromwell in 1540 (see page 130) and the apparent success of the pro-Catholic conservative faction (see page 131) also seemed to mark a new stage in developments. From 1540 until 1547 Protestants were persecuted and their ideas attacked. However, they were not wiped out. Cranmer remained Archbishop of Canterbury, surviving attempts by the conservative faction to discredit him in the eyes of the king. Henry's last wife, Catherine Parr, also gave the Protestant movement renewed vigour. She maintained an interest in reforming ideas and encouraged the education of Prince Edward and Princess Elizabeth by Protestant scholars like Richard Coxe and John Cheke.

By Henry's death, his Reformation had reached a stalemate. The preaching of Protestant ideas was suppressed, but the country remained entirely separated from the Pope's control. The monasteries had disappeared, the Bible was still available in English, and limited reforms against the worship of saints and other superstitious practices had survived. Henry's Reformation had brought about the political consequences that he had desired, but had left English religion in an uneasy state – Catholicism without the Pope. The logic behind this position was weak. Henry had overthrown the Pope's power in England, but relied on bishops who preached the Pope's doctrines to maintain the split. Given that Prince Edward had been brought up to be sympathetic to Protestant reforms and given the background of religious divisions elsewhere in Europe, no one really expected this situation to last for long.

Working on The Beginnings of the English Reformation

How historians have approached the topic

Writers dealing with the early part of the English Reformation have been divided about how quickly and how deeply change had occurred by 1553. According to A. G. Dickens in *The English Reformation* (1964), the Lollard movement and the popularity of simple Protestant teachings led communities to accept the Reformation quickly and enthusiastically. Local case studies of the spread of the Reformation have been used to support this argument.

However, other historians have challenged the idea that the Roman Catholic Church in England was vulnerable to change and have particularly criticised the notion that Catholic *faith* was in decline. Writers such as Eamon Duffy in *The Stripping of the Altars: Traditional Religion in England, 1400–1580* (1992) have mounted a defence of the view that popular Catholic traditions remained strong, arguing that Protestantism made less headway than has been suggested by selective case studies of local changes. To Duffy and others, the Reformation was brought about by political pressure from the king's ministers, rather than as a result of a popular groundswell of opinion.

Figure 25
Outline of the
beginnings of
the English
Reformation,
1520–47.

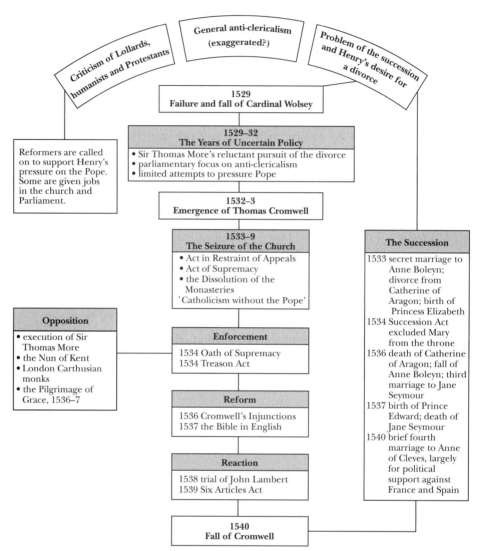

Answering Extended Writing and Essay Questions on The Beginnings of the English Reformation

Essay questions and extended writing tasks tend to focus around certain key issues and concepts. One of the important concepts which you will use frequently on your History course is **causation** – why things happened. If you think about how you would reply to this sort of question in everyday life ('Why did you do that?', 'Why do we have to take exams?' and so on), the ordinary response is to say 'Because ...'

and start to give reasons (or factors, as historians like to term them). What you would not do is start to say everything you knew about the subject, because others might think you were odd!

It is the same in History examinations. If you are asked why something happened, you are expected to focus on the reasons (which historians call causal factors) and to select details from the surrounding story to illustrate what you are saying. In other words, factors come first, the story comes second. From this, we can create a skeleton paragraph that you can use to define and set out each causal factor. Writing your essay in paragraphs like these will always keep you focused on the question and avoid getting factors and facts muddled:

▼ Your first sentence needs to give a reason. Use straightforward language to make the point clear (such as 'One of the factors which caused ... was ...')

▼ Continue by explaining ('unpacking') the factor more fully ('This meant that ...')

▼ Choose factual material which will support the relevance of the factor to the question.

To put this into practice, look at the following question:

1. **a)** Why did Henry VIII want a divorce from Catherine of Aragon?
   b) Describe the steps that he took to achieve his divorce.
   c) Why did this problem develop into a breach with Rome and the establishment of the Church of England?

On pages 81–2, we established the reasons why Henry wanted a divorce from Catherine:

▼ the marriage had failed to produce a son
▼ Henry had grown infatuated with Anne Boleyn
▼ Henry began to believe that God was punishing him for marrying his brother's widow.

These will provide the first sentences of each of our paragraphs to answer part (a). We then need to explain each factor more fully and to give relevant factual information, as in this example:

'One of the reasons why Henry wanted to divorce Catherine of Aragon was her failure to provide him with a son. [= *the factor*] Henry thought that this was essential for a stable succession after his death. [= *unpacking the factor*] He had a daughter, Mary, but there was no recent experience of a female ruler in England. More importantly, the crown had been very unstable in the fifteenth century, with rulers challenged by powerful nobles. [= *factual material to support the factor*] Henry believed that a female succession might revive these conflicts, undoing his and his father's successful work in securing the Tudor dynasty.' [= *unpacking the factor*]

Of course, as you become more familiar with writing this sort of answer at a higher level, you will be able to vary the way you write opening sentences and other elements of the paragraph to create a more elegant piece of writing, but you should try not to ignore the general structure we have established here.

You can take your answer to part (a) further by trying to make links between the factors that you include, to show how they worked together or interacted to bring about the results that you are trying to explain or describe. In this case, you might arrange the list of factors so that you can show that Henry's desire for a divorce began with his need for a son, and that he was able to justify wanting an immediate divorce by his belief that no son had been born because God was angry at the marriage.

To practise further, try planning some or all of the paragraphs that you would need to answer part (c), as well as the order in which you would put them to create a logical sequence. Here are some factors to get you started:

▼ the attitude of the Pope towards the divorce
▼ the influence of Thomas Cromwell
▼ the problems of the church
▼ the role of Emperor Charles V
▼ the influence of Protestant reformers.

Other questions to help you practise this topic include:

▼ Did Henry VIII want to reform the church?
▼ How popular were the religious changes of the 1530s?

Answering Source-Based Questions on The Beginnings of the English Reformation

One of the types of questions which you will have to tackle on every examination paper is 'cross-referencing'. This means comparing and contrasting the information contained in two or more sources.

Source G From a report by Richard Layton, one of Cromwell's commissioners, on a visit he made to the priory of Maiden Bradley in 1535.

I send you relics – God's coat, Our Lady's smock, part of God's supper – and all this from the priory at Maiden Bradley. There, you will find a holy father who has six children. His sons are all tall men who wait on him, and he thanks God that he never meddled with married women, but only with maidens (the fairest that could be got). The Pope, considering the holy father's fragility, has given him a licence to keep a whore.

The abbeys in the north parts gave great alms to poor men and have laudably served God. Now that they have been suppressed the divine service of Almighty God is much diminished and a great number of Masses are unsaid, much to the distress of the faith. The temple of God has been pulled down and the ornaments and relics of the church irreverently used. Many of the abbeys were in the mountains and desert places where people were in ungodly conditions and they gave people not only refreshment to their bodies but also spiritual refuge by their information and preaching. And such abbeys that were near the danger of the seas were great maintainers of sea walls and dikes, maintainers and builders of bridges and highways and other such things for the common good.

Source H From the evidence given by Robert Aske in his examination after the Pilgrimage of Grace; quoted in *Tudor Rebellions* by A. Fletcher and D. MacCulloch, 4th edn (1997).

▼ QUESTION ON SOURCES

How do Sources G and H differ in their view of the value and role of monasteries? **[5 marks]**

To answer this question, you need to look at what the point behind the comparison is. What is the question asking you to compare?

Then, you need to read each source carefully and come to a judgement about what points it is making (or seems to imply) that would be relevant.

Then, you need to see if any of the points from each source can be matched together because they agree or contradict each other about the same precise issue (e.g. the value of relics or the spirituality of life inside the monasteries). This will help you to avoid just writing a summary of each source without seeing the links between them.

The following answer has all the right points in it, but they are not organised very effectively. How would you advise the candidate to restructure the answer?

'Source G shows just how bad the monasteries had become by 1535. The writer thinks that they have lost all value because they have become places where superstitious practices, such as collecting together relics, are common. He also thinks that the prior lives improperly because he is not following his religious duties but has fathered children and keeps a mistress. Source H is written after some of the monasteries in the north had been dissolved. Robert Aske regrets the dissolution. He says that the monasteries had provided an important spiritual function, especially in parts of the country where people had not had much contact with the church. Their religious ornaments and relics were being mocked and abused. We can also deduce that the monasteries were places where Christian values were very strong because Aske is concerned that the number of masses and acts of charity within the community have declined sharply.'

You can also use these sources to practise other sorts of source-based questions:

1. Read Source H and use your wider knowledge.
In what ways were the monasteries an important part of community life before the Reformation? **[5 marks]**

2. Read Sources G and H.
Both sources tell us something about the state of the monasteries before the Reformation. Why might a historian be cautious about using each of them? **[8 marks]**

(See pages 32–3 for advice on answering this sort of question.)

Further Reading

Books in the Access to History series

You will find a more comprehensive survey of the events covered by this chapter in *Henry VIII and the Reformation in England* (second edition) by Keith Randell. To place the English Reformation into a wider European context, and to find out about the links between English and continental reformers, refer to *The Sixteenth Century Reformation* by Geoffrey Woodward.

Other books

If you are studying this topic in preparation for a source-based examination, you will find a collection of useful documents, with questions to test your knowledge and understanding, in *History at Source: The English Reformation* by Peter Servini (Hodder and Stoughton). There are excellent chapters on the early Reformation in most textbooks on the Tudors. Particularly useful is the section in John Guy's *Tudor England* (Oxford University Press, 1988). For more detailed analyses of the causes and progress of religious reform, the standard works are A. G. Dickens's *The English Reformation* (Fontana, 1964) and J. J. Scarisbrick's *Henry VIII* (Penguin, 1968). Some of their ideas have been developed or challenged by recent authors, most notably Eamon Duffy in *The Stripping of the Altars* (New Haven, 1992) and Christopher Haigh in *English Reformations* (Oxford University Press, 1993).

POLITICS IN THE AGE OF WOLSEY AND CROMWELL

CHAPTER 4

POINTS TO CONSIDER

Whereas Henry VII had dominated the politics of his reign, Henry VIII preferred to pursue the pleasures of being king and leave the day-to-day routines of government to his chief ministers – Cardinal Thomas Wolsey (from 1515 to 1529) and Thomas Cromwell (from 1532 to 1540). As we shall see, however, that did not mean that Henry played no part. He set the tone and aims of government and he could be ruthless in dispensing with those who did not meet them, as both Wolsey and Cromwell were to discover to their cost. In this chapter we will look at Henry's style of government, and how it differed from his father's, and then examine the impact of his chief ministers on the shape and direction of policies. In particular, you will need to focus on the debate surrounding the 1530s – did Thomas Cromwell's pursuit of power for Henry result in a 'revolution in government'? It is important also to recognise the religious dimension to policies. These are touched on here, but developed in more detail in Chapter 3.

1 The Early Years of Henry VIII's Reign, 1509–15

Figures 26 and 27 The portrait of Henry VII by Michael Sittow was painted in 1505, four years before the king's death, and is the best surviving portrait. It shows the 48-year-old Henry looking at the viewer with a serious and shrewd sideways glance. He is dressed conservatively, with few of the symbols we associated with kingship, such as a crown or sceptre. In fact, the only 'prop' shown in the painting is the red rose that Henry is holding, a reminder to contemporaries of his Lancastrian ancestry. The painting of Henry VIII is also a simple portrait, showing the young king in about 1510 or 1511.

ISSUE:

How far were Henry VIII's personality and early policies different from his father's?

The contrasts between Henry VIII and his father could not have been more marked. Henry VIII succeeded to the throne when he was 18, a young, athletic and charismatic figure who, if not born to be king, had known that this was his destiny since his brother's death in 1502. Where Henry VII had endured years of poverty and exile, succeeding to the throne only through luck and military success, Henry VIII had known only wealth and expectation, if tinged with insecurity. His accession was popular. He represented the union of the Houses of York and Lancaster, a symbol of domestic peace and harmony, and the dawn of a new era after the years of mistrust and financial oppression that had overshadowed his father's relationship with his nobility. In the words of Sir Thomas More, 'This day is the end of our slavery, the fount of our liberty; the end of our sadness and the beginning of joy.'

Source A From a letter written by the Venetian ambassador, Guistiniani, in 1521.

His Majesty is twenty-nine years old and extremely handsome. Nature could not have done more for him. He is much handsomer than any other sovereign in Christendom; a great deal handsomer than the King of France; very fair and his whole frame admirably proportioned. He is very accomplished, a good musician, composes well, is a most capital horseman, a fine jouster, speaks good French, Latin and Spanish, is very religious, hears masses three times a day when he hunts, and sometimes five on other days. He is very fond of hunting, and never takes his diversion without tiring eight or ten horses. He is extremely fond of tennis, at which game it is the prettiest thing in the world to see him play, his fair skin glowing through a shirt of the finest texture.

Q What qualities do you think made Henry a popular monarch, and different from his father?

Q What do you think that Henry intended to show by abolishing the Council Learned in Law?

a) Henry's First Decisions

The difference was reinforced by Henry VIII's first actions and the nature of the court that he established. Within days of his accession he ordered the arrest of his father's chief financial enforcers, Empson and Dudley of the Council Learned in Law, and abolished this hated court. His second announcement was that he would honour his promise to marry Catherine of Aragon. Since Arthur's death in 1502 she had been kept at court by Henry VII whilst he conducted the apparently complicated negotiations needed to secure both the Pope and her parents' approval for the remarriage. In reality, Henry had deliberately delayed permitting the marriage until he could be certain that it would bring diplomatic advantage to England. Henry VIII's decision to enact the marriage was a typically honourable and chivalrous thing to do. The early years of his reign provide abundant evidence that he took the concepts of knightly valour and honour seriously. Catherine, however, would live to see an entirely different side to his character as Henry passed from youth to middle age.

b) Henry's Court

The image and reality of the new king was also reflected in the court that he created around himself. The royal court was not only the centre of politics and government, it was also a projection of the king's personality and the aura of majesty that he sought to create. Henry VII had maintained a lavish court, with generous hospitality and patronage of scholars and explorers. The court of Henry VIII was dedicated to pleasure and refinement. While the king's favourite activities were hunting and the sports of tennis and jousting, at which he excelled, he was also intelligent enough to enjoy the company of scholars steeped in the new learning of the Renaissance. Henry also enjoyed music, and composed some creditable pieces of his own (albeit with some expert help which he kept quiet about). He also increased the number and quality of royal residences.

Figure 28 The royal palace at Nonsuch in Surrey, in an engraving from 1582. The palace was intended to show the glory and power of Henry VIII through its impressive size and architectural style.

c) Treatment of the Nobility

Henry VII had controlled the ambitions of the nobility more by threatening their status and wealth than by making concessions to them. Some historians have even gone as far as to wonder whether he intended to undermine the power of the nobility to the point where he could replace them in government with talented administrators. Henry VIII's attitude towards them seemed different from the outset. Early gestures of goodwill included disbanding the Council Learned in Law and cancelling 175 bonds and recognisances that were still owing. There is no doubt that the young king regarded the nobility as his friends and associates, with whom he could share his sporting and artistic pleasures. By gathering important men around him, Henry also enhanced the prestige of his court.

However, Henry shared his father's suspicion of possible rivals among the ranks of the nobility. Although the Yorkist threat was substantially weaker by 1509, there were still members of the greater nobility who carried royal blood in their veins, and who might be tempted to challenge the claims of the Tudors. The main candidate of the 'White Rose' party, as the Yorkists had come to be known, was Edmund de la Pole, the Earl of Suffolk. When Henry came to the throne, Suffolk was already imprisoned in the Tower of London. In 1513, Henry had him executed for treason, but his younger brother, Richard, remained free and in French service until his death at the Battle of Pavia in 1525. Although the French exploited his claims during negotiations with Henry, and even recognised him as 'King Richard IV', there was no serious attempt to replace Henry from abroad.

d) Style of Government

Henry VII's style of government had been personal and extremely conscientious. He took major decisions himself, without the aid of a powerful chief minister. He moved the administration of finances into his private rooms at court, out of the Treasury and Exchequer. He largely ignored Parliament and showed time and again that he was not prepared to trust members of the nobility until he was certain that they could be forced to obey him. Henry VIII adopted some of his father's tactics. He continued to use Justices of the Peace to carry out his wishes in local government rather than rely on the nobility. He also followed his father's practice of encouraging talented advisers and administrators from outside the nobility.

However, there were crucial differences. In the first place, Henry VIII never gave the affairs of government the personal attention that his father had exercised, tending instead to delegate far greater

Figure 29 Henry VIII dining in the Privy Chamber. This was one of the rooms within the royal palace which the king used as his private quarters. Only his most intimate advisers and courtiers were allowed to attend him there, a sure sign of who was 'in' and who was 'out' in courtly politics.

power to his chief advisers. The adult years of Henry VIII's reign were dominated by two men – Cardinal Thomas Wolsey, who was the king's chief minister between 1515 and 1529, and Thomas Cromwell, who occupied the same role between 1532 and 1540. This was a new development in government. Henry VII's close personal control of the day-to-day running of the country did not suit his younger and more secure son. Although Henry VIII kept overall control, he preferred to act out a combination of medieval and Renaissance images of kingship – the medieval 'good lord', who exhibited courage and honour, and the Renaissance 'universal man', as skilled in courtly etiquette and the arts as in warfare. He did not share his father's dedication to the unglamorous side of ruling, so left much of this to his chief ministers. However, as the careers of both Wolsey and Cromwell show, they depended heavily on maintaining the king's favour to survive. By allowing ministers to assume more power, Henry also encouraged what his father had largely avoided – **factionalism** at court.

FACTIONALISM

The royal court, not Parliament, was the centre of political power and influence during the Tudor period. Courtiers advanced by attracting the king's attention, often with the help of someone who was one of his friends or supporters. In this way, groups of ambitious courtiers clustered around powerful nobles and ministers. Rivalry developed between these groups – or factions – as all were keen to win what limited royal patronage there was.

e) Foreign Policy

The accession of Henry VIII in 1509 opened a new phase in foreign policy. Henry VII's foreign policy had been that of an insecure adult; Henry VIII's began as the actions of a confident teenager. Unlike his father, Henry VIII came to the throne peacefully, and with money in the royal treasury. His priorities were therefore different: he was keen to establish his presence in international affairs and to demonstrate his strengths to his subjects.

The easiest way to accomplish these aims was to revive hostilities with France. In 1511 Henry invaded northern France and in 1512 engaged the French army in the 'Battle of the Spurs', the result of which was the capture of the town of Tournai. Henry received personal satisfaction from this victory, but the gains of the 1511–12 campaign were minimal and expensive to uphold. Both Spain and the Empire had used England to distract France but had failed to support Henry when it came to realising English aims. Although plans were drawn up for a new invasion in 1513, both Spain and the Empire came to terms with France, forcing Henry to abandon his own raids and to make peace in August 1514.

Henry VIII and Scotland

By the time of his death, Henry VII had secured the neutrality of the Scots by agreeing a peace treaty in 1502 and a marriage alliance between his daughter and King James IV in 1503. However, problems in the relationship soon re-emerged in Henry VIII's reign. In 1512 France was able to secure an alliance with Scotland which was intended to distract Henry from his campaign to capture Tournai. A large Scottish army mounted serious border raids in northern England during 1513, but was comprehensively beaten at the Battle of Flodden in September. At the battle, over 10,000 Scots were killed, including a number of the nobility. Shortly after this crushing defeat James IV also died. This left a power vacuum since his son was only a child. Yet again, the continuity of Scottish politics was to be disrupted by a long regency. On this occasion, however, it worked to Henry VIII's advantage since his sister Margaret was left in charge. For the time being, Henry could turn his attention elsewhere.

ISSUE:

How did Wolsey rise to become Henry's chief minister?

2 The Rise of Thomas Wolsey

Thomas Wolsey was born in 1472 or 1473, the son of a butcher in Ipswich. He won a scholarship to Oxford, where he began to study towards the priesthood. Wolsey was outstandingly able, receiving his first degree at Oxford at the age of 15. Whilst at Oxford he became the bursar (treasurer) of his college, a position which allowed him to develop his talent for organisation until a disagreement about whether he had obtained proper permission to authorise a large building project forced him to leave. He then tried, with little success, to find a powerful patron who would introduce him at court. Finally, he was recommended to Henry VII as a possible royal chaplain.

The new atmosphere at court under Henry VIII encouraged ambitious men like Wolsey to get themselves noticed. He won the support of Richard Fox, one of Henry's advisers, and was promoted to the office of Royal Almoner, an official responsible for distributing left-over food from the palace kitchens to the needy poor who gathered outside each day. It was his organisational abilities and his ability to guess what the king wanted to hear that allowed him to progress further. Since his accession Henry had been frustrated by the cautious advice of his father's ministers, especially in the field of foreign policy, where he wanted to make his mark. In 1512 the king entrusted Wolsey with the organisation of the following year's expedition to France. This meant organising transport, supplies and equipment for the 30,000-strong army which Henry proposed to lead himself. It was a big task, but Wolsey showed tireless energy and commitment to achieving it. The expedition went well and Wolsey was drawn into the peace negotiations which followed.

Henry was deeply impressed by Wolsey's efficiency in delivering success in Europe and engineered his rapid promotion to high office.

WOLSEY'S RISE TO HIGH OFFICE

1513 became **Dean of York** and **Bishop of Tournai** (conquered in the French campaign that year);

1514 made **Bishop of Lincoln** and then **Archbishop of York** (the second highest post in the English church);

1515 made **Cardinal** by Pope Leo X (a high-ranking position in the Catholic Church, above any English churchman); also became **Lord Chancellor** in Henry's government when William Warham resigned;

1518 appointed **Papal Legate** by Leo X (which allowed him to deputise for the Pope and exercise papal powers).

3 Wolsey's Personality

With such an impressive array of titles and positions, it was not difficult for Wolsey to elbow aside the king's noble advisers on the Royal Council and to become *alter rex* (the 'other king').

> The Cardinal is the first person who rules both the King and the entire kingdom. On the ambassador's first arrival in England he used to say to him, 'His Majesty will do so and so', but, by degrees, he began to forget himself and started to say, 'We shall do so and so'. Now he has reached such a height that he says, 'I shall do so and so'.

Wolsey's enemies – and he had many of these – came to see him as arrogant and vindictive. On the one hand, he flattered and apparently manipulated Henry, offering him lavish gifts and tokens whilst working him around to his ideas. At the same time, he used his legal powers as Lord Chancellor and a network of informants to intimidate anyone he saw as a rival. A good example of this was the treatment received by the Duke of Buckingham. Edward Stafford was the only man to hold the title of duke by the end of Henry VII's reign. In 1520

ISSUE:

Why did Wolsey's personality and behaviour create opposition to him?

Source B The Venetian ambassador, Giustiniani, writing about Cardinal Wolsey in 1519.

Figure 30 Cardinal Wolsey.

he was investigated by Wolsey after rumours that he had said in a private conversation that Henry might not be king for much longer. In 1521 he was ordered to London, arrested and imprisoned in the Tower. He refused to plead for his life, was tried for treason, and beheaded. Contemporaries believed, rightly or not, that Wolsey had played on Henry's insecurity to convince him to order these actions, and had used Buckingham's fate as a warning to anyone who might be contemplating an attack on the cardinal's power.

Wolsey was certainly capable of taking revenge on anyone who offended him. He had been humiliated by Sir Amyas Paulet when he was a young priest, so on becoming Lord Chancellor, he summoned Paulet to London on a trumped-up charge and kept him there, demanding his daily attendance at the Court of Chancery for five years. The case was never heard, but the delays and expense virtually ruined Paulet.

Wolsey also amassed a large personal fortune and displayed his wealth ostentatiously. His household extended to over 500 servants and he usually travelled with a large escort of richly dressed attendants bearing his emblems and livery:

Source C From a report by the Venetian ambassador, Guistiniani, written in 1519.

He has a very great reputation – seven times more so than if he were the Pope. He has a very fine palace, where one crosses eight rooms before reaching his audience chamber, and they are all hung with tapestry, which is changed once a week. In his own chamber there is always a cupboard with silver vessels to the amount of 30,000 ducats, this being customary with the English nobility. He is supposed to be very rich indeed, in money, plate and household stuff. The archbishopric of York yields him about 14,000 ducats. From gifts, which he receives in the same manner as the King, he makes some 15,000 ducats.

ISSUE:
What influenced Wolsey's approach to government?

4 Government under Wolsey

Henry tended to leave Wolsey with day-to-day control of government, although Wolsey was careful never to assume that this meant that he could ignore the king. Indeed, he spent much of the time trying to keep Henry informed about what was going on whilst making sure that other courtiers did not replace him in the king's favour. A particular problem he faced was that Henry liked to surround himself with favourite nobles of his own age – his 'minions'. These men had access to the king's private rooms in the palace, so they could influence Henry from behind the scenes as well as prevent others from getting to see him.

Some of Wolsey's reforms of government were designed more to undermine potential political opponents, such as the minions, rather than to ensure good government. However, in general, Wolsey made few changes to the structure of government. Instead, he expended his energies in bringing out specific changes to aspects of royal policy that either dissatisfied him, or which were not working to Henry's best advantage.

a) Legal Reforms

How did Wolsey develop the legal system?

As Lord Chancellor, Wolsey was responsible for overseeing the legal system. His main concern was to tackle the problem of slow and often unfair delivery of justice. By 1516 he was already planning reforms to the system to improve matters. The centrepiece of his plans was a strengthened Star Chamber. Henry VII had established this court, which was staffed by members of the Privy Council, to deal out justice on his behalf, often in cases involving the nobility. However, it had not been particularly active, probably hearing only about a dozen cases each year. Wolsey used Star Chamber much more frequently to attack nobles and local officials who abused their power. He encouraged commoners to bring their complaints before the court and in doing so, increased the number of cases heard each year to about 120. This gave him the reputation of being a friend to the poor:

> He alone transacts as much business as that which occupies all the magistrates, offices and councils of Venice, both civil and criminal. He is thoughtful and has the reputation of being extremely just. He favours the people exceedingly, and especially the poor, hearing their cases and seeking to despatch them instantly. He also makes the lawyers plead without charge for all paupers.

Source D From a report by the Venetian ambassador, Guistiniani, written in 1519.

b) Financial Reforms

How did Wolsey attempt to increase royal revenues?

Shortage of money was a serious problem for Henry VIII. His father had made do by avoiding an expensive foreign policy, but this was not in keeping with the new king's desire to get himself noticed and respected by other rulers. Wolsey realised that existing forms of finance (see Chapter 2, pages 55–6) could not be exploited much further. In particular parliamentary grants, which were based on property taxes called fifteenths and tenths, had settled to a fixed sum, so were unlikely to rise much in the future. To overcome this, Wolsey proposed a more flexible tax – a subsidy. This would still be

THE 'AMICABLE GRANT'

In March and April 1525 the government sent out commissioners to order the collection of the Amicable Grant. They were instructed to tax the laity at between one-sixth and one-tenth of the value of the goods they owned, and to tax the clergy at one-third of the value of their goods. They gave people just ten weeks to find the necessary money. Resistance was immediate and widespread, forcing Wolsey to begin admitting exceptions to the tax. As news of these spread, more regions demanded that they too should be exempted. Henry responded to the unrest caused by the tax by stepping in to suspend it. It was an embarrassing climbdown for both the king (who hoped to use the money raised for renewed warfare in France) and Wolsey.

How far did Wolsey protect the livelihoods of poorer people against their landlords?

collected on Parliament's authority, but was based on income rather than property, similar to modern income tax. The subsidy was collected four times in all – between 1513 and 1515 and in 1523, each time to help pay for war in France.

Wolsey also examined the possibility of asking for further loans from taxpayers. In 1522 he undertook the first systematic investigation into national finances since the Domesday Survey of 1086. From this, he concluded that there was sufficient wealth to demand new loans. In 1525, he proposed an '**Amicable Grant**' from both the church and ordinary taxpayers based on his valuations of their property. The reaction to this demand was to provoke the only significant rebellion in the first half of Henry VIII's reign.

c) Economic Policies

It was not usual in the Tudor period for governments to have coherent economic policies, if only because there was little that could be regarded as a national economy and little that counted as industry beyond woollen production. However, Wolsey involved himself in the growing problem of enclosures. There had been tentative attempts to tackle the issue under Henry VII, but Henry had been too concerned not to annoy landowners unnecessarily whilst he was still vulnerable to opposition to sort matters out effectively. Wolsey had no such concerns, and held the view that the conversion of arable land to sheep pasture by enclosing fields destroyed village life and jobs.

In 1517 Wolsey began a national enquiry to find out how much land was enclosed and what effects it was having. From this, legal cases were drawn up against landlords who were judged to have enclosed land without the proper permission. Further investigations were conducted in 1518, although opposition from landowners in Parliament in 1523 forced him to suspend these enquiries temporarily until 1526.

d) Wolsey and the Church

So far, we have focused on Wolsey the politician. However, he also pursued a career in the church, ultimately as the Pope's representative in England. From this position, he was uniquely placed to give leadership or to reject those who wanted to reform the church in England. The origins of the Reformation during the 1520s are examined more closely in the previous chapter, but in summary, it is fair to say that Wolsey made some attempts to encourage reform, although these were not significant enough to quieten the demands of Protestants. In his capacity as papal legate, Wolsey was able to instruct English bishops to carry out their duties more scrupulously and to order inspections of the quality of religious life in monasteries and other religious

What changes did Wolsey make to the Church in England?

institutions. As a result, over two dozen religious houses were dissolved (closed down and their assets confiscated).

Wolsey was also interested in promoting religious learning to improve the quality of the clergy. He planned to fund a school in his home town of Ipswich and to establish Cardinal College in Oxford, but had fallen from power before these could be properly established.

As a Catholic cardinal, Wolsey was strongly opposed to the spread of Protestant heresy in England. He encouraged Henry to take a stand against the new ideas of the German reformer Martin Luther, which led to public burnings of Lutheran texts and executions of people suspected of Protestant sympathies.

However, Wolsey's position in the church did not always bring him praise. To some, he embodied everything that needed changing. He had already collected together a range of religious titles during his rise to power, and he continued adding to them during the 1520s. He became Bishop of Durham in 1523 and Bishop of Winchester in 1529, both important positions which attracted good income. He was also appointed abbot of St Albans, one of the wealthiest monasteries in England. Of course, Wolsey could not hope to fulfil his religious duties in any of these posts, so he was permanently absent whilst a deputy acted for him. Because of this, Wolsey attracted criticism for the twin vices of absenteeism and plurality (the holding of more than one office at a time).

ACTIVITY

A popular examination question theme about Wolsey's period in power concerns his popularity, as in this example:

Show how Wolsey's position, and his policies, brought him widespread unpopularity.

When planning an answer, you need to be careful to avoid just telling the story of Wolsey's policies. Instead, you need to select and organise your answer so that three things become clear:
▼ **What** Wolsey did that caused his unpopularity
▼ **Who** disliked him
▼ **Why** his policies offended them.

To do this, re-read sections 2, 3 and 4 of this chapter and use them to compile a list of things about Wolsey himself, and what he did, that were likely to offend the nobility, taxpayers, sheep-farmers, religious reformers and others. In each case attach the reason to a particular group and explain the link.

For example, you might mention that his *rapid rise to power between 1513 and 1515* [= **what**] was likely to cause jealousy among the *existing advisers* [= **who**] of Henry VIII because Wolsey was *winning the king's favour and sidelining them even though he was not of noble blood* [= **why**].

You will find that a number of the reasons you think of are connected to the nobility. This should not be surprising since Wolsey was effectively taking their place in the king's affection and any reforms to taxation, the law or land ownership were most likely to affect them.

5 Wolsey's Foreign Policy

Figure 31 A detail from a larger painting of Henry VIII's foreign policy triumphs. To understand what is going on you need to view the painting as three horizontal slices. In the bottom half, Henry is meeting Emperor Maximilian I.

Above this is a thinner band showing the English and French cavalries clashing in the 'Battle of the Spurs', and at the very top is a representation of the siege of Tournai (with the town on the left and the English army to the right).

By 1513 Henry VIII's dreams of glory in Europe had stalled. His advisers had cautioned him not to rush headlong into military commitments that would be expensive, and which might distract him from the business of ensuring a stable transfer of power from his father. When Henry had finally won the argument for war in 1511 and sent troops to France in 1512 the result had been an embarrassment.

Wolsey changed all this. The invasion of northern France in 1513 was seen as a great victory: the English had easily driven off the French in a cavalry encounter dubbed the 'Battle of the Spurs' and had gone on to capture the fortress of Therouanne and the town of Tournai. In 1514 the achievement was sealed in the Treaty of Saint Germaine-en-Laye, negotiated by Wolsey, which left England in possession of Tournai and Henry with a handsome annual payment for agreeing to give up his claims to the French throne.

a) The Problem of Foreign Policy

What conditions made it difficult for England to play a significant part in European affairs? How did Wolsey try to overcome these problems?

Although the victory of 1513–14 gave Henry what he wanted in the short term – a quick military adventure to bring him popularity at home and respect abroad – it was hardly the beginning of a new era of English greatness in Europe. The campaign had been expensive and had wiped out the surplus of money that Henry VII had so carefully gathered in his later years. It had also resulted in little real achievement beyond the satisfaction of defeating France. Tournai was not an impressive spoil of war – it was described by Wolsey himself as an 'ungracious doghole'.

The difficulty facing Wolsey was how to establish an effective role for England in European affairs. The resources at his disposal were limited. England could not compete in size or wealth with the French and Habsburgs monarchies. England was well placed to threaten the supply lines that the Habsburgs used to connect their scattered possessions in Spain and the Netherlands, or to threaten northern France; but she was relegated to a minor role whenever the focus of French–Habsburg rivalry shifted to the Italian peninsula. At the same time, Wolsey's survival as chief minister depended on him building Henry's reputation and delivering further victories.

Before Wolsey could discover the solution to this problem the European balance of power shifted with the deaths of King Louis XII of France in 1515, Ferdinand of Aragon in 1516 and Emperor Maximilian I in 1519. Suddenly, Europe was populated with new, young monarchs who could compete personally with Henry to be the centre of attention. The 21-year-old successor to the French throne, Francis I, showed this by immediately invading northern Italy to recapture Milan from the Habsburgs. His resounding victory over Swiss mercenaries in the Battle of Marignano gave him a reputation far in excess of what Henry had won by capturing Tournai. To make matters worse, the deaths of Ferdinand of Aragon and Maximilian I had allowed their grandson, the 16-year-old Charles, to assume the titles of King of Spain and Holy Roman Emperor in addition to his existing position as Duke in the Netherlands. Charles now commanded a vast empire stretching from the Americas through western and central Europe down into north Africa. There was no chance that Henry could compete with Charles on a equal footing.

Wolsey's response to these changes was to create a new role in Europe for his master. Since Henry lacked the resources to wage war alongside these giants, Wolsey established England as the peacemaker between them. At the same time, he was careful not to ignore Henry's desire for military glory, especially at the expense of Francis I who was far too similar in character and ambition to Henry himself not to be regarded with jealousy.

Was the Treaty of London a 'glittering success'?

b) The Treaty of London, October 1518

Leo X, who had become Pope in 1513, had called for a general crusade to halt the spread of Ottoman power in eastern Europe. There was little chance of this happening, but Wolsey saw in the scheme an opportunity to place England at the centre of European diplomacy. Rather than focusing on the crusade, he called for all the major powers of Europe to settle their differences and live under 'universal peace'. Over two dozen countries signed the resulting treaty, which committed them to avoid war or risk being attacked by the rest of the signatories. In this way, a crude balance of power was to be established across western Europe which would prevent conflicts of the type seen since 1494 in Italy.

Henry VIII was the pivotal point in this balance of power. Wolsey had arranged that each country should sign the treaty separately with England, rather than having everyone sign the same document. The treaty was, says Susan Doran, 'a glittering success', because it brought immediate fame to Henry, upstaged even the Pope, and dispelled English isolation. Henry and Wolsey attempted to play out their roles as power-brokers in European politics for the next couple of years, but another turn of events again wrecked their plans.

Once Charles's election as Holy Roman Emperor in 1519 had completed the transfer of Maximilian I's lands and titles to him, the Treaty of London's call for 'universal peace' began to look decidedly shaky. The problem lay in the change that Charles's election brought to relations with France. He was now ruler of the Netherlands, King of Spain and Holy Roman Emperor. His lands virtually encircled France and threatened to choke any efforts Francis made to win more glory through conquest. His election also threatened French control in northern Italy. Charles did not just inherit the title of emperor, but also his grandfather's commitments, one of which was to pursue the imperial claim to control over Milan, currently in French hands after Francis's victory at Marignano. Francis and Charles were now in direct opposition to each other and war was only a matter of time.

c) Support for the Habsburgs, 1520–25

How did England react to the renewal of war between France and the Habsburgs in the 1520s?

Henry and Wolsey were gripped by the dilemma of having to choose one side over the other, when both choices carried risks. For the time being, they tried to preserve their image as neutral power-brokers by arranging meetings with both sides. Henry met Francis at the Field of the Cloth of Gold in June 1520 and also conferred with Charles twice, before and after the French meeting. Ultimately, though, Henry could not afford to remain shackled to a peace treaty that was so obviously collapsing, nor could he lose prestige by allowing England merely to stand on the sidelines and watch during any Franco-Habsburg war.

Of the two sides, Spain was the more attractive. Henry was married to Catherine of Aragon, Charles's aunt, and he still dreamed of making substantial territorial gains in France. In 1522, England declared war on France, despite Wolsey's reservations. Once again, military action on the continent achieved next to nothing, but cost a fortune. In 1525 imperial forces captured Francis I after the Battle of Pavia. Henry hoped that this could be exploited; he called on Charles to help him end French independence once and for all by dividing the country into an English and a Spanish zone. Charles, however, was reluctant to pursue English interests when they did not match his own, and Henry again saw his plans thwarted.

d) Support for France, 1525–9

The results of English support for Charles in the early 1520s had disappointed both Henry and Wolsey. It appeared to them that Charles had used England to distract France but had given England nothing in return. In particular, Henry had felt that Francis's crushing defeat at Pavia had removed any obstacle to his long-held ambition to revive England's claims to the French throne. Charles's refusal to help infuriated him, but Henry was unable to raise the finances for an army to take action himself. Instead, Wolsey joined negotiations between France, the Pope, Venice and Florence for an anti-Habsburg alliance – the League of Cognac, hoping still to play the peacemaker by using the talks to pressure Charles into being more reasonable.

Events soon dragged England into war against Charles, however. At the same time that Wolsey was trying to steer a course between France and Spain, Henry's decision to seek a divorce from Catherine of Aragon made neutrality impossible. Charles was Catherine's nephew, so was unlikely to view divorce proceedings favourably. Worse, Charles's army had followed up its victory at Pavia by taking control of most of the Italian peninsula, leaving the Pope a virtual prisoner. Since Henry required the Pope's approval for the divorce, Wolsey was forced to take a more direct stand against Charles. England and France concluded an alliance in 1527, and in 1528 both were at war with the Habsburgs.

The English contribution was again ineffectual, and in June 1529 Charles once again defeated the French, at the Battle of Landriano. It was only at the last moment that Wolsey was able to ensure that England would be included in the resulting peace treaty, which was signed at Cambrai in August 1529. A fortnight later, Wolsey fell from power.

ACTIVITY

Cardinal Wolsey's foreign policy aims have been the subject of some debate among historians:

▼ According to the early twentieth-century historian A. J. Pollard, Wolsey wanted 'to hitch England to the Holy See'. He suggests that England matched the Pope's foreign policy, because Wolsey wanted to be rewarded with the title of cardinal and ultimately the papacy.

▼ J. J. Scarisbrick, whose biography of Henry VIII in 1968 challenged Pollard's views, argues that Wolsey sought peace because war was expensive and against his humanist principles.

▼ However, others take a more pragmatic line. Further analysis by historians since the 1970s has led to claims that Wolsey followed whatever path would bring him personal advancement and power (which meant satisfying both the king's need for glory and the Pope's interests).

Use the material in this section and your further researches either to test some or all of these interpretations or to develop your own explanation of what Wolsey hoped to achieve.

---

6 Wolsey and the King's Divorce

Wolsey's biggest challenge came in the late 1520s, when Henry decided that he needed to divorce Catherine of Aragon in order to allow him to marry Anne Boleyn and try to obtain the male heir his first wife seemed incapable of bearing (see Chapter 3). He spoke of the problem to Wolsey in 1525, who tackled it in three ways:

a) Scriptural Arguments

First, Wolsey drew up a complex line of argument based on the scriptures to justify the divorce in the eyes of the Catholic Church. He argued that the validity of the marriage relied on Catherine's word that her first marriage to Prince Arthur had never been consummated (see page 61). However, if this was not the case, Henry had been misled and the marriage had never been valid. Armed with this justification, Wolsey was confident that he could persuade the Pope to agree to the annulment.

b) Diplomatic Manoeuvres

The second line of attack was against Emperor Charles V. As Catherine's nephew he was unlikely to support a divorce and it was doubly inconvenient that at the moment Henry wanted it, Charles was in control in Italy. Wolsey tried to free the Pope from Charles's influence by using an alliance with France and the renewal of warfare in Italy to distract the Emperor. This policy failed, however, because Charles was too strongly entrenched in the peninsula to be evicted by France.

c) Legal Efforts

Finally, Wolsey hoped to side-step the whole problem of Charles V and his control over the Pope by holding the divorce hearings in England where he, as papal legate, would make the judgment. However, the Pope was still concerned not to offend Charles V, so although he agreed to set up a commission to hear the divorce case, he sent Cardinal Campeggio to England with strict instructions to delay the hearing and to make sure that a decision was never reached. When the court finally met in June 1529 to discuss the case, Catherine immediately refused to recognise it and appealed to the Pope to move the hearing to Rome. Since this offered him another opportunity to frustrate the divorce whilst not openly offending either Charles or Henry, the Pope agreed and the English court was wound up. As it did so, it became clear to Henry that Wolsey had run out of options for solving this problem.

7 The Fall of Wolsey

ISSUE:
What brought about Wolsey's fall in 1529?

Wolsey maintained his power and position because he served Henry well. When he ceased to do so, he fell from power. His two great failures were the collapse of his anti-Habsburg strategy in Europe, forced on him by the success of Charles V in Italy after 1525, and his inability to obtain a divorce for the king. Neither of these objectives could be achieved at the time, but it was Wolsey who paid the price for failure.

In the summer of 1529 Henry used Wolsey's position as papal legate to accuse him of Praemunire – working in the interests of the Pope rather than his king. He was stripped of his powers and possessions, and exiled to his diocese of York. During the months that followed Henry twice sent tokens of friendship to his former minister, raising Wolsey's hopes that he might be reinstated, but, instead, he was summoned to London in 1530 to answer further charges. Wolsey

Figure 32 Why Wolsey had lost Henry's confidence by 1529.

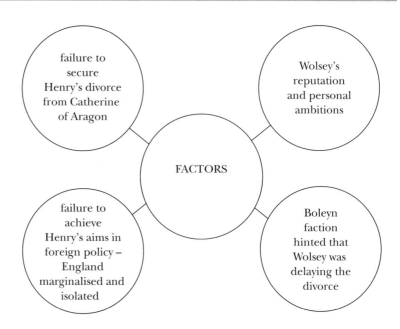

Figure 32 Why Wolsey had lost Henry's confidence by 1529.

THE BOLEYN FACTION

The modern historian David Starkey links the rise of Anne Boleyn to the beginnings of serious factional intrigue at court. Until Anne captured the king's eye and heart, Wolsey's enemies did not have a strong figure near to the centre of power who could be used to dislodge the chief minister. Starkey argues that Wolsey had been largely successful in neutralising any enemies, but that his relationship with Anne became one of bitter rivalry from 1527 when both tried to insert their supporters into key government posts. The Royal Council, which Wolsey had dominated for so long, became more difficult to control as Anne's brother, her father and other nobles who hitched themselves to the Boleyn family's rise came to dominate it.

believed, perhaps correctly, that the king's mind had been poisoned against him by the **Boleyn faction**, who blamed him for his failure to win approval for the royal divorce. This was exactly the kind of threat that he had always feared and tried to prevent by restricting access to the king. Now he was in no position to do so. His ill-health led to his death on the journey southward, at Leicester on 29 November 1530, saving him the disgrace of being tried for treason. In a little over a year, the man who had apparently ruled England for the previous 15 years was destroyed.

8 The 'Years Without a Policy', 1529–32

Wolsey was replaced as Lord Chancellor by Sir Thomas More. Although he was an able scholar, he was a poor replacement for the multi-talented Wolsey. Perhaps the most marked difference between the two men was that whereas Wolsey had been prepared to seize opportunities and to act flexibly in the interests of his royal master, More was a man of high and rigid principles, especially in religious matters. Since the question of the king's divorce remained unresolved when he became chief minister, this was to cause real difficulties in his relationship with Henry. More finally resigned in 1532, having spent a couple of years unenthusiastically trying to argue a case he had little sympathy for.

SIR THOMAS MORE (1478–1535)

-*Profile*-

Sir Thomas More has gained a reputation for being a man who put his principles before everything else. He held strong humanist beliefs which he revealed in a number of books, most famously *Utopia* (1516). On the fictional island of Utopia, the natives live in a state of innocence. More used the arrival of visitors from the outside world as an opportunity to write a bitingly satirical contrast between real 'Christian' society and the fictional perfection of Utopia. One of his targets was the landowning élite: More accused them of selfishly exploiting their tenants and allowing 'sheep to devour men' through the enclosing of land.

More's writings became a favourite with Henry VIII. He produced a history of the career of Richard III which helped to foster the myth of the Yorkist king as an evil, murdering monster. At court, More was deeply sympathetic to the plight of Catherine of Aragon and grew concerned at Henry's treatment of her and at the king's willingness to support those who wanted a deep reformation of the church to get his divorce. More was critical of some aspects of the Catholic Church, but like other humanists he remained convinced that reform could be achieved by steady persuasion rather than by drastic action. He was intolerant of opinions which did not match his own and was instrumental in the harsh persecution of reformers in 1528 and 1530–31.

After the fall of Wolsey in 1529, Henry invited More to become Lord Chancellor. In this position, he was able to attack Lutheran influences within the church, but found his work frustrated by Anne Boleyn's presence at court and by the messy question of the royal divorce. As Henry moved towards a break with the Pope, More resigned because his conscience would not let him support such a move. He refused to swear an oath accepting that Anne Boleyn's daugher was the legitimate heir to the throne whilst Catherine of Aragon's daughter was completely excluded, since this was tantamount to saying that the royal divorce was legal even though the Pope had not sanctioned it. More was imprisoned because Henry could not allow such a powerful critic to voice his opinions freely and, after a trial characterised by false evidence against him, he was executed in 1535. His courage and a favourable biography written by his son-in-law (see page 94) made him a hero to some Catholic writers.

1478 born;

1513 began work on a history of the reign of Richard III which attacked the king for tyranny;

1516 publication of first book of his major work, *Utopia*;

1528 conducted heresy trials against suspected Lutherans (but intervention of Anne Boleyn protected some from execution);

1529 appointed Lord Chancellor after the fall of Wolsey;

1531 initiated further persecutions of Protestant reformers;

1532 resigned after the king won approval for the 'Submission of the Clergy';

1534 refused to take the Oath of Succession recognising the legality of Henry's divorce;

1535 convicted of treason, and executed.

CROMWELL'S TITLES AND PROMOTIONS

1532 became **Master of the King's Jewels**, a position which gave him access to the king's private rooms in the palace;

1533 became **Chancellor of the Exchequer, Master of the Rolls** (which gave him a leading role within the legal system);

1535 appointed **Vice-gerent for Spirituals** (a government post which Henry created to give Cromwell the power to institute church reform);

1536 became **Lord Privy Seal** and **Principal Secretary** on the Royal Council; also rewarded with the title **Baron Cromwell**;

1540 became **Lord Great Chamberlain** and **Earl of Essex** shortly before his fall.

INNS OF COURT
The Inns of Court were residences in London where barristers received training and where they could lodge whilst studying.

9 Thomas Cromwell and the 'Revolution' of the 1530s

Cromwell was born in about 1485, in Putney in London. Very little is known about his early life, but his origins were certainly humble. His father was probably a cloth-worker and ale-house keeper. During his teens, Thomas seems to have been in some kind of trouble which led him to make his way to the Netherlands. He later described himself as having been 'a bit of a ruffian' in his youth. From the Netherlands he moved to Italy, where he served as a soldier, and where he probably came into contact with the radical political ideas which influenced his later life. After a period of service to a Venetian merchant, he returned to England in 1516, married, and found employment in the household of Cardinal Wolsey.

Wolsey seems to have recognised Cromwell's ability because, by 1519, Cromwell had achieved an important position in his household. Cromwell also learned enough about law to attend the **Inns of Court** in 1524 and to develop a successful legal practice. In 1529 he was elected as a Member of Parliament, in which capacity he played an active role in attacking abuses within the church. Whether he was already known to the king, or brought to his attention at this time, he soon found himself in royal service and, in 1531, became a member of the Royal Council. Unlike many others, he combined this advancement with loyalty to his old master. He defended Wolsey in Parliament and remained loyal until his death.

By 1532 Cromwell had effectively taken over the management of the king's divorce. Like Wolsey he realised that the key to success was to anticipate Henry's needs and to give him what he wanted. Also like Wolsey, he collected titles and promotions (this time outside the church) rapidly. Between 1532 and 1536 he devised the strategy for the divorce and drafted a series of Acts that destroyed the power of

Rome, created the Church of England and gave Henry unprecedented power and status as a monarch (see Chapter 3, page 88).

a) Reform of Government

One of the most contentious issues among historians over the past half-century has been whether or not Cromwell brought about changes in the structure of government that amounted to a revolution. Those who believe that he did regard Cromwell's actions as modernising the system of government into one that was distinct from the medieval idea of 'personal monarchy' (where the monarch was directly involved in decision-making through his or her offices in the royal court), and which would be recognisable today as 'bureaucratic government' (where specialised departments and trained officials manage the routine matters of government). The argument was originally made by Geoffrey Elton in 1953, in a book entitled *The Tudor Revolution in Government*. Since then, writers (including Elton himself) have watered down and modified some of his key arguments. The result is a view of political reform in the 1530s which accepts that new institutions arose and that government expanded to cope with the changes brought about by Henry VIII's decision to break away from the Pope's control to get the divorce he needed. However, this view questions how far these changes were planned by Cromwell, and how far they were new.

i) The Royal Council
In the era of personal monarchy during Henry VII's reign, the king met regularly with his Royal Council of advisers. The council was a large group (although not everyone attended every meeting) including leading noblemen, clergy and members of the king's household staff. During Henry VIII's reign a more professional Privy Council emerged. Historians disagree, however, about whether it appeared at all in the 1530s or was in fact a creation of the early 1540s after Cromwell's fall. It was different from the old one because it contained fewer people, perhaps no more than 20 members, and was mainly composed of professionally trained lawyers and bureaucrats, rather than notables from the wider ruling class.

ii) Financial Management
The Tudors had generally continued the system introduced by Edward IV of managing national finances not through the slow workings of the Exchequer and Treasury, but from offices in their private rooms in the palace – the Privy Chamber. This gave monarchs significant control over day-to-day decisions about all aspects of income and expenditure. Cromwell created new financial institutions alongside the Privy Chamber to manage the new revenues generated by

Figure 33 Thomas Cromwell.

the break with Rome. In all, four new departments were created:
▼ The Court of Augmentations
▼ The Court of First Fruits and Tenths
▼ The Court of Wards and Liveries
▼ The Court of General Surveyors.

So, by 1540, increasing specialism had apparently been introduced into the management of royal finances, although Cromwell recognised that the Privy Chamber remained an important part of the system and continued to work through it.

iii) The King's Advisers

As a result of the bureaucratic changes described above, professional administrators rather than untrained members of the nobility and clergy were needed to maintain the system. Both Wolsey and Cromwell represented this new breed of government official – hard-working, and often from humble origins. Unlike the nobility, these men depended on the king for their promotions and titles, so formed an utterly loyal band of royal servants.

b) The Power of the Crown

Another feature of the debate about the significance of the 1530s has been what effect it had on the power and authority of the monarchy. In the introduction to the Act in Restraint of Appeals in 1533, Cromwell wrote that:

Source E From the introduction to the Act in Restraint of Appeals, 1533.

Q

What is meant by the phrase 'England is an Empire'?

> This realm of England is an Empire and has been accepted so in the world, governed by one supreme head and King, having the dignity and royal estate of the imperial crown, unto whom a body politic is bound and who [the King] is owed, next to God, a natural and humble obedience without any restraint from any foreign power or potentate of the world.

Cromwell's purpose in writing this was to set up the argument that Englishmen should not have the automatic right to appeal to Rome to give them judgments in religious cases, because the king was supreme in his own lands. However, the passage has also been taken to mean something more. Cromwell seems to be suggesting that England was an independent political body ('an Empire' that had been 'accepted so in the world') and that it was a single, unitary state, with all power derived from the monarch.

This view contrasted with the reality of England in 1533. First, the king was subject to the Pope's views in matters of religious doctrine, and was supposed to seek the Pope's permission when choosing bishops and other high-ranking religious officials. Secondly, parts of England held 'liberties' which gave them semi-independent status (see page 53). Finally, Wales no longer had independence, but neither had it formally been made part of the English system of government. The consequence was that royal authority was spread unevenly across the country.

Cromwell dealt with this by using the occasion of the break with Rome (which sorted out the first problem) to extend royal power more firmly across the kingdom. In 1536 an Act of Union with Wales reorganised local government in the principality and the borderlands of the marches. At the same time an Act against Liberties and Franchises removed and restricted the special powers exercised by regional nobles in the more remote parts of the kingdom, such as those held by the Bishop in the Palatinate of Durham. Cromwell's aim was not merely to limit the power of the magnates, but to provide consistent application of the law.

c) The Role and Importance of Parliament

During the 1530s Cromwell used Parliament extensively to enact the legislation needed to legalise the break with Rome and to strengthen royal authority in outlying regions. Until then, Parliaments had not been a regular part of government, and although **statute law** had long been recognised as the highest form of law in England, kings were still able to make law by **proclamation** on many issues. The role of, and power exercised by, Parliament tended to depend on the state of royal finances. In the fourteenth and fifteenth centuries, when the Hundred Years' War was exhausting royal revenues, Parliaments had been called frequently and were able to exercise considerable influence over the choice of royal advisers and the measures taken by them. It should be stressed, however, that the House of Lords tended to take the lead, and in many ways these Parliaments were an extension of noble politics. The restoration of royal finances under Edward IV and Henry VII had reversed this trend. Parliaments were rarely called, and operated in partnership with the crown. The expenses of Henry VIII's foreign policy under Wolsey had led to some friction with Parliament, and Wolsey chose not to call it unless it was unavoidable. There was, therefore, nothing to indicate the role that Parliament was to play in the 1530s when it was summoned at the fall of Wolsey in 1529.

The Parliament that met in 1529 was to be unlike any that had gone before. It remained in being for seven years, and passed a quantity and range of laws unseen before that point in parliamentary history. This stability and workload helped Parliament to develop its procedures and gave MPs a level of experience that was rare. For

> **STATUTE LAW**
> Laws made by Parliament with royal consent. By the sixteenth century statute law was generally regarded as the highest form of law in England.

> **PROCLAMATIONS**
> Decrees by the king on policy matters either falling outside the scope of parliamentary authority or made when Parliament was not in session to cope with an unusual circumstance or emergency. In 1539 the Proclamations Act gave these royal decrees equal force with parliamentary statutes, but also said that proclamations could not contravene existing statutes.

KING-IN-PARLIAMENT

The term 'King-in-Parliament' needs to be fully understood to avoid confusion. It does not mean the same as king *and* Parliament, which implies two separate powerful institutions. King-in-Parliament refers to government by the king, but implies that some of his functions, in particular the making of law, are carried out in Parliament rather than by the king alone. Through Parliament, the king could make statute law, the highest form of law: a statute (Act of Parliament) that had been agreed by both houses and signed by the king took precedence over any earlier law or custom, and could only be changed by another statute.

example, the process for passing a bill after three readings in both Lords and Commons became standard practice. Equally significant, Parliament legislated in areas of government and the church where it had never previously been involved. By the end of the 1530s it was recognised that statute law made by the **King-in-Parliament** represented ultimate authority in England and Wales, and could be applied to virtually any aspect of life and society. Moreover, if any future monarchs wished to change the laws that had been made, they would have to do so in co-operation with Parliament.

Cromwell chose to use Parliament in a way that his predecessors had not because he needed the status of statute law to strengthen the changes that he was making in church and government. Parliament contained representatives of the 'political nation' – the governing class – on whom the king relied to make his policies happen. The House of Lords contained 51 peers, 21 bishops and about 29 abbots, representing the nobility and the church. The House of Commons had 310 members, 74 representing the English counties and 236 representing towns and boroughs. The county members and some of the borough MPs were members of the lesser nobility, whilst borough members included merchants and royal administrators. With such a cross-section of the political nation present in Parliament, any changes it enacted were likely to be implemented smoothly, whilst any resistance from Parliament could be an early warning sign of trouble in implementing the king's wishes.

The Composition of Parliament

The composition of Parliament changed considerably as a result of developments in the 1530s. After the dissolution of the monasteries the abbots disappeared and the number of bishops increased slightly with the foundation of four new cathedrals, while the number of peers increased to 55 by 1534. This meant that the clergy were now in a minority in the House of Lords. In the Commons, 14 new boroughs were given the right to elect MPs, while the increased status and importance of the chamber brought a growing tendency for gentleman landowners to seek election.

ACTIVITY

It is clear that the events of the 1530s affected Parliament in a number of different ways. Its composition, procedures, power and functions were all affected by the part that parliamentary statute played in enabling Henry to take control of the church. Re-read section, and draw up a diagram to show the effects. Then write a brief explanation of how all of these changes might combine to make Parliament more important or independent in the future.

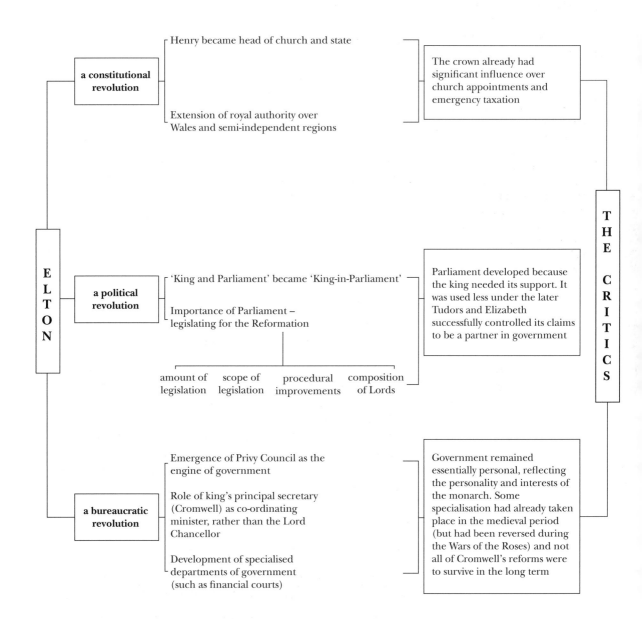

Figure 34 Summary of the 'Tudor revolution in government' historical debate.

ISSUE:
**Why did Cromwell fall
from power in 1540?**

10 The Fall of Cromwell

In 1538 Cromwell's position in government seemed secure. He had organised a transformation in the relationship between church and state; extended the reality of royal power to the borders of the kingdom; overhauled the machinery of government; and consistently demonstrated his capacity for hard work and loyalty to the king.

a) Royal Marriages

Henry had finally achieved his divorce from Catherine of Aragon in May 1533, two months after he had secretly married Anne Boleyn and shortly after the Act in Restraint of Appeals (see page 86) had been passed, preventing Catherine from appealing the decision to Rome. He had been forced to follow this odd order of events because Anne had become pregnant at the turn of the year. Henry was desperate to make sure that the child would be born legitimately, so that he (Henry was convinced it would be a son) could become the royal heir. Henry was to be bitterly disappointed. Anne gave birth to another daughter – Elizabeth – in September 1533. She became pregnant again, but miscarried in January 1536. Henry became convinced once more that God was displeased with the marriage and he engineered her downfall by accusing her of adultery (see the box about Anne on page 83). Anne was executed on 18 May 1536. Within a fortnight, Henry had married his third wife, Jane Seymour. It was to be a short marriage, however, because Jane Seymour died whilst giving birth to Henry's son, Edward, in 1538.

In 1538 the Pope finally excommunicated Henry, and peace between France and the Habsburgs raised the possibility that he might go further and call for the invasion of England. In a bid to strengthen England's relationship with other Protestant countries in Europe, Cromwell arranged a marriage between the king and Anne, sister of the Duke of Cleves in Germany. Unfortunately, Cromwell had been badly misinformed about Anne's appearance, so when she arrived in England in 1539 Henry took a violent dislike to her and demanded that the marriage should be cancelled. Although Cromwell complied, the fiasco weakened his relationship with Henry at a time when the king was already becoming unhappy with the tone of Cromwell's religious changes.

b) Religious Policies

The reforms that Cromwell had made in the 1530s went further than just placing Henry at the head of the English church. In 1535 he had been made Vice-gerent of Spirituals, which gave him the authority to make religious decisions in the name of the king. Cromwell had used this power to set out a more Protestant view of the church in the Ten Articles and a set of instructions to bishops (see pages 92–3). In doing so, he had encouraged the Protestant minority openly to preach doctrines that were too radical for Henry.

The influence of religious conservatives at court like Bishop Stephen Gardiner reinforced Henry's own dislike of Protestant theology, and set the scene for a Catholic reaction. Henry revealed his intentions in November 1538 by presiding at the trial of the Protestant heretic John Lambert, and Lambert's conviction and death were followed by a proclamation against heresy. This was followed by the Six Articles Act in June 1539 which reversed Cromwell's changes and restored essential Catholic teachings.

c) Enemies at Court

Cromwell accepted his defeat on religious policy and might have survived if his enemies at court had not made good use of the collapse of the Cleves marriage. Henry's distaste for Anne was heightened by his growing desire for Catherine Howard, the pretty, young and flirtatious niece of the Duke of Norfolk. The duke was Cromwell's bitterest rival on the Privy Council and used this opportunity to poison Henry's relationship with his chief minister. As Cromwell worked towards securing the king's divorce from Anne, Catherine was instructed to spread rumours that he was not carrying out the task quickly enough. The final blow came when Norfolk suggested that Cromwell was protecting a group of Protestants in Calais (at that time an English possession). With indecent haste, Cromwell was arrested and imprisoned in the Tower before his execution on 28 June 1540.

The fall of Cromwell came suddenly, but his power had always depended on his absolute obedience to Henry's wishes, and his ability to provide Henry with the answers that he required. In 1539–40 his political skills failed him on both counts. The Protestant alliance, his own religious preferences and the Cleves marriage created the suspicion in Henry's mind that his chief minister was pursuing his own interests rather than his king's. This suspicion combined with Henry's embarrassment over the marriage fiasco to create a desire to punish Cromwell, which his enemies at court were well placed to exploit. Although Henry was usually able to maintain control of the rival groups at court, it seems that on this occasion his anger at Cromwell and his desire for Catherine clouded his judgement. Certainly, he seems to have realised quite quickly that he been deprived of his best and most faithful servant.

▼ Working on Politics in the Age of Wolsey and Cromwell

Figure 35 Key events and developments in the age of Wolsey and Cromwell.

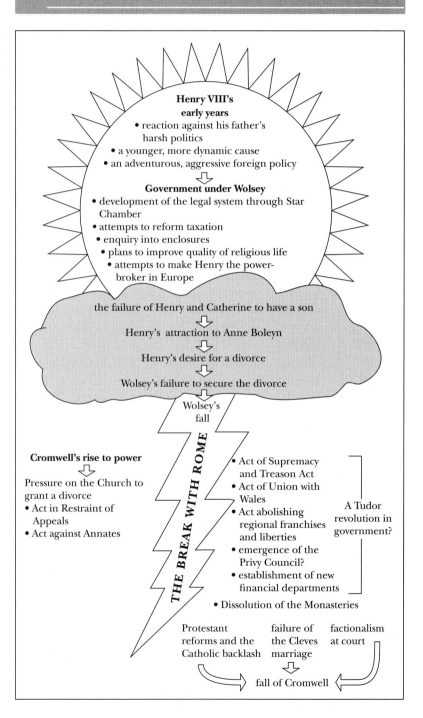

How historians have approached this topic

Until the mid-twentieth century, historians generally accepted the idea of a 'New Monarchy' developing under the Tudors (see page 62). For them, the developments of Henry VIII's reign were the natural extension of his father's achievements. Henry VII had laid the foundations of strong central government and a revitalised monarchy. Now, Henry VIII used these strengths to position himself as one of England's strongest kings. He was able to extend his control to include the church during the 1530s, push royal authority outwards into the provinces and Wales, and manage a spectacular court by a combination of charm and ruthlessness.

As we saw above (see Figure 34), Geoffrey Elton challenged this view in *The Tudor Revolution in Government* (1953). He shifted attention away from the period 1485 to 1529 and onto the 1530s as the vital era of political change. He also played up the importance of Henry's chief minister, Thomas Cromwell, as the architect of reform.

This analysis has proved to be very contentious and historians still debate how far the 1530s were 'revolutionary'. Moreover, interest has also shifted to include discussion of how far Henry was actually in control of events. J. J. Scarisbrick's biography *Henry VIII* (1968) began this trend by suggesting that Henry kept broad control but did not have the patience or attention to detail needed to translate ideas into achievements. For this, he needed men such as Wolsey and Cromwell. Other writers, such as David Starkey in various books since the 1980s, have gone further by researching the extent of factionalism at Henry's court and by showing that the king was often the victim rather than the master of these rivalries.

Answering Extended Writing and Essay Questions on Politics in the Age of Wolsey and Cromwell

Essay questions and extended writing tasks tend to focus on certain key issues and concepts. Those relating to Henry VII are often focused on how successful his policies were, and the same questions are often asked about the early part of Henry VIII's reign. The 1530s, however, were clearly a very successful period for the monarchy, since Henry got his divorce, gained control of the church, and saw significant extensions of royal power and very positive changes in the methods of government. Questions therefore tend to focus on how he was able to do this, and on describing and assessing the effects of what was done in both the short and long term.

Question

1. Describe any THREE policies which Thomas Cromwell followed to strengthen royal power in the 1530s. **[30 marks]**

2. Which policy do you think was his greatest achievement? Explain your answer. **[60 marks]**

To answer the second part of this question, you need to think carefully about the idea of an 'achievement'. In particular, you need to consider whether the question is asking you to judge Cromwell's achievements from our modern perspective, or whether you should be looking at them through Henry VIII's eyes. Of course, there is nothing to stop you doing both (and gaining higher marks as a result!)

How do you decide which was the most important achievement? To do this, you will need to compare the effects that each had. Did it produce a positive change? Did it produce a lasting change or just a short-term benefit? Think about the increased revenues from the dissolution of the monasteries, for example. The massive amount of wealth that Cromwell's commissioners were able to find and remove from them certainly pleased Henry and enabled him to revive his flagging foreign policy ambitions during the 1540s and to compete on more equal terms with his great rival, King Francis I of France. From Henry's perspective, this was a significant achievement (especially after the embarrassments earlier in his reign when he was refused the 'Amicable Grant' by his subjects), but the benefits did not last. The wealth of the monasteries encouraged him to spend unwisely, and he began to sell off their lands to raise money (especially as price inflation grew worse). By the end of the century the wealth of the monasteries had been squandered and the monarchy was in a worse financial state than before the Reformation. For historians, then, the organisation and efficiency of the *Valor Ecclesiasticus* (see page 91) might be commendable, but the policy of dissolving the monasteries did not bring a lasting benefit to the monarchy.

Now see if you can adopt a similar approach to the other policies you have identified, by looking at the achievement first from Henry's short-term point of view, and then from a longer historical perspective.

For further practice, here is another question for you to attempt:

(a) What aspects of English government and politics changed during the 1530s?

(b) Why were these changes so significant?

Answering Source-Based Questions on Politics in the Age of Wolsey and Cromwell

In some of the examinations you will sit, especially in the second year of the course, you are likely to find source-based questions which are set mainly or wholly on secondary sources. Often, their point will be either to tackle issues about the way writers have approached a topic, or to examine changes over a longer period of time.

In 23 years Edward IV summoned only six parliaments which sat for 84 weeks in all, while in 24 years Henry VII summoned seven which sat for 72 weeks. Neither Henry nor Edward saw the need to initiate a large body of legislation; their commonest acts were attainders against political enemies. Parliament's main judicial function had by this time been taken over by various legal offshoots of the Royal Council. And, most significantly, neither king had to ask for war taxation nearly as frequently as in the time of the Hundred Years War [1337–1453].

Source F Adapted from Alexander Grant, *Henry VII* (Methuen, 1985).

All through the 1530s every important step was embodied in statutes. Parliament legalised the Reformation. But the matter goes further than that. The Reformation statutes in the 1530s demonstrate that the political sovereignty created in the 1530s was to be a parliamentary one. The highest authority of the land was recognised to lie in that assembly of king, lords and commons whose decrees commanded complete and universal obedience and could deal with any matter on earth.

Source G Adapted from G. R. Elton, *England under The Tudors* (Methuen, 1955).

Parliament was a royal institution, whose function was not to obstruct the King or limit his power, but to facilitate government with laws and taxes. Therefore the dates of summons, the duration of sessions, prorogations [when Parliament was dismissed for a period without calling a fresh election] and dissolutions [when the crown called a general election] all depended on the will and needs of the monarch. During 1529–59 there were almost annual sittings: 27 sessions in 21 of the 30 years. Under Elizabeth, however, parliament settled back into the pre-Reformation rhythm, averaging a meeting every three and a half years.

Source H Adapted from Michael Graves, *The Tudor Parliaments, 1485–1603* (Longman, 1985).

▼ QUESTIONS ON SOURCES

1. Use these sources to trace the development of Parliament's role in government during the Tudor period. **[12 marks]**

2. How far can it be argued that the 1530s marked a turning point in the relationship between crown and Parliament? **[18 marks]**

You will see from the number of marks that these are questions which require extended answers. Also, Question 2 does not specifically tell you to use only the sources, so you ought to bring in any additional knowledge that you think is relevant.

Here is a plan of a student's answer to Question 2. Do you think that it will adequately answer the question? What advice would you offer about:

a) organising the answer?

b) which points from this plan to include and which to leave out?

c) additional information that would be relevant?

▼ Source G by Elton – biased because it's about the Tudor Revolution and he thought 1530s was significant. Can't trust what he has written.

▼ G says parliamentary law became supreme

▼ extra information – Parliament passed more laws than at any time before C19th, passed laws about lots of different issues, began to make its procedures better, abbots removed from the Lords so became more secular

▼ F – Parliament not very important before 1530s, so 1530s were important after all

▼ extra information – Henry VII only went to war with France once, so didn't need much money, Henry VIII was always at war with France, so had to call Parliament a lot. Amicable Grant? Henry got money from the monasteries so didn't need Parliament as much after 1540

▼ H says that Elizabeth didn't need Parliament – she rarely called it.

Further Reading

Books in the *Access to History* series

The politics of Henry VIII's reign can be traced through Keith Randell's *Henry VIII and the Government of England* (second edition, 2001). Because religious affairs were so closely linked to political developments it would also be worth looking at the same author's *Henry VIII and the Reformation in England* (second edition, 2001). To follow up the rebellions during Henry VIII's reign, consult *Disorder and Rebellion in Tudor England* by Nick Fellows.

Other books

J. J. Scarisbrick's biography *Henry VIII* (Penguin, 1968) has long been regarded as the main reference work on Henry's reign. However, there is plenty of literature available on both the king and his chief ministers. David Starkey's

The Reign of Henry VIII (Collins and Brown, 1991) uncovers much of the factionalism of the period as well as reassessing the 'Tudor Revolution in Government' debate. A further assessment of the reign by David Starkey can be found in *Henry VIII* (Pimlico, 2001). There are excellent short chapters about aspects of Henry's reign in A. G. R. Smith, *The Emergence of a Nation State* (Longman, 1994) and John Lotherington's *The Tudor Years* (Hodder and Stoughton). Foreign policy receives special treatment in Susan Doran's *England and Europe 1485–1603* (Longman, 1996). For a very engaging read about the personalities of the period and of the workings of courtly life, try *The Six Wives of Henry VIII* by Alison Weir (Pimlico, 1997) and *Henry VIII: King and Court* by the same author (Jonathan Cape, 2001). Henry's ministers have not escaped the attentions of historians, either. Two of the most recent biographies are *Thomas Cromwell* by Geoffrey Elton (Plantagenet, 1991), which is worth reading to compare the author's treatment of the 1530s to that in his earlier works, and *The Life of Thomas More* by Peter Ackroyd (Vintage, 1998).

CHAPTER 5

A MID-TUDOR CRISIS, 1540–58

POINTS TO CONSIDER

One of the big questions which historians have asked of the Tudor period is whether there was a period of dangerous instability in the middle of the sixteenth century which threatened the achievements of the Tudor state. Those who argue that there was a 'mid-Tudor crisis' usually locate it in the 1540s and 1550s (although there are disagreements about the precise start and end points). They suggest that a series of changes came together during the reigns of Edward VI (1547–53) and Mary I (1553–8) to create a sense of great uncertainty which threatened to overwhelm the weak governments of these monarchs. In this chapter, we will examine the evidence for this claim so that you can reach your own judgement about the nature and extent of the crisis.

ISSUE:
What were the elements of the mid-Tudor crisis?

1 Defining the Crisis

By drawing on material in other chapters of this book, we can identify the broad changes which form the elements of the instability of the mid-Tudor period. These are set out in Table 7.

Table 7 The forces of instability in mid-Tudor England.

Type of change	Source of instability
Political	• After two strong Tudor monarchs, the succession of weak rulers in 1547 and 1553, raising fears of instability and a power struggle between rival groups within the court and the wider nobility • The growing interference of government in people's everyday lives (especially to regulate the economy, to support the needy, and to transform religious beliefs)
Social	• Population increase • Strengthening of the gentry class, possibly at the expense of the traditional landowning aristocracy • Growing numbers of unemployed poor, and crime among the 'idle poor' • The drift into towns, with attendant employment problems
Economic	• Attempts to exploit the boom in the woollen industry by enclosing land • Price inflation
Religious	• Closure of monasteries and other local Roman Catholic religious houses • Introduction of Protestant ideas into worship

Few historians doubt that these changes were occurring. Where they disagree is assessing the seriousness and extent of the consequences. We can group the kinds of effects associated with the political, religious, social and economic changes of the 1540s and 1550s under five broad headings:

▼ **uncertainty** – about work, about faith; a weakening of the means by which people gained their identity (church, community)

▼ **threats to the Tudor state** – weaker government than under the first two Tudors; a loss of reputation abroad; rivalry and factionalism at home

▼ **re-ordering of society** – establishing the gentry class; the importance of merchant activity

▼ **new economic arrangements** – a transition from feudalism to capitalism?

▼ **unrest** – the problem of the poor; localised rioting; larger rebellions.

> **Q** What does the word 'crisis' mean? Is it too emotive to be useful as an analytical term?

Why have Historians Taken Different Approaches to the Question of a Mid-Tudor Crisis?

Coming between such well-known and strong rulers as Henry VIII and Elizabeth I, it is easy to exaggerate the weakness of the governments that lay in-between. Also, by looking for patterns that suggest a 'crisis', historians may be seeing links and connections that were not apparent to people at the time, or they may be in danger of focusing only on problems and missing the achievements of this period.

Some interesting recent opinions about the period have almost turned the idea of a crisis on its head by asking not how close to disaster the country came, but what was so strong about the Tudor state that enabled it to avoid disaster.

To navigate through the arguments surrounding the mid-Tudor crisis, it will be helpful if you think about and discuss the following sub-questions as you read about the period from 1540 to 1558:

▼ In which areas of life can you detect a 'crisis': in political affairs? social structure and relationships? religious beliefs? economic relationships?

▼ Do you think that the degree of 'crisis' was the same in each area?

▼ How long did the 'crisis' last – was it evident throughout 1540–58, or were there particularly significant moments?

▼ Was the crisis a national one, or were particular regions affected more than others?

ISSUE:
How important was factionalism to politics in this period?

HENRY'S FINAL YEARS

1540 married Catherine Howard; execution of Thomas Cromwell; English Bible to be placed in all churches;

1541 Act declared Henry king of Ireland;

1542 execution of Catherine Howard; defeat of Scots at Battle of Solway Moss; death of James V of Scotland created succession crisis which Henry hoped to exploit;

1543 Act extended English law across Wales; conservative faction plotted against Cranmer; Henry married Catherine Parr;

1544 first debasement of coinage;

1545 Chantries Act passed but not implemented;

1546 Anne Askew burnt for heresy; Sir Anthony Denny became Chief Gentleman of the King's Privy Chamber; Henry's last will excluded Gardiner from the Regency Council;

1547 execution of Earl of Surrey; death of Henry VIII; establishment of Regency Council.

2 Henry VIII's Final Years, 1540–47

The last years of Henry VIII's reign were dominated by an intensification of the rivalry between the conservative and reform factions. The king's decision not to appoint a chief minister to follow Wolsey and Cromwell encouraged this development, as did Henry's increasingly poor health. This has led historians to question whether Henry was actually in control of events; some have downgraded the king's importance to that of a sickly bystander. It is difficult to know precisely how influential the king was between the fall of Cromwell and his death in 1547: some decisions towards the end of his life were clearly taken without his consent, whilst others show that Henry was still capable of wrong-footing his advisers. Wherever the balance lies, it is important to understand that political development was being driven by the intensity of factionalism at court during this period.

What makes factionalism intriguing, especially in the 1540s, is that the king was fully aware of the manoeuvrings of his courtiers and even encouraged them. To some extent this was sheer egotism – the enjoyment of watching noblemen and counsellors fighting for royal attention – but it also prevented one view of politics from dominating and encouraged discussion of important matters such as religious change. This dimension means that it is difficult to discount completely the political importance of Henry, even in the last years of his reign, as the manipulator of courtly politics.

Conservative faction	Reform faction
Accepted the break with Rome, but opposed doctrinal changes	Accepted the break with Rome, seeing it as an opportunity to introduce Protestant doctrines into the church
Led by the Duke of Norfolk (Thomas Howard) and Stephen Gardiner (Bishop of Winchester)	Led by Edward Seymour (Earl of Hertford and later Duke of Somerset) and Archbishop Cranmer
Associated with ● passage of the Six Articles Act, 1539 ● fall of Thomas Cromwell ● Catherine Howard, Henry's fifth wife ● plot against Cranmer (1543) ● plot against Catherine Parr (1546)	Associated with ● foreign policy success in Scotland ● fall of Catherine Howard ● Catherine Parr, Henry's sixth wife ● plot against Gardiner (1544) ● arrest of Norfolk (1546)

Table 8 Factions during the 1540s.

In 1540, the conservative group were able to feel self-satisfied and confident. They had recently won three key victories (see page 131): the Six Articles Act had enshrined in law their belief that religious innovation should be limited; they had seen their greatest enemy, Thomas Cromwell, fall from power; and they had increased their access to Henry through his new wife, Catherine Howard (who was the niece of the Duke of Norfolk). However, their success was to be short-lived. The first blow was the loss of Catherine. Although Henry was besotted with her (he called her his 'rose without a thorn'), there was a significant age difference between them – he was 49, she was 19. It was quickly obvious to all but Henry that she had other admirers at court and in 1541 the king was finally presented with the extensive evidence of her unfaithfulness. His response was fury: the men implicated in her adultery were executed and Catherine herself was beheaded for treason. Although the Duke of Norfolk proclaimed his outrage at what his niece had done to his royal master, the incident did serious damage to the conservative group.

Worse was to follow. When the conservatives tried to break the friendship of Henry and Cranmer in 1543 by suggesting that the archbishop was dabbling in Protestant heresy, the king not only rejected these allegations against his friend but put Cranmer in charge of the investigation into the claims. He also married Catherine Parr, the sister of the Earl of Essex, in July 1543. This was an important decision since Catherine was close to the Seymour family and was a Protestant sympathiser. She gathered scholars around her at court and allowed them to manage the education of Henry's youngest children, Edward and Elizabeth. Although the conservative faction struck out at her by accusing members of her household of heresy, Henry supported his wife.

By the final year of Henry's reign the reform faction was dominant. Catherine Parr had survived and Edward Seymour had built his position at court both as Prince Edward's uncle and as successful military commander in the war against Scotland. By contrast, Gardiner's career was in decline. He had been accused by the reformers of suggesting that the Pope should be reinstated as head of the church and only quick thinking had enabled him to avoid the Tower. He had also made a crucial miscalculation by becoming embroiled in the plot against the queen in 1546. This, together with a trumped-up accusation that he was refusing to grant some of his lands to the king, was enough to push him out of the inner circle of royal advisers. In the meantime, reformers occupied important positions at court. In October 1546 Sir Anthony Denny was made Chief Gentleman of the King's Privy Chamber. As Henry's illnesses during his last years kept him largely confined to his private apartments, Denny's role became crucial. He tended to Henry's needs and spent much time with the

Q Why did the reform faction replace the conservatives as the dominant political group?

Figure 36 Henry VIII in his declining years.

king. He also decided whether Henry was fit to receive visitors and
who should be admitted.

Events in Scotland, 1540–47

During the 1540s, Henry again returned to the problem of the
security of his northern frontier with Scotland. James V had
intensified the potential threat his country posed by pursuing an
actively pro-French line – he married Mary of Guise, a relative of
the French king, in 1538, for example. Henry attempted to nego-
tiate an agreement with James which would have guaranteed
England's security, but James refused, humiliating Henry in the
process by failing to turn up for the pre-arranged talks.

By 1542, Henry was sufficiently concerned and irritated by
events to send the Duke of Norfolk to invade Scotland. The campaign was a military success: at Solway Moss (November 1542) the
Scottish army was defeated decisively. Within a week of the defeat,
James V died, leaving the crown to his week-old daughter Mary.

In the Treaty of Greenwich, Henry proposed to strengthen
English influence in Scotland through the marriage of his son
Edward to Mary, but this was too much for the Scots and the
treaty collapsed. With it came the renewal of war as Scottish
nobles again looked to France for assistance in maintaining their
independence from English control. In 1544 and 1545, the Earl
of Hertford (reform faction leader and later Protector
Somerset) took the English army on a series of raids in the border region. People at the time referred to these attacks as
Henry's 'rough wooing' of Scotland, but the Scots were only
alienated further by them.

By his death, Henry had prevented Scotland and France from
combining against him, but at great financial cost. Only repeated requests to Parliament for subsidies, reductions in the silver
value of coins and the sale of monastic lands kept the crown solvent. These short term measures, however, contributed significantly to the financial difficulties of the mid-Tudor and
Elizabethan periods.

Whilst the reform faction worked its way into positions of authority
at court, the conservative group was finally broken apart by the arrests
of the Duke of Norfolk and his son the Earl of Surrey. Rumours had
been circulating for some time that Surrey had spoken openly about his
family's claim to the throne (a very sensitive issue given Henry's illness
and the age of his only surviving son). To make matters worse, Surrey
foolishly put part of the royal coat of arms of his ancestor King Edward

I onto his own family emblem, despite having no official authority to do so. This seemed to suggest that his designs on the crown were serious, so he was arrested for treason and executed a week before Henry's death. Norfolk was also arrested, but escaped execution because Henry died before giving the order. With the influence of both men eliminated, Bishop Gardiner removed from the Regency Council and **Henry's will** in their hands, the reform faction had triumphed.

ACTIVITY

The factionalism of the 1540s gives us our first piece of evidence to test the 'mid-Tudor crisis' theory. Did these intrigues, and Henry's worsening health, create an atmosphere of conflict and uncertainty which threatened the effectiveness of Tudor government? Much depends on whether you accept the arguments of historians such as Ives, who argue that the king's control weakened and left him the victim of these rival groups, or the arguments of others such as A. G. R. Smith, who suggest that for the most part Henry knew what was happening and played the groups against each other. Consider some of the important incidents of this period, such as the conservatives' attack on Cranmer in 1543 and the queen in 1546, to decide which interpretation you think is best.

---

3 Henry's Legacy

a) The Succession

Well before his death, Henry had taken steps to ensure his son's safe succession. He had dealt with the lingering possibility of rival claimants by executing members of the Pole family and by his violent response to the Earl of Surrey's ham-fisted attempts to promote his family's interests. Henry had also ensured that the succession of Edward was secure in law. The Succession Act of 1544 named Edward as heir, with Mary, then Elizabeth, as next in line should he fail to survive or to produce children. Since Edward was only a boy, Henry also made provision for a regency. Decisions on this were critical because regencies had proven notoriously weak in the past. Without a strong male figure as head of state, the greed of the nobility might reassert itself, bringing unrest and unravelling Henry's successes and reputation.

By the terms of the will, the regency was to be managed by a council of 16 men, named by Henry. The reform group dominated the membership of the council, especially since the Duke of Norfolk and Bishop Gardiner had been ejected. In the secrecy surrounding Henry's death, it appears that the council began immediately to dis-

---

HENRY'S WILL

Sir Anthony Denny's position gave him access to an important political instrument – the Dry Stamp. Instead of bothering the king with every trivial document that needed signing, the holder of the stamp could make an impression of the royal signature onto the paper, then ink in the outline to create an almost perfect copy of the king's handwriting. Using the stamp, the reform faction could legalise any document they chose – including an altered version of Henry VIII's will which they published shortly after news of the king's death. The revised will left the succession as Henry had intended, but added provisions that strengthened the power of the Regency Council established to rule on Edward VI's behalf.

ISSUES:
What arrangements had been made for the succession?
How far were they followed?

cuss how best to implement the regency. His plan of government by committee was a clever way of protecting his son's interests, but it was too ambitious and unusual a scheme to work. The Earl of Hertford seemed the best placed for leadership. He was Edward's uncle, an important figure within the reform faction with a successful military career to commend him. Three days after Henry's death, the council appointed Hertford as Lord Protector, reviving the traditional idea of a regency led by someone close to the king-in-waiting. Following this, Hertford took the title Earl of Somerset and used the power granted to the council in Henry's will to promote supporters with new titles and positions in government. Finally, Somerset began to appoint his own Privy Council, drawing on a wider circle of men than the will had envisaged. By the time of Edward's coronation procession in mid-February, Somerset's hold on power was virtually complete, a 'bloodless coup' as Mark Nicholls has described it.

b) The Condition of England in 1547

ISSUES:
What problems did the new government face? Did these amount to a crisis?

Henry VIII's death had clearly left England with a political problem, but it had also left the country vulnerable at a time when wider changes were becoming apparent. You will find more details of the changes in the thematic chapters of this book, but the main developments were:

▼ a noticeable rise in population, which put pressure on the food supply, jobs and rents and which contributed to inflation as the price of essential items rose

▼ a change of land use from crop production in open fields to sheep-farming in enclosed fields in some regions, leading to the disruption of traditional village life

▼ resentment at the growth in government activity in everyday life, from making decisions about personal faith to regulating the economy and trying to manage the problem of poverty

▼ an over-ambitious foreign policy based on a jealous rivalry with France and a desire to exercise greater influence in Scotland which had led Henry VIII into disastrously expensive wars against France and Scotland in the 1540s. This had resulted in policies such as the debasement of the coinage and the sale of crown lands which threatened financial stability

▼ the gathering pace of religious debate. On the continent, Protestant faiths had emerged and were beginning to establish themselves in Germany, Scandinavia and Switzerland. In England, debate in universities and at court about the future shape of the church and doctrine was beginning to widen out into the community. Although most people remained loyal to traditional religious ideas, Protestant influences were taking root in some parts of London and the south-east as well as in ports such as Hull which had trade links to Germany and Scandinavia.

EDWARD VI (1537–1553)

You might be surprised to see little reference to Edward himself in this chapter or in other textbooks that you consult. Although Edward was the rightful successor to Henry VIII, his age – he was nine in 1547 – meant that he could not take the crown immediately. Instead, a Regency Council was appointed to conduct business on his behalf. In this way, the story of Edward's reign tends to be more about what the regency governments did, rather than the part the king himself played.

Edward was born in October 1537, the son of Jane Seymour and third child of Henry VIII. He was the male heir that Henry had so desperately wanted, but was under-sized and sickly. Portraits such as the one on this page serve only to emphasise how young and vulnerable Edward seems.

As a child, he seemed very serious and committed to his studies. He was educated in the Christian Humanist tradition and became proficient at Greek, Latin and French. His tutors also introduced him to Protestant ideas and Edward became very interested in theological questions:

> Believe me, my esteemed friend, you have never seen in the world for these thousand years so much learning united with piety and sweetness of character. Should he live to grow up with these virtues, he will be a terror to all the sovereigns of the earth. He writes a copy with his own hand of every sermon that he hears, and most diligently requires an account of them after dinner from those who study with him.
>
> *Source A* From a letter by John Hooper, the Bishop of Gloucester, to the Protestant reformer Bullinger, 27 March 1550.

There seems little doubt that Edward was a clever student, but also that he felt a great responsibility as the heir to the throne; because of this he has been described as 'old beyond his years'. Edward's writings help to reinforce this impression of a rather isolated, but dutiful, young man. Even when writing of painful family matters, the style of his diary remained detached and factual to the point of coldness:

> January 1552: Today, the Duke of Somerset had his head cut off on Tower Hill.
>
> *Source B* Edward's succinct description of the execution of his uncle, Edward Seymour.

-Profile-

1537 born, son of Jane Seymour;

1543 marriage to Mary Queen of Scots was discussed;

1547 succeeded to the throne;

1551 began regular attendance at meetings of the Privy Council; discussion of marriage to the daughter of Henry II of France;

1552 contracted measles then smallpox, raising fears that he would not reach adulthood;

1553 signed an order excluding his Catholic sister Mary from the throne a few weeks before he died of tuberculosis.

In short, the elements of a crisis were apparently present; a weak and uncertain government faced deep-rooted problems across a range of issues. However, the triumph of the reform faction within the Regency Council offered at least some political stability. So too did the emergence of Somerset as Protector, since the use of a regent to solve the problem of government was a traditional one, accepted by the majority of people. Despite fears of unrest, the careful preparations and quick actions of the council ensured that Henry VIII's passing was uneventful.

ACTIVITY

Understanding the range of problems facing the governments of Edward VI and Mary is important if you are to avoid the mistake of interpreting the mid-Tudor crisis as being purely about politics. To reinforce your understanding of the wider context, follow these page references:

social problems	population change	Chapter 1, pages 5–8
economic problems	inflation	Chapter 1, pages 22–5
	enclosures	Chapter 1, pages 16–18
	debasement of coinage	Chapter 1, pages 22–3
religious problems	debate about Protestant ideas	Chapter 3, pages 77–8

ISSUES:
What problems did Somerset face? Why did he fall from power in 1549?

4 Protector Somerset

Protector Somerset's reputation among historians has declined from the image of the 'Good Duke' whose policies reflected a genuine concern for the Protestant faith and the needs of his people, to the modern image of an arrogant man whose poor choices brought the country close to ruin in 1549. To some extent, Somerset faced an impossible task. He had considerable power as protector (since he could issue proclamations in the king's name which had the force of law), but could never be more than a caretaker until Edward came of

Decisions facing Protector Somerset's government	Why the government should take the decision	Why the government might regret the decision
1. Should the war with Scotland be resumed?	• Henry VIII had revived this conflict partly to prevent France from using Scotland to weaken England. The weak succession in 1547 kept this danger alive • Over £2 million had already been spent on the war, for no real result. Could the new government afford to lose national pride by withdrawing now? • Nobles and the gentry had raised forces and led troops in the campaigns of the 1540s. They were anxious to see the war continue to win personal fame. Could the new government afford to alienate these powerful families?	• Henry VIII had already gone into debt and brought England close to bankruptcy to pay for the war. Could the country afford to continue? • By attacking Scotland, it was likely that France would be drawn into the conflict. Could the government risk an invasion in the south whilst dealing with the Scots in the north?
2. Should religious reform along Protestant lines be encouraged officially?	• The reform group dominated the council and key government posts. Could Somerset afford to do nothing? • There was a Protestant minority in parts of the country, especially in London and the south-east, who were anxious to see further change. Could they be ignored?	• In the regions, most people followed traditional Catholic rituals and practices. Would the government create open rebellion by using the law to change people's faith? • Too much change might alarm the Catholic powers of Europe (especially Emperor Charles V) at a time when England was already at war with France and Scotland
3. Should the government make economic and financial reform a priority?	• There was good evidence of growing popular discontent over issues such as enclosure, price rises and the breakdown of traditional village communities. Action would perhaps satisfy people that something was being done	• Making changes, particularly to enclosure rights, would attack the gentry class on whom the government depended for support • Trying to improve national finances by raising more through taxes would certainly be unpopular and lose the new regime what support it could rely upon

Table 9 The dilemmas facing Protector Somerset in 1547.

age. He also had to deal with a weak inheritance from Henry VIII, especially the long-term structural changes that were taking place within society and the economy. As Table 9 reveals, all the key decisions which needed to be taken were fraught with problems.

ACTIVITY

Based on the information in Table 9, what would be your recommendations to Protector Somerset for each of the policy decisions he needed to take?

ISSUES:
Was Somerset right to place such a high priority on the war in Scotland? How successfully did he resolve it?

GOVERNMENT OF PROTECTOR SOMERSET

1547 Jan: succession of Edward VI; Edward Seymour (Earl of Hertford) became Lord Protector;

1547 Feb: Seymour took the title Duke of Somerset;

1547 Sept: defeat of Scots at Battle of Pinkie;

1547 Nov: Parliament repealed anti-Protestant Treasons Act; passage of new Poor Law (the 'Slavery Act'); Act abolishing chantries;

1548 June–July: French army landed in Scotland; Mary Queen of Scots moved to France;
June: creation of Enclosure Commission;

1549 Act of Uniformity; new Prayer Book; taxes increased on sheep and cloth;
June: outbreak of Western Rebellion in Devon and Cornwall and Kett's Rebellion in Norfolk;
Oct: fall of Somerset; power struggle to replace him.

a) The War in Scotland

Somerset made the decision to continue the war in Scotland his first priority. It is easy to criticise him for failing to pay more attention to England's domestic problems, but we must remember not only the protector's background as military commander, but also the over-riding concern within the Tudor state about security. Regencies did not have a distinguished history: they revealed a weakness at the centre of political power and encouraged greed and ambition amongst the leading nobility. The war against Scotland had to be completed, not only to prevent France from exploiting this difficulty, but also to demonstrate the strength of the Protectorate.

At first, everything went well for the new government. The protector himself led the royal forces into battle against the Scottish army at Pinkie (September 1547) and won a decisive victory. However, the battle came too late in the campaigning season to be followed up, giving time over the winter for the Scots to look to France for support. Although Somerset tried to strengthen England's presence by ordering fortifications to be built along the Anglo-Scottish border and on the east coast of Scotland (where a French fleet was most likely to land), the policy quickly collapsed. The fortifications were hugely expensive to maintain because they were largely garrisoned by mercenaries. Moreover, they failed to keep the French out: soldiers began arriving in summer 1548 and the heir to the Scottish throne, Mary, was moved to France in preparation for her marriage to the French heir, Francis.

In all, Somerset spent about £600,000 on the Scottish campaign for no real return on his money. Critics of the protector point out that his policies had increased the economic crisis in England, distracted government attention away from these problems at home, and worsened security by creating the one thing that English policy had sought to avoid – a dynastic union between France and Scotland. These criticisms are valid, but need to be moderated by the fact that Somerset did not conduct the campaign alone. He discussed the war strategy with other councillors and took decisions based on their advice. The failure in Scotland contributed to the unease and sense of crisis, but it was a failure of government rather than of the protector.

b) Religious Reform

ISSUES:
What was Somerset's attitude to religious reform? How did national policy reflect his views?

Somerset had some personal sympathy with the more extreme Protestant ideas of John Calvin. As Lord Protector, however, he recognised the sensitivity in making religious changes and tried to adopt a moderate and cautious approach. This was not easy in the face of the pressures building up:

▼ as soon as news of Henry VIII's death reached the continent, exiled Protestants who had fled persecution in the 1530s and 1540s began returning from the Netherlands and Germany. They settled in towns and villages along the east coast, where their radical demands caused frequent clashes within the local community

▼ the reform faction was in control of the government, and keen to see reform get under way, but English bishops were split fairly evenly on whether to support further changes

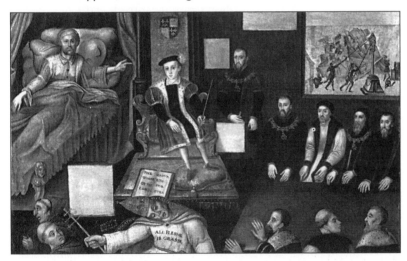

Figure 37 This is a famous depiction of the Edwardian Reformation. It is an allegorical painting, which means that it should not be seen as a photographic likeness of any event, but contains messages and special meanings for its audience, in this case the triumph of Protestant 'truth' over Catholic 'error'. In bed, an ailing Henry VIII points to his successor, Edward, who sits on the throne beneath the royal coat of arms. Standing to Edward's left is Protector Somerset and seated next to him are members of the Privy Council. Through the window we can see people pulling down religious idols associated with Catholicism and burning them. The Pope has tumbled awkwardly at the front of the picture, hit by a copy of the Bible bearing the inscription 'The Word of the Lord Endureth Forever'. By contrast, the phrase 'All Flesh is Grass' is printed on the Pope's robe, denying his claim to be head of a timeless church. Frightened monks and priests flee the scene at the bottom left.

▼ the relaxation of press censorship (encouraged by the government) led to a massive increase in the number of pamphlets and writings against Catholicism and to the free circulation of the writings of Martin Luther and John Calvin, to the horror of religious conservatives.

At first, the government adopted a logical policy, which helped to stall for time. A full-scale enquiry into the state of the Church of England was launched, with commissioners sent out to investigate what was happening in every parish. In addition, measures were introduced which undid the Six Articles Act and strengthened rules that provided for services and Bibles to be in English. When Parliament met in November 1547, it was again used to enact religious change, but legislation did little more than to underline what was already happening. The Treason Act repealed the Six Articles Act and the heresy, treason and censorship laws which had stifled religious debate in the closing years of Henry VIII's reign. The Chantries Act abolished a particular type of Catholic religious house, but more to raise money for the Scottish war than for religious reasons. It was not until that war was over that the government felt secure enough to take firm action to sort out the confusion over religious policy by passing the 1549 **Act of Uniformity**.

Alongside the Act, Archbishop Cranmer introduced a new Prayer Book setting out the form that services should take. It was a masterpiece of vagueness. Whilst not entirely denying the central Catholic idea that the priest transformed the bread and wine of the mass into the 'real presence' of Christ – His body and blood – the Prayer Book none the less gave the impression that the priest was simply commemorating an event, thus reassuring Protestants.

Although the attempt to impose the Act of Uniformity and the new Prayer Book contributed to the rebellions which ruined Somerset's career in 1549, it is difficult to see what else he could have done. During his brief time in power, he dismantled the obstacles to religious change that had been erected by the conservative faction in the late 1530s whilst avoiding an open religious schism. Given England's precarious international position and the political weakness inherent in regency government, Somerset's religious policies were all the more impressive.

c) Economic Reform

Traditionally, the reputation of Somerset as the 'Good Duke' rested on his apparent desire to help those in economic difficulties. In reality, Somerset might have felt that some assistance was necessary to defuse protest, but he could not afford to go too far without jeopardising revenues for the Scottish war. This pushed him into a dangerous and ultimately disastrous policy. By seeming to be sympathetic, he raised the hope of reform without being able to deliver it.

ACT OF UNIFORMITY

The Act was designed to impose a single (uniform) standard of worship across England, to end the religious confusion and argument that had been growing since 1534. Among its terms were requirements that English was to be used as the language of worship and that congregations should be offered both the bread and wine during communion (this was a clear breach with the Catholic tradition of reserving the wine for the priesthood). However, it did not go so far as to create a full Protestant church. Services were conducted along familiar lines (apart from the language) and by priests who dressed and behaved as always.

ISSUE:
Why did government efforts to limit enclosures prove so unpopular?

Somerset's government chose enclosures as the crusading issue. In fact, it was more important to tackle inflation if real economic improvements were to be made, but Somerset shied away from this because the policies needed to control inflationary pressures would have reduced the taxes he needed to fight the Scottish war. A commission was established to investigate the legality of recent enclosures. Once more, government inspectors toured the country. This time, they were welcomed by families in the Midlands and the south who had lost their lands and customary rights when landowners had converted fields from open strips for crop production into fenced-off pastures for sheep grazing. There was a real expectation that the commissioners would order a reversal, and bitter disappointment when they did not.

However, not everyone welcomed the arrival of enclosure commissioners. Gentry landowners who had made their wealth from sheep-farming feared a loss of their livelihood, and were further angered by new laws, passed in 1548–9, which raised the tax on sheep and cloth. The investigation of enclosures was a well-meaning policy, but led to frustration and fury among both rich and poor.

d) The Crisis of 1549 and the Fall of Somerset

By summer 1549 the elements of crisis were in place. Somerset's foreign policy had driven the Scots into the arms of the French. His concern for the economic hardships facing some regions had produced a flurry of activity, but no real results. His religious policies, whilst appropriate in the circumstances, had failed to satisfy radical Protestants yet had alarmed traditional Catholics. It might have been possible for Somerset to have survived all this, but he had few supporters left in government.

i) The Western Rebellion
The first stirrings of popular rebellion can be seen well before summer 1549. As the government sent its agents out to check on the state of the church and the progress towards limited reform from 1547, there were signs of resistance to change from local communities. In Helston in Cornwall, William Body was killed by a mob who resented his attempts to order the removal of traditional Catholic statues and images from local churches. In Somerset and Bristol mobs tore down the fences and hedges that had been erected to enclose pastureland. Similar stories of spontaneous local rioting were reported outside the south-west.

The Western Rebellion grew out of these riots in Cornwall and Devon. When the government ordered that the new Prayer Book should be used in churches from Whitsuntide onwards, groups were formed to resist and a full-scale rebellion had begun by mid-June.

Q Was Somerset's desire to show the government's understanding of people's economic hardships genuine, cynical, or simply foolish?

ISSUE:
Why did major rebellions break out in summer 1549?

INTERPRETATIONS OF PROTECTOR SOMERSET
Historians now regard the 'Good Duke' as an arrogant and aloof figure, who became increasingly unwilling to consult or to listen to advice from the Privy Council. His personal style of government was shown most clearly by the increasing use of proclamations. These allowed Somerset to use royal prerogative to make policy without going through Parliament. Had his policies been more successful, he might have been forgiven his high-handed style of ruling, but their failure magnified the accusations that he was incompetent and dangerously powerful.

The rebels gathered at Crediton, where they were met by a local landowner. He treated them unsympathetically and the accidental burning of part of the rebel defences finished any chance of a quick settlement. The rebels then advanced past Exeter and set up camp. There was no attempt to march towards London to protest their grievances to the government; instead, the rebels brought the south-west to a standstill and waited for the government to come to them. News of the rebellion travelled slowly and Somerset almost certainly underestimated the seriousness of the situation at first. It was diffi-cult, however, for the government to respond. Troops were needed to defend the north against Scotland and the coast against France. By the time the rebels had gained control of the lands around Exeter, the government also faced a second major protest in the east.

ii) Kett's Rebellion

In Norfolk, gangs emerged in May and June 1549 to break enclo-sures. Robert Kett was one of the landowners whose property was attacked, but he agreed to end enclosure on his estates and offered to lead the rebels to secure their rights. Kett's Rebellion followed a similar pattern to the Western Rising. The rebels did not march towards London, but set up camp on Mousehold Heath, near Norwich. From there, they ran a largely peaceful campaign to end enclosures, improve local government and (unlike the Western Rising) secure better quality clergymen. At the height of the camp, Kett boasted that he could call on 15,000 men if the army attacked.

These rebellions threatened a complete breakdown of govern-ment in two regions of England. In both cases, Somerset's response was slow almost to the point of paralysis. The western rebels were finally beaten by the royal army in mid-August, whilst the Earl of Warwick put an end to Kett's Rebellion in a bloody confrontation at the end of the month. Neither revolt had forced the government to change its policies either on religion or enclosures, but they shook government to the core and gave those who were aggrieved at Somerset's style of government their opportunity to strike. Somerset was arrested on the orders of the council on 11 October and impris-oned in the Tower. He was released in February 1550 and was allowed to rejoin the Privy Council (his only real crimes had been incompetence and panic). However, rumours soon began to circu-late that Somerset was gathering support to take power back from the council. He was arrested again and tried on charges of treason, specifically of plotting to assassinate some of his rivals on the council, and executed in January 1552.

ACTIVITY

If there was a mid-Tudor crisis, historians have pointed out that it hap-pened in 1549. You should aim to write clear notes about the **causes**, **nature** and **results** of what hap-pened in the summer of that year.

Did the 1549 rebellions pose a genuine threat to the government? How might a historian measure the seriousness of the crisis?

5 Northumberland's Government, 1549–53

ISSUE:
How did Northumberland's government differ from Somerset's in its priorities and policies?

The man who benefited most from Somerset's difficulties in the summer of 1549 was the Earl of Warwick. In his campaign against Kett's Rebellion he had shown himself to be an effective military commander and his supporters in government felt that he would be more willing to rule with their advice than Somerset had been. None the less, Warwick had to struggle for power and only gained the upper hand in February 1550 after securing clear backing from Edward. He soon took the title Duke of Northumberland, but was not granted the position of protector. Instead, he was named **Lord President of the Council**.

At the same time that Somerset's reputation has declined, Northumberland's has risen. He was once thought of as a ruthless opportunist, but historians now paint a less extreme picture of a greedy yet skilful politician who drew government back together after the disasters of 1549. This achievement has to be set in the context of the time. Northumberland came to power after the most serious public disturbances of the sixteenth century. Although the worst was over, there were still signs of unrest across the country which were sparked by bad harvests and a slump in the cloth trade in the early 1550s. Religious differences were also by no means healed by the events of 1549 – if anything, as time went on Protestant influence created more uncertainty in communities traditionally loyal to Catholicism.

For these reasons, Northumberland pursued different policies from Somerset, as Table 10 reveals.

LORD PRESIDENT OF THE COUNCIL
This title gives some clue as to how Northumberland governed. Unlike Somerset, who was the king's uncle, he lacked the personal authority that a close connection with Edward would have brought. Instead, he was forced to govern through the authority of the Privy Council. This exposed Northumberland to more day-to-day pressure than Somerset had faced, but meant that he could not make his predecessor's fatal mistake of becoming remote from the government he led.

Table 10 A comparison of Somerset and Northumberland's priorities in government.

Somerset's policies, 1547–9	Northumberland's policies, 1550–53
• continue military action in Scotland to break apart the French-Scottish alliance and improve England's influence in the north	• bring the expensive and unsuccessful war with France to an end and repair relations in case the Catholic Emperor and ruler of Spain, Charles V, grew more hostile to the spread of Protestantism in England
• pursue a cautious religious policy of weakening Catholicism whilst introducing only a moderate form of Protestantism	• advance the Protestant faith (according to the wishes of Archbishop Cranmer and the reform faction) by making a more decisive statement of national beliefs
• resolve economic and social problems by focusing on enclosures	• resolve economic problems and restore government finances by shifting attention to strengthening the currency and tackling a wider range of social grievances

ISSUES:
Why did Northumberland attempt to change the succession in 1553? Why did he fail?

In foreign policy, Northumberland changed direction almost completely. He saw the war against France as a distraction from urgent domestic problems and was willing to sacrifice influence over Scotland to achieve a peace in the Treaty of Boulogne in March 1550. At this point, English policy began to regard Spain and the Holy Roman Empire as the greater threat, since these powers represented hard-line Catholicism. Northumberland wisely saw that France could be useful as a counterweight against Spain, foreshadowing developments in Elizabeth's reign.

At home, Northumberland largely abandoned the government's interest in challenging the enclosure movement and tried to revive royal finances. Under Sir Thomas Gresham, schemes were established to cut government spending and to chase up debts more efficiently. There were also policies to restore the value of the currency (by 1550, successive debasements had meant that the silver content of coins had been reduced to 25 per cent of the 1530s level). The government has also earned something of a reputation for its awareness of social concerns. The 1552 Poor Law placed greater responsibility on parishes to collect money to help the deserving poor, whilst the Act Concerning Tillage taxed all land that had been recently converted from crop farming to pastureland.

Perhaps the greatest achievement of the Northumberland government, however, was to clarify the religious situation. Somerset's legislation in 1549 had created a national church, but one based on half-changes and vague statements. It had not satisfied those who saw the break with Rome as leading naturally to the establishment of a distinctively English church. Legislation in 1552–3 went much further. A new Prayer Book, composed by Archbishop Cranmer, made fundamental changes to the meaning and structure of church services, pushing them firmly into the Protestant tradition. In July 1553 this change was reinforced by the publication of a new statement of national faith which drew heavily on the ideas of continental reformers. In the short term these changes incurred the anger of Mary Tudor, who reversed them all when she became queen in 1553; but in the longer term, they were valuable in establishing ideas that became the basis of the Church of England in Elizabeth's reign.

6 The Succession Crisis of 1553

During 1552–3 Edward VI's health began to deteriorate. He caught and survived both measles and smallpox in the spring of 1552, but soon afterwards the first signs of tuberculosis appeared. It was clear that, short of a miracle, the 14-year-old would not live to be crowned king.

Under the terms of the 1544 Succession Act, Edward's heir was the Princess Mary. This posed a problem for the Northumberland government: Mary was a committed Catholic and had drawn close to her cousin, the Emperor Charles V. If she succeeded to the throne, the policies pursued since 1550 would be swept aside along with the men who had promoted them. To protect both himself and the Protestant faith, Northumberland tried to alter the succession before Edward died. He based his plans on two facts:

▼ Mary had been made illegitimate when Henry VIII's marriage to Catherine of Aragon had broken down. Similarly, Elizabeth had also been made illegitimate by the collapse of Henry's marriage to Anne Boleyn. Although both women had been officially restored to the succession, these changes had been damaging.

▼ Henry VIII's will had directed the succession towards his own children, but had not set aside the claims that his younger sister's family might make. From these two strands, Northumberland decided to ensure that Edward's will did not pass the crown to either Mary or Elizabeth, but to Lady Jane Grey (who married Northumberland's son in May 1553, six weeks before Edward's death).

The events of 1553 showed that, for most people, it was important that God's rightful choice of monarch – Mary – should take the throne rather than a usurper. Moreover, there was still significant support for traditional ways outside London, so the provinces backed Mary to disrupt the drift towards Protestantism noticeable for the last decade. The events surrounding Mary's succession, then, show both how vulnerable the country could be to political disruption, and yet how secure the Tudor dynasty had actually become.

ACTIVITY

Here is another moment when a political crisis might have overwhelmed the government. By challenging Mary's claim, Northumberland was acting against the terms of Henry VIII's will and against what most people considered to be the natural line of succession. You will need to judge whether Lady Jane Grey could realistically have become queen against the claim of Mary. If you believe that it was possible, then you are accepting the notion of a profound political crisis. Consider the following statements to help you judge:

1. Northumberland won the Privy Council's approval for Lady Jane Grey's claim to the throne, but only after much pressure and hesitation.
2. There was virtually no popular support for Jane – only the local authorities in Berwick and King's Lynn backed her.
3. Northumberland ended the coup himself when he surrendered to Mary near Cambridge.

-Profile-

LADY JANE GREY (1537–1554)

Lady Jane Grey is a fascinating victim of Tudor politics. Her involvement in the disputed succession of 1553 reveals both the ongoing insecurity of the Tudor dynasty and its inherent strengths in being able to survive this opportunistic challenge.

On Edward's death in July 1553, the contents of his will revealed that the crown should be passed to Lady Jane Grey. The Privy Council hesitated, but finally recognised that this was the king's instruction so proclaimed her queen and ordered the arrest of Mary. This was the dreadful moment that had haunted Tudor politics since Henry VII had seized the crown in 1485 – a successful challenge to the crown from a royal pretender. In this case, Lady Jane Grey had good credentials:

▼ she was the granddaughter of Henry VIII's sister Mary, so was related to the Tudor dynasty through the female side of her family

▼ she had been named as heir by Edward VI

▼ she was a Protestant, so offered a religious continuity which Mary did not.

There was little support in the country for her claim, however. When Northumberland led the royal army north to arrest Mary he saw the strength of support that she enjoyed because she was the legitimate heir and bowed to the inevitable. By 3 August, Mary was in London and Northumberland, his son and Lady Jane Grey were all in the Tower.

Mary was initially reluctant to execute Jane Grey because she recognised her as an innocent pawn in Northumberland's plans, but she also realised that the pretender queen would continue to represent a hope for English Protestants as long as she remained alive. Confirmation of this came in the form of an attempted rebellion led by the Duke of Suffolk, Lady Jane Grey's father. For this reason, she was convicted and beheaded on the charge of treason.

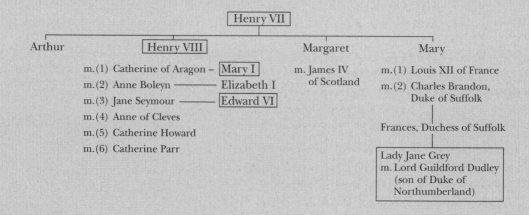

Figure 38 Lady Jane Grey's claim to the throne.

7 The Reign of Mary Tudor, 1553–8

ISSUES:
How did Mary change the direction of government policy after 1553? Why did this make her increasingly unpopular?

That Mary threw away the genuine wave of support that carried her to the throne was the result of her failure to recognise that the country had been undergoing significant social, economic and religious change for about a generation, and that altering direction in any of these areas had to be done slowly and cautiously. Instead, Mary appeared to be impatient to make changes. She interpreted the popularity which greeted her succession as a sign that her subjects were welcoming the return of Catholicism rather than as a reaction against Northumberland and Lady Jane Grey. In this way, her sharp reversal of the religious policies promoted by the reform faction during the 1540s and early 1550s and her equally dramatic decision to marry her nephew Philip, heir to the Spanish throne, turned her early popularity into doubt and dislike in the minds of many Englishmen.

a) Religious Reform

ISSUE:
Why did Mary reverse the drift towards Protestantism?

The major aim of Mary's reign was to reinstate traditional Roman Catholic doctrines in the church. As a child, Mary had been brought up by her mother, Catherine of Aragon, as a strict Catholic. When her father had manipulated religion to divorce her mother, and when he had denied the authority of the Pope and seized control over the church for himself, Mary had been horrified. She saw the break with Rome as a sinful act and was determined to correct it. The destruction of church property and the rewriting of the Prayer Book to include heretical ideas of what happened to the bread and wine in the mass had only confirmed her desire to set things to rights.

Early in her reign, Mary approached Parliament for help in overturning the Reformation. The obedient majority of the House of Commons voted to repeal all doctrinal legislation passed since 1529. Since this included the 1534 Act of Supremacy, it meant the reinstatement of the Pope as head of the church. It did not, however, mean the restoration of church lands and property, for this was too complex and too divisive an issue to be resolved easily. Although there was opposition to this sudden change of direction, Mary remained convinced that Protestantism lacked the deep roots in English culture that would allow it to survive.

Having achieved the reunion of England with the Roman Catholic Church, government policy now divided into two distinct strands – education and persecution. To ensure that Catholicism took root once more, emphasis was placed on better training and supervision of parish priests. Bishops were instructed to set up local training

MARY'S REIGN

1553 July: Mary proclaimed queen after failed coup of Northumberland;

1554 Jan: marriage treaty with Spain;
Feb: Wyatt's Rebellion;
July: Mary married Philip of Spain;

1555 Jan: legislation reversed Edwardian reforms of the church and restored papal supremacy;
Feb: first executions of Protestant heretics;
Sept: second worst harvest of 1550s;
Dec: Cranmer removed as Archbishop of Canterbury;

1556 Jan: Philip became King of Spain;
March: execution of Cranmer;
Sept: worst harvest of sixteenth century; beginnings of influenza epidemic;

1557 June: war against France to support Spain;
Aug: Anglo-Spanish victory over France at Saint-Quentin;

1558 Jan: loss of Calais;
Militia Act; Arms Act improved the condition of the army;
Nov: death of Mary; smooth accession of Elizabeth I.

Source C The burning of bishops Latimer and Ridley in Oxford in 1555. This account is taken from John Foxe's *Book of Martyrs*.

How did Mary justify what seems to modern eyes to have been a cruel and extreme policy of religious persecution?

schools and to make regular visits to observe the work of priests in their area. National decrees laid down the standards expected from priests and new editions of the Prayer Book and Bible were issued for guidance.

However, the policy of persecution has been much more widely reported by historians, and has created the reputation of 'Bloody Mary'. Leading Protestant churchmen, including Archbishop Cranmer, were arrested and others replaced by committed Catholics. Within a year of her succession, the senior clergy had been purged of Protestant elements and work had begun on ordering parish priests who had married to either give up their families or leave their jobs. Once Parliament had revived the heresy laws which had operated during Henry VIII's reign, Protestants who would not renounce their faith were burned at the stake in their local community as a warning to others. The executions began in February 1555 and claimed both high-ranking victims such as Cranmer and many ordinary people who were unable to escape abroad. About 300 suspected Protestants were burned in total.

Then the smith took a chain and fastened it about both Ridley and Latimer's middles. Then his brother brought him gunpowder in a bag and tied it around their necks. Then they brought a faggot, kindled with fire and laid it down at Ridley's feet. Latimer turned to him and spoke in this manner: 'Be of good comfort, brother Ridley, and play the man. We shall this day light such a candle by God's grace in England as I trust shall never be put out.' And so the fire being kindled, Latimer cried out, 'O Father of heaven, receive my soul' and reached to the flame as if embracing it. After he had stroked his face with his hands, and, as it were, bathed them a little in the fire, he soon died, with very little pain. But Ridley lingered longer by reason of the badness of the fire, which only burned beneath him. He asked for them to let the fire come to him, saying 'I cannot burn'. This was apparent for after his legs were consumed, he showed his other side towards us, shirt and all untouched by flame! In which pain he suffered til one of the standers-by moved the faggots. When Ridley saw the fire flame up, he leaned himself to that side. And when the flame touched the gunpowder, he was seen to stir no more, but burned on the other side, falling at Latimer's feet.

Mary regarded the executions as necessary to cleanse the country of Protestant heresy. Her advisers were less convinced. As the death toll mounted, signs of opposition to the policy began appearing. By executing her subjects in such a graphic way in their own community, Mary inadvertently turned many into public heroes. Instead of

Figure 39 The burning of bishops Latimer and Ridley, from an illustration in John Foxe's *Book of Martyrs* which documented the Marian persecutions.

frightening people back to Catholicism, the burnings raised questions about what was so powerful and important about Protestantism that people were prepared to die for it. This was picked up by English Protestants who had fled abroad. They produced propaganda which associated Catholicism with intolerance and an over-powerful government. The Marian persecutions might not have increased the number of English Protestants but they certainly had the unintended consequence of creating an organised and committed resistance to Catholicism which gained ground across the country and which seriously undermined Mary's popularity.

The people of London are murmuring about the cruel enforcement of the recent acts of Parliament on heresy which has now begun, as shown publicly when a certain Rogers was burnt yesterday. Some of the onlookers wept, others prayed to God to give them strength, perseverance and patience to bear the pain and not to recant; others gathered the ashes and bones and wrapped them in paper to preserve them; others threatened the bishops. The haste with which the bishops have proceeded in this matter may well cause a revolt. Your Majesty might inform the bishops that there are other means of chastising the obstinate at this early stage, such as secret executions, banishment and imprisonment. The watchword should be *secure, caute et lente festinare* [to hasten safely, cautiously and slowly].

Source D Simon Renard, the imperial ambassador in London, writing to Mary's husband King Philip II of Spain, February 1555.

Do you think Renard's advice would have worked?

b) The Spanish Marriage

Mary came to the throne aged 37 and unmarried, raising the possibility that her reign would be no more than an interlude before her Protestant younger sister Elizabeth took the crown. Mary reasoned that if Catholicism was to survive beyond her reign, she must marry and produce an heir – the age-old Tudor problem. As Catherine of Aragon's daughter, she was close to her Spanish relatives and had been considered a possible wife for Charles V. In 1553, she discussed the possibility of marriage to Charles's son Philip with Simon Renard, the imperial ambassador and a close personal friend. The two worked out the details of the marriage alliance without consulting the Privy Council. Because of this, the scheme was a disaster in the making – Mary did not take into account the likely reaction of her subjects to the plan.

Opposition to the marriage centred on two concerns. First, Philip was a staunch Catholic. Protestants feared that he would add strength to Mary's determination to reverse the Reformation in England. Secondly, Philip was heir to the throne of Spain and its vast empire in Europe and the Americas. It was assumed – correctly – that he would use England as a tool to further Spanish ambitions and would have little regard for the interests of the country. There was also the question of how France would react if England and Spain drew together so closely, and what this would mean for relations with Scotland.

Figure 40 A painting celebrating the marriage of Mary Tudor to her nephew, Prince Philip of Spain.

Wyatt's Rebellion, 1554

Sir Thomas Wyatt was a member of the gentry in Kent. He led what has been rather romantically seen as a nationalist, Protestant rebellion against Mary in February 1554. As news of Mary's plan to marry Philip of Spain leaked out from the court, Wyatt and others plotted to overthrow the queen and to replace her with Edward Courtenay, the great-grandson of the fifteenth-century Yorkist king, Edward IV (and the only male claimant to the throne to hand). Courtenay, to strengthen his thin connection to the Tudor crown, was to marry Princess Elizabeth.

The original plan was for four rebellions against Mary to begin in March 1554: one in Devon where the Western Rebellion had taken place; one in Leicestershire led by Lady Jane Grey's father; one on the Welsh border; and one in Kent, led by Wyatt. However, it was difficult to keep these plans secret and the plotters had to advance their timetable to the beginning of February to keep the element of surprise. Three of the four uprisings simply failed to materialise. Only Wyatt was able to gather sufficient men – about 3,000 in total. He marched his rebel army into London, but found London Bridge closed against him. In the confusion that followed, Wyatt failed to convince Londoners to join him and the rebellion collapsed within a week.

Unlike the Western Rising and Kett's Rebellion of 1549, Wyatt's actions were serious because he threatened the capital. However, the failure of the City to support him meant that the danger posed by the rebels was reduced. Mary ordered the execution of Wyatt, Lady Jane Grey and her husband, and about a hundred other conspirators. Princess Elizabeth was also arrested on suspicion of complicity, but released after no solid evidence could be found to implicate her.

Q Why, even after Wyatt's rebellion, did Mary still fail to realise that her plans were unpopular?

THE MARRIAGE ALLIANCE

Although Mary was desperate to marry her nephew, she was careful enough to limit his power within England. By the terms of the marriage agreement, Philip was to be called king, but he had none of the powers associated with the title. He was also forbidden from bringing foreigners into English government and had no claim to the throne in the event of Mary's death. In effect, the agreement created a marriage of convenience and wisely limited the damage that could be done to English interests.

None the less, Mary pressed ahead with the marriage, which took place in July 1554. She always valued the relationship with Philip more than he did. Once he became King of Spain in 1556, Philip paid Mary only one brief visit and that was largely to persuade her to join him in waging war against France. The extent of Mary's desperation and self-delusion about the state of the marriage can be seen in the two false pregnancies that she had in 1554 and 1557.

c) Foreign Policy

Although few Englishmen wanted it, the natural outcome of Mary's marriage was war. Philip had made no secret of wanting England's

ISSUE: What was so disastrous about Mary's foreign policy?

help against France in the final stages of the Habsburg–Valois struggle and put Mary under considerable pressure to declare war. By doing so, Mary undid the diplomacy of Northumberland and put English foreign policy back onto its traditional anti-French footing. She declared war on France in June 1557 and sent troops across the Channel to join her husband's forces. Together, they achieved victory in the battle of Saint-Quentin, but Spain was too exhausted financially to follow this up.

Within a year, France had not only recovered but had seized Calais from the English. This was a terrible blow to national pride, for Calais represented the last outpost of the great medieval empire that had encompassed England and half of France. It severed England from the continent and seemed to symbolise the limited role that the country could play in European affairs. For Mary personally, it was a humiliating example of how her marriage had become more of a convenience for Spain than for England. Popular feeling was such that, when she died ten months later, few people mourned her.

d) Mary's Reputation

ISSUE:

Was Mary's reign a complete failure?

BOOK OF RATES
All goods leaving the country were taxed and the income passed to the crown as part of ordinary revenues. The Book of Rates (1558) set out the level of tax on a wide range of products but had not been updated since the beginning of Henry VIII's reign and therefore took no account of mid-Tudor inflation. The effect of updating rates was to treble crown income from customs duties, but provoked hostility from the merchant community since the new rates coincided with a collapse in the cloth market.

It is very tempting to leave the story of Mary's reign at that – misjudged religious and foreign policies which sacrificed English interests to win the approval of Spain – and to portray Mary as something between a sad victim and a self-deluding idealist. To do so, however, would ignore the accomplishments of her reign. These have been overshadowed by the high-profile disasters, but are important if we are to gauge the extent of the 'mid-Tudor crisis' in the 1550s. Behind the scenes, a quiet strengthening of government and royal finances was taking place:

▼ the role of the Privy Council in managing the daily running of government was becoming more established, and committees were used to deal with specialised issues (such as the war against France)

▼ efforts were made to make revenue collection more efficient (Northumberland had begun this campaign in 1552 by setting up a royal commission) by transferring more responsibility to the Exchequer

▼ a new **Book of Rates** was introduced in May 1558 to improve crown income from customs duties

▼ plans were drawn up to revalue the currency after the 'Great Debasement' of the 1540s.

Mary's government has also been credited with reviving England's great military and naval tradition, providing Elizabeth with the means to resist Spain later in the century. During the Northumberland regime, standards of maintenance of the royal fleet had been allowed to slip, and a number of ships had been decommissioned, leaving Mary with just three serviceable warships. A major programme of rebuilding and refitting was begun under Mary and by 1558 there had been a return to the fleet level of the end of Henry VIII's reign. The government also modernised the army. The 1558 Militia Act laid down a system of Commissioners of Muster with responsibility for organising the recruitment of regional militias in wartime, whilst the Arms Act of the same year established better procedures for supplying weapons to the royal forces.

ACTIVITY

Mary has traditionally received a bad press among historians, and her failures have been regarded as contributing to the sense of crisis in the middle years of the sixteenth century. Produce your own evaluation of Mary by discussing the following questions:

1. What did Mary do that has attracted so much criticism from both contemporaries and historians?
2. Is there any way to justify Mary's actions?
3. What other factors should be taken into account when judging her reign?
4. How do these additional considerations alter our impression of Mary and her achievements?

▼ Working on A Mid-Tudor Crisis

Summary: Themes and Developments, 1540–58

Date	Developments in			
	Politics	**Religion**	**Society/Economy**	**Foreign policy**
1540	fall of Thomas Cromwell; Henry VIII's fifth marriage, to Catherine Howard	order that English language Bibles should be placed in all churches		
1541	Henry declared King of Ireland			
1542	execution of Catherine Howard			defeat of Scots at Battle of Solway Moss; death of King James V
1543	Henry's sixth marriage, to Catherine Parr; English law extended across Wales	conservative faction plot to discredit Archbishop Cranmer		
1544	Succession Act		'Great Debasement' of coinage began	border raids on Scotland – 'the rough wooing'
1545		Act abolishing chantries (but not implemented)		

Date	Developments in			
	Politics	**Religion**	**Society/Economy**	**Foreign policy**
1546	conservative faction plot against Catherine Parr			
1547	death of Henry VIII; establishment of Regency Council under Edward Seymour	repeal of the Treasons Act; abolition of chantries	new, far harsher, Poor Law (nicknamed the 'Slavery Act')	defeat of Scots at the Battle of Pinkie
1548			enclosure commission established by Somerset	Mary Queen of Scots taken to France
1549	fall of Somerset	Act of Uniformity; Revised Book of Common Prayer	serious harvest failure; Western Rising; Kett's Rebellion	
1550	emergence of Warwick as Lord President of the Council			Treaty of Boulogne with France
1551	Warwick became Duke of Northumberland		further failure of harvest; collapse of export market for woollen cloths	
1552	execution of Somerset	Revised Book of Common Prayer created a fully Protestant form of worship	new Poor Law	
1553	Death of Edward VI; Northumberland's attempt to place Lady Jane Grey on the throne; accession of Mary			
1554	Wyatt's Rebellion to depose Mary; marriage between Mary and Philip of Spain			marriage treaty with Spain
1555		legislation to reverse Edwardian reforms and to restore papal supremacy; first executions of Protestant heretics; Cranmer removed as Archbishop of Canterbury	second worst harvest of 1550s	
1556		execution of Cranmer	worst harvest of the sixteenth century; influenza epidemic began	Philip II became King of Spain
1557				England declared war on France; victory in Battle of Saint-Quentin
1558	death of Mary; succession of Elizabeth I			loss of Calais

How historians have approached this topic

If you read this section in each of the chapters so far, you will notice one consistent theme: that the interpretations of older generations of historians (broadly meaning anyone writing before the 1950s) have gradually been reversed by so-called 'revisionist' writers. The same is true of the debate surrounding the 'mid-Tudor crisis'. Traditionally, the 'Little Tudors' – Edward VI and Mary I – received far less attention than Henry VIII and Elizabeth I. Their reigns were short and their achievements few. Although Protector Somerset was hailed as the 'good duke' for his attempts to continue the Reformation and improve the social and economic conditions in England, the Duke of Northumberland was characterised as a self-seeking and ruthless politician. Mary I's reign was often dismissed as simply disastrous. She transacted an unsuitable marriage, lost England's last continental possession and nearly wrecked the Protestant Reformation.

More recently, writers have found more positive things to say about the period 1547–58. They have noted that government was never in serious danger of collapse during these years and that many of the reforms credited to Elizabeth were in fact foreshadowed by Northumberland and Mary. For these reasons, historians such as David Loades and Robert Tittler have downplayed the idea of a mid-Tudor crisis, although they still recognise the difficult social and economic conditions of the time.

Making judgements about the mid-Tudor crisis

As you have worked through this chapter, you will have begun to decide for yourself if the evidence is sufficient to suggest a mid-Tudor crisis. To come to a judgement you will have to engage in what examination boards call a 'synoptic' activity. This means that you will have to use knowledge and skills drawn from across the whole of your study of the Tudor period, rather than from just one section of it. So, your judgement will need to be taken in the light of information about Henry VIII's reign from the 1530s (Chapter 4), Edward VI and Mary's reigns (this chapter), the beginning of Elizabeth's reign (Chapter 6), and the wider religious, social and economic changes examined in Chapters 1 and 3. You will also have to think about why historians have come to different conclusions about the same events. Among the reasons which you might consider are:

▼ some historians focus on one aspect of the mid-Tudor period, such as religious change or the structure of government. Do these different interests lend themselves to different conclusions?

▼ some writers have studied the 1540s and 1550s in the light of what had already happened in Henry VIII's reign; others judge the crisis years in view of what Elizabeth went on to achieve. How can these forward-looking and backward-looking perspectives lead to different conclusions?

▼ historians may have personal views, particularly of the treatment of Protestants in Mary's reign, or the general plight of the poor at this time. Can historical judgements, particularly on dramatic or controversial subjects, ever be free of personal opinion?

Answering Source-Based Questions on A Mid-Tudor Crisis

The following extracts and questions will help you navigate through all these considerations:

Historians and the 'Mid-Tudor Crisis'

Source E A. G. R. Smith, *The Emergence of a Nation State, 1529–1660*, published in 1984.

It is doubtful if the Tudor State was ever in quite as serious difficulties as the word 'crisis' implies. Between 1540 and 1558 the throne was occupied successively by a sick and rapidly ageing bully, a boy who was too young to rule and a woman of limited political abilities. In these circumstances what is significant and remarkable is not the weakness of government, but its relative strength.

Source F Edward Towne, in *The Tudor Years* by J. Lotherington, published in 1994.

The crisis theory overlooks the fact that the government never lost control, even in 1549. This may have been partly because the two rebellions in 1549 had limited aims and did not intend to topple the government. The Council functioned effectively from 1540 despite undoubted factional turmoil from time to time. At the centre ministers kept the show on the road, assisted in the provinces by the mass of JPs. The governing elites survived the most dangerous moment in 1553 when they decided to back Mary's legitimate descent.

Source G Geoffrey Elton, *The English*, published in 1992.

Two real crises did occur in the sixteenth century. The first (in the 1540s and 1550s) sprang from a massive inflation of prices, provoked by a repeated debasement of the coinage. The new income from monastic lands in the end did not suffice, and the unrestrained greed of the governing order with neither an effective king nor a Thomas Cromwell to control things produced the economic collapse of the mid-century. It was aggravated by a temporary but serious slump in the export of cloth, the market having been saturated before. The rebellions of 1549 arose from this complex of difficulties and distress.

Was there a crisis in religion between 1547 and 1563? Given the confusion, rebellion, plotting and faction that religious change created, it is hard to deny that there was indeed a crisis. It is quite clear that religious change struck at the heart of traditional concepts of authority, at high and low, central and local level. Henry's assault on the Pope and his dissolution of the monasteries dismantled an entire edifice of traditional authority. The changing role of priests, monks and nuns, the changing definitions of the Mass and the attempt at Catholic restoration all confused and undermined previously accepted roles and authorities. From the humblest parish priest to the burning of Cranmer, the highest priest in the land, we see one of society's long-standing props – clerical respect – called into question.

Source H Paul Thomas, *Authority and Disorder in Tudor Times, 1485–1603*, published in 1999.

▼ QUESTIONS ON SOURCES

1. Identify the type of crisis – social, economic, political, religious or other – discussed in each of these extracts. **[4 marks]**

2. Use the extracts and your own ideas from this chapter to complete the following chart. **[16 marks]**

Type of crisis	Evidence to support the crisis theory	Evidence to challenge the crisis theory
Political		
Religious		
Economic		
Social		

3. Use the chart to write your own summary, in no more than 50 words, of what the 'mid-Tudor crisis' was. **[10 marks]**

Answering Extended Writing and Essay Questions on A Mid-Tudor Crisis

One type of extended writing task you will come across in some examinations takes a single source, or a small group of sources, as its starting point. Whereas the tasks we discussed at the end of earlier chapters simply gave you a question and asked you to recall information and arguments in response to it, this type of question uses sources as a stimulus to get you started and to focus your approach.

Because the mid-Tudor period is the subject of a significant discussion between historians about the problems facing the country and their significance (did they create a 'crisis'?), questions are likely to focus on these issues also.

The Mid-Tudor Crisis: Events in 1549

Source I From a letter by William Paget to Protector Somerset, 7 July 1549; quoted in *Tudor Rebellions*, by A. Fletcher and D. MacCulloch, 4th edn (1997).

I told your Grace the truth, and was not believed. Well, now your Grace can see the truth for yourself and what do you see? The king's subjects are all out of discipline, out of obedience, caring neither for Protector nor king. Society consists of, and is maintained, by means of religion and law. Look whether you have either religion or law at home, and I fear you shall find neither. The use of the old religion is forbidden by law and the use of the new is not yet settled in the stomachs of even one twelfth of the realm. Put no more so many irons in the fire as you have this year – war with Scotland, with France, commissions out for this matter and that, new laws for this, proclamations for that.

1. What, according to Paget, were the problems facing the government in summer 1549? **[4 marks]**
2. What effects did these problems have during 1549? **[8 marks]**
3. Do you think that the events of 1549 amounted to a 'crisis' in government and wider society? Explain your answer. **[18 marks]**

Planning
Question 1 seems to be the most straightforward – almost a 'warm-up' question. It is an important one, however, because by answering it you are **defining** the 'crisis' that the other questions are asking about. The question asks you to outline what Paget says, so it expects you to use the source extensively. Use a highlighter, or underline, each phrase that suggests a problem, then rewrite each into your own words to show that you understand what it means.

Question 2 is about **consequences**. You will notice that the source does not tell you much about what was actually happening; it just suggests that there were significant difficulties. You will need to draw on your knowledge of the topic to fill in this missing information. Look at how you have defined the problems in Question 1. Some of the points you have made will have a direct consequence (such as the 'war with Scotland' adding to economic and financial difficulties and failing to prevent France growing more influential). Others may have more indirect or general consequences. Make a list of all the consequences you can think of – and note how the question is written. It says 'during 1549', so you would need to go beyond the summer of rebellion to mention Somerset's fall in the autumn.

Question 3 asks you to **make a judgement**. It is a very direct question: '*Do you think ...*' , but be careful not to rush in too quickly. There are two parts to consider when you make your decision – 'in government' and 'in wider society'. You should also try to avoid a simple, one-dimensional response. Perhaps *in some ways* there might have been a crisis, but in *others* there was less difficulty, or perhaps the crisis seemed more real than it actually was. Judgements such as these show that the situation was not black and white, but subtle and complex. You will always gain more marks for showing the different opinions that might be possible rather than merely grabbing at the most obvious point of view that you can think of instantly. A good way of planning these sorts of questions is to treat them as a mini-discussion. Try to find evidence and ideas for and against the argument suggested in the quotation or question:

	Evidence that would support ...	Evidence that would challenge ...
... a crisis in government		
... a crisis in wider society		

Writing Your Answers

Once you have planned you material, you need to shape it into clearly and carefully presented pieces of writing. In this question there are a number of pitfalls which you need to avoid:

▼ in Question 1 it might be very tempting to put in a lot of quotations from the source. Try to limit this, otherwise you might just as well copy out the source entirely as your answer! Examiners want to see if you have understood what Paget is warning Somerset about, not whether you can copy accurately. It is always better either to rewrite a quotation in your own words, or to follow a short quotation with a sentence or two of explanation.

▼ in Question 2 you might feel that just writing a story of what happened in 1549 will answer the question. You would be right, but you would not get many marks, because your answer would not be organised around consequences. It would be better to let each of the points you made in Question 1 trigger a comment about consequence in Question 2 so that the answer is more focused than a simple narrative of events would be.

▼ in Question 3 it would be easy to start writing about whether there really was a crisis or not and to leave an overall assessment until the conclusion. This would mean that you could work up to the judgement, thinking about it as you write. However, it would leave the examiner in the dark until the very end about what you think. If you have planned well, you should know what conclusion you have reached before you start writing. A better way of constructing the answer, therefore, would be to use the introduction to define the key issues and arguments and to give a potential judgement, then to use the main part of the essay to weigh up the evidence for and against your opinion before coming to a final, balanced choice in the conclusion.

Further Reading

Books in the *Access to History* series

The final years of Henry VIII's reign are covered in Keith Randell's *Henry VIII and the Government of England*, while the reigns of Edward and Mary are dealt with in *Edward VI and Mary: A Mid-Tudor Crisis?* by Nigel Heard. This book also breaks down the elements of the supposed 'crisis' into political, economic and religious themes, so provides a different way of analysing the problem from that explored in this chapter. Religious change can also be explored further by consulting *The Sixteenth Century Reformation* by Geoffrey Woodward.

Other books

Debating the nature and extent of the mid-Tudor crisis is a popular theme in most textbooks on the sixteenth century, so you will find helpful sections in *The Tudor Years*, edited by John Lotherington (Hodder and Stoughton, 1994), *The Emergence of a Nation State* by A. G. R. Smith (Longman, 1984), *Tudor England* by John Guy (Oxford University Press, 1988) and *The Later Tudors, England 1547–1603* by Penry Williams (Oxford University Press, 1995). More specific works dealing with the period 1547–58 include *The Reign of Mary* by Robert Tittler (Longman, 1983) and *The Mid-Tudor Crisis, 1545–1565* by David Loades (Macmillan, 1992). Little has been written just about Edward VI, but the balance has been somewhat redressed by *The Boy King: Edward VI and the Protestant Reformation* by Diarmaid MacCulloch and *Edward VI* by Jennifer Loach. These writers present Edward as a confident, intelligent young man with clear views about the future of the church. Alison Weir also presents a portrait of Edward in *The Children of Henry VIII* (Ballantine, 1997). This book is also useful if you would like to find out more about Lady Jane Grey. Apart from Robert Tittler's biography of Mary Tudor, you might like to consult Carolly Erickson's *Bloody Mary: The Life of Mary Tudor* (Dobson Books, 1995) which sets out to examine why the queen has received such a poor press.

POLITICS IN THE AGE OF ELIZABETH I, 1558–1603

CHAPTER 6

POINTS TO CONSIDER

When Elizabeth came to the throne England had been governed by the Tudors for nearly 75 years. Systems of government had evolved which kept the monarchy secure and the country free of damaging civil wars. To people living in the troubled seventeenth century, Elizabeth's reign seemed to be the perfect image of what a well-governed state should be like; cultured, prosperous and respected abroad. In reality, life in Elizabethan England was much less glamorous, so in this chapter we will examine the effectiveness of Elizabethan government, especially in the latter years of the queen's reign.

Each new Tudor monarch presented a clear contrast to his or her predecessor. Henry VIII's youthful ambition was a clear change from Henry VII's caution and insecurity. In 1547 the 'ageing tyrant' gave way to a minority government and in 1553 the first female monarch for 400 years took the English throne. Elizabeth's accession in 1558 fitted into this pattern of contrasts. She had an assertive and confident approach to government, sharply different from her sister's emotional agenda. She had been raised in the Protestant faith and had taken note of the growing concern expressed at the Marian persecutions. If anything, Elizabeth was her father's daughter – schooled in the tradition of the strong royal government of the 1530s. She certainly needed to make a strong impact quickly, if this pessimistic list of the troubles facing England in 1558 is to be believed:

> The Queen poor, the realm exhausted, the nobility poor and decayed. Lack of good captains and soldiers. The people out of order. Justice is not executed. All things are dear. Divisions among ourselves. Wars with France and Scotland. The French king bestriding the realm, having one foot in Calais and the other in Scotland. Steadfast enmity but no steadfast friendship abroad.

Source A From a report by Armigail Waad, Clerk to the Privy Council, summarising the problems confronting the government at Elizabeth's accession.

ACTIVITY

Look carefully at the points the writer of Source A makes. Can you explain any of them further?

1 The 'Virgin Queen'

Elizabeth recognised that, as a female monarch, she was in a weaker position than if a man ruled. On a practical level, there were doubts about whether she could become head of the church (since there was no scriptural authority for women to take doctrinal decisions) and on a personal level, there was speculation about whether a female ruler could have the authority needed to impose her will in the male-dominated world of politics. The Presbyterian leader in Scotland, John Knox, had no doubts on the matter:

Source B From John Knox's *The First Blast of the Trumpet against the Monstrous Regiment of Women*, 1558. Knox was the leader of the Protestant Reformation in Scotland and had been a strong critic of Mary I who he believed lacked the authority to enact religious changes.

> To promote a woman to bear rule, superiority, dominion or empire over any realm, nation or city, is repugnant to nature, contumely to God, a thing most contrarious to His revealed will and approved laws; and finally, it is the subversion of good order, or all equity and justice.

Historians generally agree that Elizabeth was a very effective ruler. Although she was over-cautious at times and had to be pushed into making critical decisions, her image was that of a woman who had put her country before her personal needs and who protected England as a mother protects her family. Such an image was carefully cultivated:

▼ She travelled the country on 'royal progresses' – at least 25 during her reign – staying in the homes of leading families, and meeting her subjects to show the human face of monarchy. Progresses were accompanied by much spectacle for the entertainment of the masses, such as fireworks displays, street decorations and a royal procession.

Source C From a report of the queen's royal progress in 1568, by the Spanish ambassador.

> She was received everywhere with great acclamations and signs of joy, as is customary in this country; whereat she was extremely pleased and told me so, giving me to understand how beloved she was by her subjects and how highly she esteemed this, together with the fact that they were peaceful and contented, whilst her neighbours on all sides are in such trouble. She attributed it all to God's miraculous goodness. She ordered her carriage to be taken where the crowd seemed thickest, and stood up and thanked the people.

▼ She deliberately toned down the extravagance at court, not only to save desperately needed money but also to portray herself as careful and hard-working. Her propaganda stressed that the queen would sooner spend money on public needs than on new palaces.

▼ Courtly rituals were emphasised, such as jousting tournaments at which the queen's champion competed in her honour. Such rituals were often medieval in origin and were designed to focus attention on Elizabeth as the provider of honours and glory.

▼ Elizabeth's reluctance to commit herself to marriage was also turned into positive propaganda. As the 'Virgin Queen', she reminded the country that her priority was politics and no doubt benefited from the associations people drew between her image and the Catholic image of the Virgin Mary.

▼ Other female icons were borrowed to flatter Elizabeth. From popular Renaissance culture came the image of Astraea, the Greek virgin-goddess who was the last of the gods to leave the earth. Mythology suggested that Astraea's return would bring a new age of prosperity and stability, which Elizabeth's propagandists converted into the illusion of the queen ushering in England's 'golden age'.

▼ Portraits and paintings drew on classical themes, well known through the spread of the Renaissance, to reinforce positive images of the queen as the bringer of peace and plenty.

Because of all this Elizabethan image-building, it is difficult to get a truthful picture of what Elizabeth was like. She was certainly hard-edged, demanding much from her courtiers and impatient with people who failed her. She deliberately created a masculine personality

Figure 41 A water pageant which Elizabeth attended during a visit to Elvetham in Hampshire, 1591. The queen is sitting on her throne to the upper left of the picture, watching re-enactments of battles and swimmers representing the gods of the sea.

to command her courtiers, but at the same time used the fact that she was a woman to charm them and throw them off-balance. It was a skilful combination, and one which allowed Elizabeth to rule over a more loyal and united court than any since the 1520s.

Q What aspects of the Armada Portrait suggest Elizabeth's power and authority? What image of the queen is being conveyed?

Figure 42 The Armada Portrait, 1590, attributed to George Gower (1540–96). To control the representation of her image, Elizabeth ordered in 1563 that all paintings of her were to be modelled on portraits supplied by her 'Sergeant Painter'. Production of unauthorised images was prohibited and offending items destroyed. This meant that a standard image of the queen appeared in nearly all paintings, unchanging over the decades even though Elizabeth grew thinner and more arthritic, and began to lose her looks, hair and teeth. This portrait shows a youthful and commanding figure, when in fact Elizabeth would have been 57 years old at the time.

ISSUES:
How had the Privy Council developed since the 1540s? How did it continue to change under Elizabeth?

2 Elizabethan Government

a) The Privy Council

The Privy Council had been established as an advisory and co-ordinating body during the reign of Henry VIII. Its composition was determined by the monarch, from whom its power derived. Membership of the council had grown to between 40 and 50 people during Mary I's reign to contain the heads of major government departments, representatives of the greater nobility and the crown's personal favourites. On her accession to the throne, Elizabeth was expected to change the personnel of the council in line with the different priorities and supporters that she had, but Elizabeth also reduced it to under 20 members to make it easier to manage and to reduce the power of the traditional nobility.

i) Personnel

Few of the pro-Catholic courtiers that Mary had installed on the Privy Council survived her death. Elizabeth's preference was for people who had proven their loyalty to the Tudor dynasty, either through personal service to her, or because they came from an established family. The number of nobles was significantly reduced, as was the trend under Mary towards appointing members of the church onto the council. In their place Elizabeth built up a core of professional men who enjoyed her confidence, so tended to serve for long periods, improving the effectiveness and unity of the council. Not all historians have seen this as an advantage. Christopher Haigh, who has been the leading critic of Elizabeth's achievements, has pointed out that by largely excluding the nobility and the church, Elizabeth made the Privy Council unrepresentative of the ruling élite as a whole, undermining its value as an advisory body and provoking resentment among courtiers at the restriction in their opportunities to advance in government. He also suggests that the council's narrow membership limited the range of debate and tended to produce a co-operative body unlikely to challenge the queen.

Figure 43 Elizabeth receiving foreign ambassadors in her Privy Chamber. Compare this rather intimate gathering with the picture of Henry VIII's courtiers gathered around him at meal-time in his private rooms (Figure 29, page 109). One of the noticeable features in this picture is that Elizabeth had female attendants in her chambers. Male courtiers, who had been used to jockeying for position as personal servants of the king, found it more difficult to get access to the queen's private rooms.

-Profile-

WILLIAM CECIL, LORD BURGHLEY (1520–1598)

There is general agreement that William Cecil was the greatest of Elizabeth's ministers. He worked with the queen for most of her reign, first as Secretary of State, then as Lord Treasurer from 1572 to his death in 1598. His family pedigree was relatively undistinguished, but he demonstrated a talent for administration which brought him to Elizabeth's attention in 1550 when she appointed him to oversee her estates. Much of his later career continued to be associated with financial management, but he exercised a much wider influence, counterbalancing the younger and more headstrong Earl of Leicester. Like Elizabeth, Burghley was essentially a conservative and a stabiliser. He promoted policies which attacked religious extremism, whether from the Puritans or Catholics, and sought to preserve England's independence abroad by treading a careful path between France and Spain. This policy brought him into conflict with Leicester who favoured a more openly anti-Spanish and anti-Catholic policy.

1520 born in Lincolnshire, son of a minor Welsh family who had supported Henry VII's claim to the throne;

1535 educated in humanist and
–41 Protestant ideas at Cambridge;

1543 became an MP;

1550 appointed Surveyor of the Queen's Estates;

1550 acted as Secretary of State in
–53 Northumberland's government;

1553 fell from power when Mary came to the throne;

1558 career revived under Elizabeth when she re-appointed him Secretary of State;

1561 appointed Master of the Court of Wards and Liveries;

1568 Earl of Leicester and the Duke of Norfolk plotted to reduce his influence at court;

1571 awarded the title Baron Burghley;

1572 became Lord Treasurer;

1598 died.

The principal person in the Council at present is William Cecil, now Lord Burghley. He is a man of mean sort, but very astute, false, lying, and full of all artifice. He is a great heretic and such a clownish Englishman as to believe that all the Christian princes joined together are not able to injure the sovereign of his country. By means of his vigilance and craftiness, together with his utter unscrupulousness of word and deed, he thinks to outwit the ministers of other princes.

Source D An unflattering portrait of Burghley, by the Spanish ambassador.

I do hold, and always will, this course in such matters as I differ in opinion from Her Majesty: as long as I may be allowed to give advice I will not change my opinion, but as a servant I will obey Her Majesty's commandment, presuming that she being God's chief minister here, it shall be God's will to have her commandments obeyed.

Source E This advice from Lord Burghley to his son, Sir Robert Cecil, was written shortly before his death and encapsulates his relationship with Elizabeth.

ii) Functions

The traditional functions of the Privy Council were maintained under Elizabeth, although the workload expanded considerably because of the need to administer the Anglican Reformation and the country's complex foreign policy. Broadly, the council had four main roles:

▼ it offered advice to the monarch. One of the key areas of debate was policy towards the Netherlands because there was no agreement amongst councillors on the best course of action to check the growth of Spanish power in the region.

▼ it administered public policy. The council maintained a network of contacts at national and local level through which its instructions were implemented (see the diagram of Elizabethan government in Figure 46, page 188).

▼ it co-ordinated the work of the different elements of government.

▼ it acted as a royal court of law through the prerogative courts which Privy Councillors staffed.

Of these functions, the advisory role was the most dramatic, because it sometimes brought councillors into direct confrontation with the queen. However, the more important part of the council's work was undoubtedly its daily administrative duties, since these kept the whole machinery of the Elizabethan state operating. The range of policy areas that the council managed can be glimpsed from the minutes of its meetings (see text box).

Examples of the Routine Work of the Privy Council

July 1565	instructions to the mayor and city corporation of Newcastle regarding the arrival of German miners
Jan 1567	instructions to the Treasury to settle debts for two plays the queen had attended at Christmas
June 1570	a request for the transfer of a prisoner to the Tower for torture to investigate his part in a murder
Feb 1574	instructions for the recall of licences issued to corn sellers in Berkshire, Bedford and Hereford who were suspected of price fixing
Aug 1574	requests for the mustering of troops in readiness for intervention in Ireland
Nov 1574	instructions to arrest Catholic troublemakers in Lancashire.

Q What do these examples tell us about how Elizabethan government worked?

Part of the increase in the variety of the council's work can be explained by the growth in the number of petitions it received. Rather than rely on the legal system, those with enough money and influence approached the Privy Council directly with their grievances. Although councillors tried to discourage this practice, they were inevitably drawn into settling these private disputes as part of their administrative control of local life. The result of the increased workload facing the Elizabethan Privy Council was a growth in the number and duration of meetings. During the crisis years of the 1590s, when England was at war with Spain and facing economic problems at home, the council often met six full days a week, compared to the three half-days that were typical at the start of the reign.

iii) Significance

Judging whether the Privy Council managed government policy depends on which aspect of its work is being considered. This was still an age of personal monarchy, where the queen was expected to take important decisions and to have the final say. In some policy areas, such as determining the succession, taking firm action to support the revolt of the Netherlands and dealing with Mary Queen of Scots, the council was unable to exert much pressure on Elizabeth. These matters concerned the queen personally, or were areas that fell within the royal prerogative, and she tended to guard her right to decide such questions jealously, even if that meant being slow and over-cautious in reaching a decision. However, she was not unreasonable, and a well-argued case could sway her. So too could threats of resignation, especially by her most trusted councillors early in the reign. William Cecil, for example, used this tactic to pressure the queen into military action against Scotland in 1560.

ISSUE:
What role did the court play in political life?

b) The Role of the Court

The royal court was the hub of social and political life, as it had been throughout the Tudor period. Under Elizabeth, however, the ritualisation of courtly life blurred its political and social functions, leaving a spectacular atmosphere that befitted the 'Golden Age' of royal propaganda. Elizabeth did not merely promote men who were loyal to the Tudor dynasty. Courtiers who attracted and flattered her were also brought into government. The most famous example is Robert Dudley (see profile).

The royal court incorporated both government offices (such as the Privy Council and the Chamber, which met in rooms in the palace) and the queen's personal household. It was a place where the business of government was conducted and was at the same time the

ROBERT DUDLEY, EARL OF LEICESTER
(1532–1588)

-Profile-

Although Dudley was the son of the late Earl of Northumberland, Elizabeth's interest in him stemmed from the close relationship the two enjoyed (it has been suggested that Dudley was her personal choice for a husband). According to one visitor to the court:

> She took me into her bed-chamber, and opened a little cabinet, wherein she kept many little pictures wrapped within paper, and their names written on with her own hand upon the papers. Upon the first that she took up was written, 'My Lord's Picture'. I held the candle and pressed to see which picture was so named. She appeared loath to let me see it; yet I prevailed for a sight of it, and I found it to be the Earl of Leicester's picture.
> **Source F** From a record by James Melville, the ambassador of Mary Queen of Scots, written during the 1570s.

It is telling that he gained so many promotions so quickly, entering the Privy Council at the relatively young age of 30. His relationship with Elizabeth was volatile – he disagreed sharply with her on some policies and voiced his concerns openly, and his relationships with other women caused public arguments with the queen. None the less, he was a capable and trustworthy minister. As Earl of Leicester he controlled large areas of land and used patronage at court to promote the careers of men with similar views to his own.

Leicester was leader of the more radical group of politicians at court and in the Privy Council. He supported active policies to defeat Catholicism at home and abroad and grew frustrated at the queen's caution and Lord Burghley's opposition. Among the policies Leicester favoured were:

▼ further reforms to the church along the lines suggested by Puritans
▼ stronger persecution of English Catholics, especially after news of their plots to replace Elizabeth with Mary Queen of Scots on the throne
▼ active military intervention to help the Huguenot and Dutch rebels
▼ an alliance with France against Spain.

1532 born, son of the Earl of Northumberland;
1535 married Amy Robsart;
1554 sentenced to death under suspicion of his role in Lady Jane Grey's coup, but pardoned by Mary;
1557 distinguished himself at the Battle of Saint-Quentin against France;
1559 appointed Master of the Horse, made a Knight of the Garter;
1560 suspicious death of his wife – rumours that Dudley had ordered her murder;
1562 joined the Privy Council; advocated military intervention in France to assist the Huguenots;
1564 made Earl of Leicester;
1585 commanded the expeditionary force to aid the Dutch rebels;
1586 angered Elizabeth by accepting the title of Governor of the Netherlands; brought back to England;
1588 appointed to lead part of the royal army against the possible Spanish invasion, but died before the Armada arrived.

private household of the queen. To achieve social status and future titles or lands, nobles had to be seen at court. To ensure that government ran smoothly, royal officials had to attend court to secure royal permission for their actions. This explains why the social and political functions of the court overlapped.

Figure 44 The dancing queen: Elizabeth I (who was reputed to be a very good dancer) is shown as the centre of attention with her partner, the Earl of Leicester.

The system of patronage was central to the operation of the court. The crown controlled appointments to offices in local and central government, the church, the law and the royal household. In addition, the monarch had land and titles to distribute, as well as economic benefits such as the right to collect taxes. The key to power, position and wealth, therefore, was the queen. As Robert Dudley discovered, catching and keeping royal attention could mean rapid promotion. Others, such as the ill-fated Earl of Essex (see below, pages 197–8) found out that losing the queen's interest could lead to an equally quick collapse of status and income. By careful distribution of patronage, Elizabeth was able to maintain control in the male-dominated atmosphere at court and could keep rivalries under control.

Historians have commented on the domestic peace during Elizabeth's reign. The two key domestic rebellions – of the Northern Earls in 1569 and of the Earl of Essex in 1601 – show that occasionally rivalries within the ruling élite could still spill out from the court into civil disturbance. For the most part, however, the court was a mechanism to contain such rivalries. The different factions disagreed about the best way to achieve the queen's aims, but were not generally disloyal. By maintaining the close support of men such as Burghley and Leicester over such long periods, Elizabeth brought stability to courtly politics and avoided the destructive factionalism that had beset the final years of her father's reign and the crisis year of 1549.

The Revolt of the Northern Earls, 1569–70

In 1568 Elizabeth, under the guidance of William Cecil, ordered the seizure of Spanish ships carrying silver through the English Channel. The Spanish government reacted furiously at what it regarded as an act of piracy, confiscating all English ships docked in ports in the Netherlands (see page 219). This incident intensified the struggle between the factions at court. Cecil's enemies tried to persuade the queen that he had given her foolish and dangerous advice and that he should be dismissed. Tied to these events was the larger and still unresolved issue of the succession. Some of those who opposed Cecil did so because they hoped to pressure Elizabeth into naming Mary Queen of Scots as her successor and into restoring better relations with Catholic Spain. These plans got nowhere but brought Cecil's enemies into temporary disgrace for trying to undermine the crown's religious and foreign policies.

Faced with the unravelling of their scheme to improve their position at court, the northern earls of Northumberland and Westmorland raised a rebellion at Durham in October 1569 and marched towards York. They hoped to gather discontented Catholics and assistance from Spain, but there was no momentum and the rebels were dispersed by the royal army in February 1570.

---

c) The Importance of Parliament

In Chapters 3 and 4, we looked at how Henry VIII's need to legalise the break with Rome in the 1530s increased the scope and importance of parliamentary work. During the reigns of Edward VI and Mary, Parliament had continued to be used to enact religious changes, including the important doctrinal statements contained in the Act of Uniformity in 1549, and had been involved in legislating to manage

ISSUE:
Did the relationship between crown and Parliament sour during Elizabeth's reign?

social and economic change. So, by 1558, it had become embedded within the political system to a degree that would have been unrecognisable to Henry VII. That is not to say, however, that Parliament had necessarily become more powerful in the process. It was still primarily an instrument to support royal policy. It was summoned and dismissed in accordance with the monarch's needs and had little power to initiate policies. Instead, it advised the monarch, voted extra taxation in emergencies, and turned royal policies into laws.

Figure 45 Elizabeth sitting on the throne in the House of Lords.

There has been much debate about whether the deterioration in relations between the Commons and the crown – which had grown to crisis proportions by the 1640s and triggered the **English civil wars** – began under Elizabeth. According to the 'conflict' view, the growing legislative importance of Parliament encouraged factionalism among MPs since the Commons had become a forum for decision making akin to the Privy Council and royal court.

This was particularly the case in religious matters, where the competence of Parliament to enact changes to both the structure and doctrines of the church had become established. Some MPs attempted to use Parliament to reform the Anglican Church created in 1559 along more radical, Puritan lines. To do this, they used Commons time to debate the condition of the church, extending their previously weak privileges of free speech.

Parliament's influence was also increased by the crown's financial problems. Elizabeth tried to control spending and to increase traditional sources of revenue (see below, pages 188–90), but was forced to rely heavily on parliamentary subsidies during the years of war against Spain. This gave Parliament financial leverage over the crown but also provoked angry exchanges at the demands that the government was making at a time of inflation and economic hardship.

Evidence FOR Conflict between Crown and Parliament

▼ By the end of Elizabeth's reign, over half of MPs had a university education, or were trained lawyers. This helped to create a more self-confident Parliament which was able to argue more strongly against the crown

▼ 1566 MPs angered Elizabeth by discussing the succession question

▼ 1553–6 A Puritan party – what the historian Sir John Neale described as the 'Puritan Choir' – emerged as an organised group of at least 40 MPs to press for more daring religious reforms

▼ 1576 Peter Wentworth was imprisoned in the Tower for demanding greater freedom of speech

▼ 1586 Norfolk Election Case – the Commons asserted its right to settle a dispute over the result of the election, even though this was traditionally the Lord Chancellor's responsibility

▼ 1584 Puritan members of the Commons reacted with fury to Archbishop Whitgift's attack on godly preachers

▼ 1593 MPs discussed a bill to reform the church, using their claim to free speech. Elizabeth ordered Lord Keeper Puckering to read out a statement to them setting out the extent to which she was prepared to allow free speech. Whilst she recognised that MPs should not be prevented from discussing legislation, the queen insisted that this did not extend to other matters which interested them

▼ 1601 Parliament clashed with the queen on the issue of monopolies. MPs successfully refused to grant her additional taxes for the war against Spain unless she agreed to withdraw many of the licences that had been issued.

THE ORIGINS OF THE ENGLISH CIVIL WARS

Between 1640 and 1642, a faction of radical MPs in the House of Commons tried to strengthen the defences of Parliament against the power of the crown. This involved attempts to strip King Charles I of some of his royal prerogatives, including the right to collect some taxes and to summon Parliament only when he wished. These efforts brought MPs into direct confrontation with a king determined to protect his heritage. War between the two broke out in the summer of 1642, dividing the country between those who feared that the king had become too uncontrollable and those who regarded traditional forms of government as paramount.

Historians have sought the origins of this crisis in the Tudor period. Some have suggested that the growth of parliamentary privileges following the break with Rome in 1534 established the importance of the Commons as a partner in government, whilst the financial weakness of the later Tudors established royal dependency on Parliament for support. By drawing the crown closer to Parliament in these ways, the scene was set for some MPs to interpret their role as guardians of the welfare of the country against a king whom they thought had exceeded his powers.

Q

On what issues did crown and Commons disagree? Were these likely to be representative of the matters discussed in Parliament?

Recently, a number of these arguments have been challenged by historians who prefer to stress co-operation rather than conflict in the crown's dealings with Parliament. According to this view, opposition in Parliament was infrequent and disunited, never posing a serious challenge to Elizabeth's authority. Moreover, there was a considerable measure of agreement on most issues between the élite who sat in Parliament and those who directed policy at court. Where disagreements existed, they did not signify a crisis within the ruling élite, but were usually a working out of policy on issues of religion and foreign matters that resolved rather than created conflict.

Evidence AGAINST Conflict between Crown and Parliament

▼ Only 13 Parliaments were summoned during Elizabeth's reign, and each sat for short periods – the average was ten weeks per session. For much of the time, Elizabeth ruled through the Privy Council and its machinery of government without the need for parliamentary legislation

▼ The Commons was an important training ground for future Privy Councillors, a place where political fortunes could be made by catching the attention of the queen

▼ The Commons did not press its demands to settle the disputed Norfolk election of 1586 and conceded the right of the Lord Chancellor in this matter

▼ Elizabeth resisted all attempts by Parliament (and the Privy Council) to force her to marry or name a successor

▼ The 'Puritan Choir' was a less united and powerful group than Neale has suggested. Religious opposition to the Elizabethan Settlement was not sustained throughout the reign, but flared up in response to particular events (as in 1584). It also failed to bring about any changes

▼ Although individual MPs like Wentworth railed against the limitation on their freedom of speech, there was no general support to win this right given Elizabeth's absolute opposition to it

▼ Elizabeth summoned most of her Parliaments to obtain money. On nearly every occasion, she received the grant that she asked for

▼ Much of the work of the Commons involved legislating on uncontentious issues, such as land disputes and town charters. This mundane work performed the important function of creating an outlet for local matters to be resolved quickly and without violence.

ACTIVITY

The debate about the importance of Parliament is not only central to understanding where power was located within the Elizabethan state, but also to the argument about the long-term origins of the English civil wars in the mid-seventeenth century.

Read the information in the two boxed sections on pages 183 and 184.
1. Rewrite the material in each box so that, as far as possible, the points are matched against each other to create an argument. For example:

Evidence of a crown–Parliament conflict	Evidence to undermine this view
▼ Peter Wentworth was imprisoned in the Tower for demanding greater freedom of speech	▼ Although individual MPs like Wentworth railed against the limitation on their freedom of speech, there was no general support to win this right given Elizabeth's absolute opposition to it

2. Using the material you have assembled, try to add a short conclusion summarising how powerful you think Parliament had become by the end of Elizabeth's reign. You will need to reach a balanced assessment by considering what 'powerful' means in this situation:

▼ What 'weapons' did Parliament possess to get its way? How often did it dictate policy?
▼ What 'weapons' did the queen possess to limit Parliament's political role? Is there evidence that these did or did not work?
▼ Is there a difference between political and legislative power? Do not fall into the trap of considering only the crown–Parliament relationship in terms of controversial subjects such as religion or the succession.

d) Local and Regional Government

ISSUE:
Who ran local government?

You will see from the examples of the work of the Privy Council on page 177 that a large portion of routine administration involved issuing instructions to those who implemented royal policies in the regions. Since the government lacked the equivalent of a modern professional civil service (and the money to buy one), it relied on men of standing in the local community to act as its agents. The growing tendency of the government to interfere in local communities (to instruct the parish priest on how to conduct his services, or to arrange poor relief, for example) was an important – but not always welcome – trend during the sixteenth century. Increasing the scope of government activity inevitably involved placing more work on this unpaid governing class. This group accepted the heavier workload because of the prestige and influence its role carried within the community.

The key figures in local government were the Justices of the Peace. They were appointed from the ranks of the gentry, or from wealthy families and the merchant élite in towns. Their responsibilities included maintaining the rule of law by settling disputes and punishing offenders, and administering a range of government policies, including the Poor Laws. Under Elizabeth the trend towards appointing more JPs continued; it has been estimated that there was an average of 50 per county by 1600. However, whether this number made local government any more effective is questionable. JPs were in the difficult position of having to live in the communities they administered. Not surprisingly, then, there were accusations that some ignored policies that they knew would be unpopular locally, or used their position for personal profit against local rivals.

ACTIVITY

Elizabethan Justices of the Peace

Know that we have assigned you to be our Justices to keep our peace and to keep and cause to be kept all ordinances and statutes published for the good of our peace. Further, we assign you to inquire of all and every felonies, poisonings, enchantments, sorceries, magic, trespasses, engrossings and extortions whatsoever, and all other crimes and offences, and of such men as go or ride armed in assemblies against our peace in disturbance of our people. Also of such as lie in wait to maim or kill our people, and of innkeepers and all others who in weights and measures or in selling offend against the ordinances and statutes published for the common good, and of such sheriffs, bailiffs, stewards, constables, keepers of jails and other officers as are lukewarm, remiss or negligent in the performance of their duties. And to hear and determine all felonies and to correct and punish the same by fines, ransoms, forfeitures and otherwise.

Source G From the instructions issued to Elizabethan Justices of the Peace.

▼ an order prohibiting Adam Hutchinson and Thomas Hodgson of Barnsley from operating alehouses because they 'are men of bad behaviour' who 'do maintain ill rule in their houses'

▼ an order requiring the parish of Halifax to provide poor relief for an abandoned baby left in the village of Southerham

▼ an order preventing brewers from selling ale at prices above one penny for 2 pints, unless they had a special licence from the JP

▼ an order requiring larger landowners in the parishes of Leeds to send horses and labourers to help repair the road from Leeds to Wikebrigg

▼ an order that Thomas Stringar should be whipped back to his home parish of Wenbridge as punishment for sheep rustling.

Source H Examples of the work of Justices of the Peace in the West Riding of Yorkshire, 1597–8.

QUESTIONS

1. Use these sources to describe the role of the Justice of the Peace in local government. **[5 marks]**.

2. Read Source G. What does it reveal about the preoccupations and concerns of the Tudor authorities in Elizabethan times? **[5 marks]**

3. How useful is the information in Source H in helping a historian to judge the work of Justices of the Peace? **[5 marks]**

In Elizabeth's reign, another type of local official grew in status. Lord Lieutenants had been responsible for raising local militias during Henry VIII's reign, but under Elizabeth they acquired additional duties. In the second half of her reign, a Lord Lieutenant was appointed permanently in nearly every county, usually from one of the most distinguished families (which in many cases meant someone already sitting on the Privy Council). He was expected to manage the raising of troops, but also to supervise the work of JPs and to report local events to the Privy Council. The title – which still exists today – carried considerable prestige, as did the office of Deputy Lieutenant, created in the 1560s to share the workload.

Beneath these impressive figures lurked a massive group of parish officials, each with their own little responsibilities. This might be to distribute poor relief, to look after the day-to-day affairs of the parish church, to arrest troublemakers, to repair local roads or to catch rats. The variety of work going on at a grassroots level should remind us that 'government' was a lot more sophisticated than it might first appear.

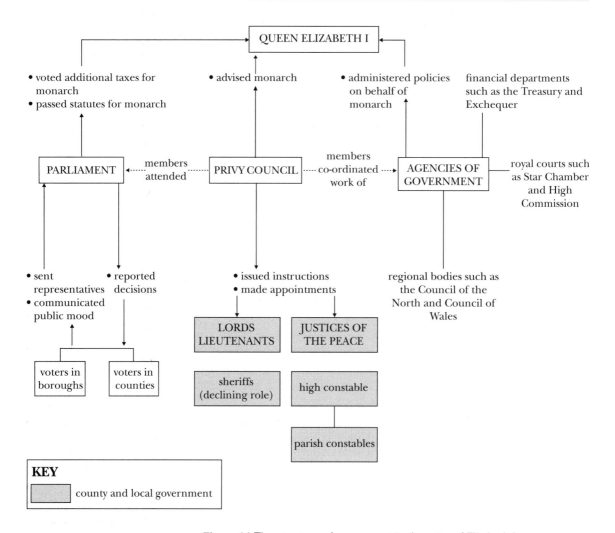

Figure 46 The structure of government in the reign of Elizabeth I.

e) The Problem of Royal Finances

Elizabeth ruled at a time of inflationary pressure on the economy. The prices of basic commodities rose, but so too did those of goods that the government consumed, such as iron for shipbuilding or provisions for the army. To remain solvent, or to stand any chance of pursuing an active foreign policy, the crown had to increase its revenue. Mary Tudor had already begun the process of examining how to achieve this (see page 162) and Elizabeth largely continued and developed this work. Between 1558 and 1603 royal income increased by approximately 50 per cent, just enough to keep pace with price inflation, but not enough to afford prolonged war against Spain after 1585. Revenues were raised by exploiting traditional sources of income rather than by innovating:

▼ the new Book of Rates introduced at the end of Mary's reign increased the income from customs duties on exports. The recovery of the cloth industry after the crash of the 1550s also helped to generate taxes

▼ as head of the church, Elizabeth claimed income from a variety of religious sources, such as the 'first fruits' tax on all new ecclesiastical office-holders

▼ Parliament was approached to grant additional subsidies to finance foreign policy

▼ crown lands, some appropriated from the church in the 1530s, were sold off to raise £800,000

▼ **monopoly rights** to produce or import particular products were sold to merchants.

Elizabeth also attempted to control expenditure. Part of her cautious approach to foreign policy, especially to direct military action in support of French or Dutch Protestant rebels, stemmed from her recognition that she lacked the money to sustain a war against Spain. Like Henry VII, Elizabeth tried to conserve her finances by using diplomacy rather than open combat. Other methods of saving money included underpaying officials and delaying the appointment of bishops when positions became vacant (so that the crown could collect church taxes).

At first sight, these policies seem to have been successful. Although Elizabeth left the crown in debt, she had enough money to defend England against the vastly superior military strength of Spain when war broke out in the last two decades of her reign (see pages 196–7). Some historians, however, have been more critical of these policies and have pointed out that Elizabeth's failure to transform radically what was essentially her father's financial system left the crown underfunded. They also challenge the idea that the growth in income was a success, arguing that Burghley, the Lord Treasurer for much of the reign, was inefficient at extracting the maximum value from the crown's assets. Looking beyond Elizabeth's reign, modern historians also note that financial weakness was a principal reason why the crown was forced to rely on Parliament in the seventeenth century. Since this created tension in the relationship between crown and Parliament and ultimately contributed to the civil wars of Charles I's reign (see page 183), it is tempting to see Elizabeth's caution as one of the long-term causes of this conflict. A. G. R. Smith suggests this connection when he writes that Elizabeth's financial policies:

MONOPOLY RIGHTS

Such rights were granted by royal charter, declaring that a particular group of merchants had the sole legal right to make or to import a commodity such as soap or sugar. Monopolies were unpopular because they were often granted in everyday products, allowing the group of merchants who controlled the monopoly to fix prices at artificially high levels to make a profit.

Source 1 From A. G. R. Smith, *The Emergence of a Nation State 1529–1660*, published in 1984.

left Burghley's successors in the office of Lord Treasurer in charge of an old fashioned financial machine which brought the government a much smaller proportion of national resources than it might reasonably have enjoyed. Even more important, perhaps, it accustomed the landed and trading classes to a situation in which they paid a very small part of their income in taxation. When they were called on to give more under the early Stuarts their reluctance and resentments caused major difficulties for the crown.

ISSUE:

How was the stability of Elizabethan government threatened?

3 The Threats to Elizabethan Government

So far, we have examined the strengths of the Elizabethan system – a talented and manipulative monarch, an effective government through the Privy Council, and a Parliament that was less hostile than once thought. These were the bases for the success and strong reputation of Elizabeth I. Through this system of government she was able to establish and maintain a unique national church that drew on the strengths of both Protestant and Catholic traditions, and to preserve national security and independence. In the troubled times of the seventeenth century, people looked back to Elizabeth's reign as a golden age of domestic peace and prosperity.

As students of history, we must be careful not to accept this sort of propaganda at face value. Behind the images of Gloriana and Astraea lay real difficulties which threatened the success of the late Tudor state.

ISSUES:

Why was the succession such an important issue from the start of Elizabeth's reign? Why did the queen resist pressure to marry?

a) The Succession Question

At 25 years of age in 1558, Elizabeth was young enough to produce children to sustain the Tudor dynasty. However, a sudden, and nearly fatal, attack of smallpox in 1562 reminded everyone that she represented the last of the main Tudor line and pressure mounted for her to consider marriage. Elizabeth was remarkably resistant to this idea for a number of reasons:

▼ marriage would limit her personal freedom. Given social conventions of the time, it would be assumed that her husband would play an active role in making decisions

▼ marriage also limited more general freedom of action to pick and choose alliances with foreign powers, because of dynastic links

▼ if she married an Englishman, she faced the prospect of unbalancing the carefully poised rivalries at court by favouring one network of supporters to the exclusion of the rest

▼ she might have taken a personal decision to remain celibate, perhaps because of her childhood experiences of her father's failed marriages, or because she feared being unable to have children.

Whatever Elizabeth's reasons, the question of the succession was too important to remain in the background for long. There was almost immediate pressure on her to marry, especially from MPs in the House of Commons. In an early collision with Elizabeth, both the Lords and Commons discussed the marriage question against the

To whom?	Why?	How serious?
Philip II of Spain	To reinforce the Anglo-Spanish alliance at the start of her reign	Not very – it would have meant losing freedom of action almost immediately and the memory of Philip's marriage to Mary Tudor still smarted among the English
Archduke Charles of Austria	He was the son of the Holy Roman Emperor	Said to have been a serious prospect, but he refused to come to England to live
Robert Dudley, Earl of Leicester	A long-standing relationship between Dudley and Elizabeth	Elizabeth was greatly attracted to him, and gave him rewards and favours at court, but a marriage would have intensified factionalism by allying the crown to one noble family. Dudley was also married when Elizabeth came to the throne. His wife died from a broken neck caused by a fall at her home in 1560, raising uncomfortable questions
Duke of Anjou	To win French support for the rebellion in the Netherlands	Failed when France became too enthusiastic to gain land from the Dutch
Duke of Alençon	To win French support for the rebellion in the Netherlands	A good prospect, but Alençon died in 1584

POTENTIAL CLAIMANTS IN 1558

Henry VIII's will had set out the line of succession through his own children, but had not excluded the possibility that his younger sister Mary's family might inherit. This had prompted Northumberland to promote the claim of Lady Jane Grey in 1553. In 1558 Jane's younger sister Catherine might have advanced her own claim, but there seemed no good reason to do so – there was little support within the nobility to revive memories of the failed coup of 1553. A potentially more serious threat came from Mary, Queen of Scots. She was the granddaughter of Henry VIII's elder sister, Margaret, and heir to the Scottish throne. In 1548 she had been moved to France at the height of the Scottish War, where she had met and married Francis, heir to the French throne.

Table 11 Elizabeth's possible marriage partners.

queen's wishes in the 1566 session. MPs even tried to force the issue by linking the grant of a subsidy to Elizabeth's answer. She refused to be drawn, however, and told the Commons that they were 'too feeble-minded to discuss so weighty a matter'. When pressed, she gave the classic response: 'I have already joined myself in marriage to a husband – namely the kingdom of England.'

At the same time, Elizabeth managed to reduce some of the pressure on her by seriously entertaining marriage proposals from the Habsburgs and the French court (see Table 11). In the 1570s, serious negotiations with the Duke of Alençon led to his arrival at court in 1578 amid a flurry of gossip and speculation about the likelihood of an early marriage. As always, Elizabeth remained cautious, aware of the personal opposition of the Earl of Leicester and conscious that public opinion had turned against France after the Saint Bartholemew's Day Massacre in 1572 of Protestants on the orders of Alençon's brother and mother.

The collapse of the Alençon marriage plan in the early 1580s signalled the end of the Tudor dynasty. Elizabeth was nearly 50 years old and unlikely to produce a child even if another eligible husband could be found. By this time, she was being flattered by a new generation of younger courtiers, especially the Earl of Essex. Her thoughts never seriously turned to the question of her successor, even in her final years. Mary Queen of Scots' son, King James VI of Scotland, was Elizabeth's closest male relative. He was a firm Protestant and an adult male, exactly the qualities needed in a successor. Elizabeth wrote teasing letters to him, seeming to offer him the crown without ever making the promise explicit. Courtiers also wrote to James in secret, realising that they needed to prove their loyalty to him even whilst Elizabeth lived.

b) Mary Queen of Scots

ISSUES:
Why was Mary Queen of Scots a threat to Elizabeth? Why did Elizabeth take so long to deal with this threat?

Relations with Mary Queen of Scots were, as we saw above, intimately connected to the succession question because Mary was the legitimate heir unless Elizabeth produced a child. At the beginning of the reign, Mary's marriage to Francis II of France posed a serious threat to English security and to the religious settlement of 1559, but Francis's sudden death in 1560 and Mary's disastrous return home significantly reduced the danger. However, Mary remained a difficulty for Elizabeth because her presence highlighted a number of the fundamental disagreements over policy being expressed during the 1560s and 1570s and acted as a rallying point for those disaffected with the tone and direction of Elizabethan government.

Some of Elizabeth's councillors called for Mary's execution to end the problem, but Elizabeth was reluctant to listen to them for personal

MARY, QUEEN OF SCOTS (1542–1587)

Mary Queen of Scots was a tragic figure in Elizabethan politics. A series of unfortunate choices alarmed both the Scots and the English, to the point where Elizabeth's advisers considered her too great a security risk to be allowed to live. Her life can be divided into three stages:

1. During her childhood, she was a pawn in the struggle between England and France for control of Scottish affairs. Her father, James V of Scotland, died when she was just a week old, leaving the country at war with England. A marriage alliance which would have wed Mary to Edward VI was discussed, but French intervention prevented this. Instead, Mary was transported to France at the age of five, where she was raised by her Catholic Guise relatives. A new marriage was arranged, this time to the heir to the French throne.

2. Following her husband's death, Mary returned to Scotland, where a pro-English government had been installed after the 1560 Treaty of Edinburgh. She was not welcome: the country was undergoing a Protestant Reformation and rival groups of nobles threatened renewed civil war. Mary felt rootless – she had no official position in France and had been rejected by Protestants at home as their monarch. To strengthen her status, she promoted her claim to the English crown. It is unclear whether she saw herself simply as Elizabeth's heir, or her immediate replacement. Either way, she exposed the vulnerability of the Tudor crown. Her marriage to Lord Darnley was a political manoeuvre to strengthen her claim – he was the great-grandson of Henry VII. The marriage was a disaster and broke down within a year. Darnley suspected Mary of having an affair with her secretary David Rizzio and conspired to kill him in 1566. Mary knew that the stabbing of Rizzio – 56 times – could hardly have been accidental and may have supported Lord Bothwell's murder of Darnley the following year. After a moment's mourning for Darnley, she married Bothwell, but this marriage also collapsed and he left for Denmark. Whilst the Scottish people followed these dramas avidly, few felt that Mary's actions made her a suitable ruler. Renewed civil war by 1568 forced her to flee to England.

3. Elizabeth kept Mary under close scrutiny and house arrest for the next 19 years. She had become a focal point for Catholic

-Profile-

1542 born, the only child of James V of Scotland;

1548 taken to France to be educated at court;

1558 married the heir to the French throne;

1559 her husband became King Francis II of France;

1560 death of Francis II;

1561 Mary returned to Scotland;

1565 married Lord Darnley (a descendant of Henry VIII's sister, Margaret) prompting speculation that she intended to claim the English throne;

1567 murder of Darnley by Mary's lover the Earl of Bothwell; marriage between Mary and Bothwell (which lasted just a few weeks);

1568 rebellion against Mary in Scotland forced her to flee to England for safety;

1569 Revolt of the Northern Earls supported Mary's claim to the English throne;

1571 implicated in the Ridolfi Plot to overthrow Elizabeth;

1582 implicated in the Throckmorton Plot to overthrow Elizabeth;

1586 Babington Plot; Mary put on trial for complicity in the plot and convicted of treason;

1587 Elizabeth signed Mary's death warrant after four months of delay; execution of Mary at Fotheringay Castle.

and noble discontent and a potential pawn of Spain or France should they seek to undermine or to depose Elizabeth. One of Elizabeth's ministers summed up the problem of Mary by saying that, 'As long as life is in her, there is hope. As they live in hope, we live in fear.' Events such as the Revolt of the Northern Earls and the Spanish-inspired plots against Elizabeth in the 1570s and 1580s were reminders of the danger that Mary posed, but Elizabeth was reluctant to take action against her cousin. Finally, Francis Walsingham produced evidence of Mary's complicity in the Babington Plot and she was put on trial. Despite a guilty verdict, Elizabeth delayed signing the death warrant for four months. Mary's execution finally came in February 1587.

and for practical reasons. She regarded Mary as a family member and felt some sympathy for the difficulties that she had endured. Moreover, Elizabeth was careful not to support harsh treatment of a fellow female monarch, especially one with a rightful claim to the Scottish throne. Politically, it was also unwise to dispose of Mary. She had close relations with the Guise family in France, so could be useful to blunt any French action against England, especially if the complex marriage negotiations with the Dukes of Anjou and Alençon failed. These were, at best, flimsy excuses given the mounting evidence that Spain and disaffected English Catholics were plotting fairly continuously by the late 1570s to put Mary on the throne. Only when the evidence of Mary's involvement apparently became overwhelming did Elizabeth finally agree to her cousin's execution in 1587.

Source J From a report sent to Lord Burghley giving details of the execution of Mary Queen of Scots, 8 February 1587.

Groping for the block, she laid down her head, putting her chin over the block with both her hands, which, holding there still, would have been cut off had they not been seen. Then she, lying very still upon the block, one of the executioners holding her slightly with one of his hands, she endured two strokes of the other executioner with an axe, she making a very small noise or none at all, and not stirring any part of her from where she lay. And so the executioner cut off her head, save for one little gristle. Once cut asunder, he held up her head to the view of all the assembly and said, 'God Save The Queen'. Her lips stirred up and down a quarter of an hour after her head was cut off. Then one of the executioners, pulling off her garters, espied her little dog which had crept under her clothes. It could not be gotten away from her except by force, but afterwards came back to lay between her head and her shoulders, until it was carried away and washed.

c) The Crisis of 1584–1604

By 1584 Elizabeth had been queen for over a quarter of a century. She had come to the throne a cautious, but intelligent, 25-year-old but as she aged, she had become more difficult and bitter. There was a definite air of decline about her reign in its closing years. The 1590s were characterised by war, rebellion, disease and famine, presided over by a queen who seemed to have lost the sureness of control that had characterised her early years.

i) Economic Problems

The 1590s were difficult years for the people of England. Although the decade began with successful harvests, the years 1594–7 saw four successive serious crop failures. One effect was to push up agricultural prices even further; during the decade, it has been estimated that prices rose by over one-third. There were also outbreaks of plague, whose severity was worsened by the lack of food. Thousands died in the first visitation of 1592–3 and the effects continued to decimate urban and rural populations for the next ten years at least. Overall, the 1590s contained some of the most miserable years of the century. Yet what is noticeable is the lack of significant popular rebellion. There were local riots, especially when it was rumoured that foodstuffs were being hoarded by merchants hoping to drive up prices still further. However, only one national revolt occurred (section iv below) and this was not caused by economic hardship.

ii) Ireland

In theory, Ireland had been an official part of the English crown since 1541, but in reality English control extended little further than **the 'Pale'**. In the rest of the island clans exercised real power based on local tradition and custom rather than English law. There had been successive attempts by English governments to strengthen their control over the clans because Ireland was regarded as strategically important to national security. Like Scotland, it offered foreign powers a tempting base from which to threaten the mainland. This potential threat grew worse under Elizabeth because Irish clans remained loyal to the Catholic Church whilst England moved towards Protestantism. Spain in particular saw the potential in this religious disagreement to make Ireland a distraction for the English crown.

Under Edward VI, clumsy attempts to export the Reformation to Ireland had resulted in the collapse of earlier efforts to extend royal control beyond the Pale. During the 1550s relations deteriorated further when settlers began arriving from England to implement the policy of **plantation**. Elizabeth therefore came to the throne with Ireland in rebellion over religious and land changes, and periodic outbursts kept the problem alive for the rest of her reign.

THE PALE
The Pale was England's foothold in Ireland, a region on the eastern coast around Dublin. It was the centre of English government on the island during the fifteenth and sixteenth centuries, heavily manned and fortified against the Irish clans who lived 'beyond the Pale'.

PLANTATION
Plantation involved settling English colonists on lands formerly owned by Irish clans in order to extend the Pale and slowly establish control over the whole island. The policy began in Edward VI's reign, but was extended under Mary with the creation of the 'Queen's County' and 'King's County' to the west of the Pale. During Elizabeth's reign further plantation was encouraged, especially in the northern county of Ulster and in the western county of Munster. Although the policy aimed to bring peace and stability by planting English settlers in Ireland, it often had precisely the opposite effect, provoking Irish clans whose lands had been seized into open rebellion.

The most serious challenge was mounted by Hugh O'Neill, the Earl of Tyrone, between 1598 and 1603. Tyrone's army of about 6,000 men easily defeated the much smaller English force at the Battle of the Yellow Ford in August 1598, threatening then to move on to dismantle all the control built up by the plantation policy. Equally dangerous were the links that Tyrone had built with Spain, which promised to double the men at his disposal. Elizabeth quickly sent over a larger force commanded by the Earl of Essex, but it was a complete failure and Essex returned home in disgrace (to lose his influence at court and drive him to rebellion, as we will see below). His replacement, Lord Mountjoy, managed to defeat Tyrone's forces by constantly harassing them in year-round campaigns. The turning point came when a Spanish relief force was defeated at Kinsale in 1602, depriving Tyrone of desperately needed assistance. From this moment, opposition to the English army rapidly crumbled and order was restored to the devastated country as the crown passed from Elizabeth to James I.

iii) The Threat from Spain

Had England been at peace in the 1590s, the Irish rebellion of Tyrone might have assumed less worrying proportions. However, from 1585 England was at war with Spain. The causes of the war are examined elsewhere (see pages 219–20), but were essentially bound up with England's desire to keep the Netherlands out of Spanish hands. In 1585 Elizabeth agreed the Treaty of Nonsuch with the Dutch rebels fighting against the extension of Spanish rule, committing England to provide troops and money to aid the Dutch cause. This action raised the stakes considerably: there had been simmering tension between Elizabeth and Philip II for some time, but the queen had always stopped just short of giving official approval for a direct attack on Spanish interests. With hindsight, it is easy to say that the war was a mistake, promoted by the Tudor 'war party' at court who saw in it their chance to achieve personal fame and fortune, but it is difficult to see what else could have been done in 1585. The Dutch rebels were nearing the point of collapse whilst France was shifting from ally to possible enemy.

The two sides were badly mismatched in terms of military manpower, equipment and national resources. Spain could call on a larger population, a long tradition of successful military campaigning which had created one of the most effective fighting forces in Europe, and a vast overseas empire rich in silver and precious spices. These strengths determined the English war effort. Direct confrontation with Spain on land, except in the rebellious Netherlands, was generally avoided, whilst at sea English ships tried to hinder the flow of bullion from the New World. Both strategies came perilously close to failing. In the Netherlands, Elizabeth's choice of the Earl of

Leicester as military commander and royal representative backfired when he proved incapable of directing his soldiers and far too willing to act independently of royal advice. In the New World, Spanish ships were harried, but Philip could still muster the resources to build a series of armadas and to maintain the war in the Netherlands.

In the end, England was successful and the mythology surrounding the defeat of the Spanish Armada of 1588 has sustained Elizabeth's reputation ever since. By intervening in the Netherlands, and by supporting Henry IV's claim to the French throne, Elizabeth denied Spain both a victory over the rebels and a possible religious ally against the English Reformation. Two points need to be borne in mind, however. First, the war was as much lost by Spain as won by England. Philip II's finances depended on heavy government borrowing, which forced him into bankruptcy in 1596. He also faced the prospect of fighting on an increasing number of fronts – the Netherlands, the seas around Spain's Caribbean colonies, and in eastern France when Henry IV claimed the crown. This was too much for Spain to manage and led to compromises such as the instruction to the Duke of Parma to divert his men from the Netherlands into France, at the point when he might have delivered a decisive blow to the rebellion.

Secondly, the war cost England dearly. It has been estimated that Elizabeth was spending twice as much as her revenues normally yielded. To cover the shortfall, she sold valuable crown lands and resorted to unpopular financial expedients such as the sale of monopolies (which provoked the opposition of the 1601 Parliament). In the short term, these raised enough money to avoid bankruptcy, but in the long run the loss of land deprived later monarchs of regular income, whilst the legacy of repeated demands on Parliament for money created a sense of grievance that was to have important repercussions for her Stuart successors.

iv) The Essex Rebellion, 1601

As we saw above (page 180), manipulating patronage effectively was central to Elizabeth's achievement. As she grew older, however, her skill at handling the different factions and interests swirling around her at court weakened. It seems to have deserted her almost completely in 1601 when the Earl of Essex rebelled.

Essex had come to the court as the stepson of the Earl of Leicester, and when Leicester died he became the leader of the group of courtiers who favoured stepping up military action against Spain. Elizabeth, however, did not favour such action and Essex found that he was unable to gain seats on the Privy Council or positions at court for his allies. Instead, the so-called 'peace party', led by Lord Burghley and his son, monopolised key posts. There is no doubt that Essex was infuriated by the queen's obstinacy and his lack of

Figure 47 Elizabeth's rebellious courtier, the Earl of Essex. According to the French ambassador, 'He was a man who did not content himself with a small fortune and aspired to greatness.'

progress. On one famous occasion, she hit him and he had to be forcibly restrained from drawing his sword.

In 1599 Elizabeth finally gave Essex a chance to show his talents and to reward his supporters by appointing him to command her army in Ireland. He threw away this opportunity, however, and fell from royal favour once again. As a result, he lost valuable monopolies and a possible government position in the Court of Wards. Nearly bankrupt by February 1601, he attempted to seize London. The 'rebellion' was a miserable failure – few people actively joined it and Essex was quickly arrested and executed for treason. What concerned Elizabeth was the fact that it had happened in the capital, close to the centre of power, and that a number of noblemen had joined Essex in his abortive coup. None of these supporters was put on trial for fear of provoking further rebellion. In her final years, therefore, Elizabeth seems to have failed to distribute patronage evenly enough to maintain the loyalty of some of her leading subjects. By favouring Lord Burghley's family and circle of supporters, Elizabeth alienated other families, but the Essex rebellion seems to have done no more than to reinforce her dependence on them.

ISSUE:

How strong was the monarchy in 1603?

4 The Tudor Legacy

The largely uncritical view of Elizabeth's reign which persisted among historians for so long has broken down in the last generation or so. Now a richer and more complex picture both of the queen herself and of her achievements is emerging. One of the key areas of debate has been whether the Tudors left England politically stable and strengthened, or whether the seeds of the seventeenth-century struggle between crown and Parliament had been planted during their reigns.

The real problem by 1603 was that rapid and profound religious, social, economic and cultural changes had taken place without a similar revolution in government. Although there were more professional administrators and fewer amateur nobles running government by 1603, the system remained in essence what it had been in 1485: a personal monarchy. Under Elizabeth the country had a capable monarch whose character and political skills were mostly sufficient to hold the political system together. However, there was no guarantee that every monarch would possess such abilities, or would even have the interest to be a strong ruler. The fragility of personal monarchy was evident throughout the 1540s and 1550s and became apparent once again in the 1590s. Elizabeth's achievement was to keep control for nearly half a century, than to create the conditions necessary for continued stability under her Stuart successors. She left James I a potentially strong monarchy, a stable society and the goodwill of most Englishmen. At the same time, she also provided him with an expensive war against Spain, financial problems and political and religious tensions.

> The report of her death, like a thunderclap, was able to kill thousands. It took away the heart from millions. For having brought up, under her wing, a nation of people who were almost all born under her, that never saw the face of any prince but herself, never understood what the strange outlandish word 'change' signified – how was it possible but that her sickness should throw abroad a universal fear, and her death an astonishment?

Source K From the writer Thomas Dekker's description of the effect of Elizabeth's death on the nation, 1603.

Table 12 The Tudor legacy: stability or instability?

Arguments for political stability	Arguments for political instability
• The image and status of monarchy had been cultivated carefully by Elizabeth's propagandists. Victories over her Catholic enemies at home and abroad in the 1580s and 1590s strengthened her position considerably	• During the 1590s social, economic and political crises came together to expose the fragility of Elizabeth's control. Her need to placate Parliament in 1601 over monopolies and the sudden rebellion by the Earl of Essex revealed that the elderly Elizabeth had lost some of her youthful charm
• Parliament met infrequently, and was summoned and dismissed according to the monarch's wishes. Despite occasional criticism, Parliament was a loyal supporter of royal policy	• By involving Parliament in legislating major constitutional changes, such as the break with Rome and the establishment of a national church and doctrine, Tudor monarchs raised the status of MPs and inadvertently created the impression that there was more of a partnership between crown and Parliament than actually existed
• There were few serious rebellions after 1549, showing the extent of the nobility's support for a monarchy which offered them stability and patronage	• By assuming control over the English church the monarchy became a focus for religious as well as political criticism. Both extreme Protestants and unreconciled Catholics remained hostile to the nature of the Elizabethan settlement

▼ Working on Politics in the Age of Elizabeth I

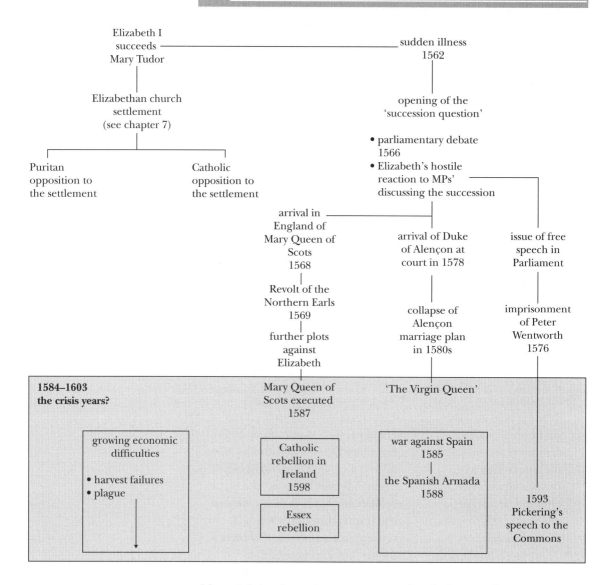

Figure 48 Political developments in the reign of Elizabeth I.

How historians have approached the topic

Until recently, most historical writing about Elizabeth I was full of congratulation for the queen and her achievements. Since her reign included the establishment of the Anglican tradition in English religion, the defeat of the Spanish Armada and the development of cultural life at court and through the writings of Shakespeare and others, it is easy to see why. It was not until the 1950s and 1960s that serious consideration was given to the role of Elizabeth's ministers (a trend which echoed the work of Geoffrey Elton and others in reappraising Henry VIII's style of government).

One of the key debates about Elizabethan politics has focused on the development of Parliament as an institution. According to Sir John Neale (who was writing in the 1930s), Elizabethan Parliaments were centres of political dispute and division, especially on matters of religion. Looking forwards to the 1640s, when civil war broke out between crown and Parliament partly over the future direction of the church, some historians saw Elizabeth's reign as sowing the seeds of this dispute. More recently, writers have challenged this connection, particularly by showing that Parliaments were much more co-operative and less fragmented than was supposed.

It is only in the last 20 years, however, that a serious attempt to challenge the overall perception of Elizabeth's reign as a 'golden age' has emerged. Christopher Haigh in *The Reign of Elizabeth I* (1984) has led the way by playing up the problems and insecurities of the reign and other historians, such as David Starkey, have begun to reveal more about Elizabeth's difficult personality and how it was shaped by her troubled early life.

Research and notemaking

A good place to start when trying to sort out the politics of Elizabeth's reign is the diagram of government on page 188 (Figure 46). Begin by identifying all the key parts of Elizabethan government from the diagram, then develop information about them as suggested in this chart:

Element of government	What its role was under Elizabeth	How it developed during her reign	How important it was in the political system

Once you have a clear idea about the organisation of government, you can then stand back and evaluate the overall strengths and weaknesses it possessed. Planning answers to the following questions will help you to think through the key issues:

1. Who controlled government? The queen? Her chief advisers?
2. What threatened political stability in Elizabethan England?
3. Were the queen or her government ever in serious danger of being overthrown?
4. Did Elizabethan government become less effective towards the end of the reign?
5. Why was Elizabeth able to rule so successfully for so long?

Answering Extended Writing and Essay Questions on Politics in the Age of Elizabeth I

Questions about Elizabethan government appear regularly on examination papers. Here are some typical examples:

1. (a) Explain the role of Elizabeth I's ministers in governing England.

    (b) How convincing is the claim that there was a decline in the effectiveness of Elizabeth I's government during the final years of her reign?

2. Consider arguments for and against the claim that the role and nature of Parliament changed little during the reign of Elizabeth I.

3. How important a figure in government between 1558 and 1603 was Elizabeth herself?

4. (a) Describe any THREE of the problems which confronted Elizabethan governments.

    (b) Which proved to be the most serious problem for Elizabeth?

The final example includes a type of question that we have not considered so far – a comparative question ('Which proved to be the *most serious* problem?'). To answer this successfully, you need to make a direct comparison between the problems. This means thinking of criteria against which to judge the seriousness of each problem, rather than simply writing about each problem in turn (which would sound like a repeat of your answer to part a).

How could you judge the 'most serious' problem? Perhaps it was serious because it threatened to topple Elizabeth from the throne? Because it lasted for so long? Because it was never resolved, so created a difficulty for James I? Because it damaged the reputation of England abroad, or created deep divisions at home?

Using some of these criteria, it should be possible to arrive at a conclusion about the seriousness of a problem such as the fact that Elizabeth was a female head of state. Although she was challenged by Mary Queen of Scots and Philip II, this was not because she was a female ruler, but because of her religious policies. No one seriously challenged Elizabeth because she was a woman – even her Catholic subjects were more inclined to support her because she was the legitimate monarch than to consider supporting the Armada or plots against her. Elizabeth's sex also did not seem to damage England's reputation abroad (in fact, other monarchs seemed to be falling over themselves to marry her!), especially after her foreign policy victories in the 1580s. So, it seems unlikely that Elizabeth herself was a serious problem for Elizabethan government – she scores a very low mark against our criteria.

Based on this example, try to write paragraphs which judge the significance of each of the other problems in the list in the question. You could divide this task up within a group then explain your findings to each other. The problem with the highest 'score' against the criteria is probably the most serious.

If you think you have got to grips with making comparisons, why not think about this question:

5. What was the most important element in Elizabethan government – the crown, Parliament, the Privy Council, or the royal court?

Answering Source-Based Questions on Politics in the Age of Elizabeth I

Sometimes, you will be required to use a set of sources to construct what is effectively a mini-essay, as in the example below. Most examination boards will set source-based exercises which include, usually as the last part of the question, a task that is worth up to half the available marks. You will need to realise this as you begin your first answer so that you can plan your time in the examination accordingly.

> I shall require you all, my lords, and chiefly you of the nobility, to be assistant to me; so that I with my ruling, and you with your service, may make a good account to Almighty God. I mean to direct my actions by good advice and council.

Source L From the Elizabethan courtier Sir John Harington's *Nugae Antiquae*, a collection of his letters and writings, published in 1769.

> Leicester, Hatton and Walsingham have endeavoured to persuade the Queen that it is desirable for her to openly take the Netherlands under her protection but they have been opposed by Cecil and Sussex when the matter was discussed in the Council, and the Queen therefore remained undecided.

Source M From a report by the Spanish ambassador to King Philip II.

> Her ministers and instruments of State were many, and were memorable, but they were only favourites and not minions, so they acted more by her princely rules and judgements than by their own wills and appetites. The principal note of her reign will be that she ruled much by faction and parties, which she herself both made, upheld and weakened as her own great judgement advised.

Source N From Sir Robert Naunton, *Fragmenta Regalia*, published in 1641.

> Her wisest and best councillors were oft sore troubled to know her will in matters of state, so covertly did she pass her judgement it seemed she left all to their discreet management.

Source O From Sir John Harington, *Nugae Antiquae*.

▼ QUESTIONS ON SOURCES

'Elizabeth I was both the greatest asset and the greatest liability to government.' Discuss this claim using these sources and your own knowledge.
[20 marks]

Planning is essential to achieving a good mark on a question such as this. You will need to unpack the question into its component tasks:
▼ The question asks you to 'discuss' the quotation, so you will need to adopt a 'for and against' approach
▼ How was Elizabeth an asset to government according to the sources?
▼ Do you know anything else that would be relevant to a discussion of her strengths?
▼ How was Elizabeth a liability according to the sources?
▼ What else do you know that would back this up?

Having planned what needs to be covered, you can then begin to search the extracts for relevant material. Remember that you are not just looking for quotations to lift out, but also material drawn from 'between the lines' – based on the tone and style of the extract. Here is what the sources have to say about Elizabeth's assets as a ruler:
▼ Source L strikes a very positive, no-nonsense tone. Here is a queen who means to rule and to rule well. She talks about seeking advice and co-operation from her leading subjects, suggesting that she wants to win their trust and support
▼ Source M shows the queen weighing the different opinions of the 'peace' and 'war' factions towards intervention in the Netherlands. By not appearing to make a sudden decision, or openly to favour one of the factions, Elizabeth is leaving herself room for manoeuvre
▼ Source N takes this point further by suggesting that Elizabeth was in control of the factionalism at court and used it to her advantage. The writer strongly suggests that Elizabeth set the tone and direction of government, not her ministers, and that their dependence on her for their positions meant that she was always the master
▼ Source O could be taken to mean that Elizabeth was careful not to impress her views too strongly on her ministers, preferring instead to let them think they were in control.

These points are a very one-sided reading of sources L–O. The nature of historical sources means that they can usually be interpreted in different ways. Look at each extract again and see if you can put a different interpretation on what the writer is saying. Once you have done this, you will need to outline both interpretations of the sources to an examiner and, for high marks, reach a judgement about which interpretation is better. You can do this by using your knowledge of Elizabethan governments, and any relevant points about the usefulness of the sources provided, to identify any significant strengths or weaknesses of the arguments.

Further Reading

Books in the *Access to History* series

Two books in the Access series deal with the reign of Elizabeth I. John Warren's *Elizabeth I and the Government of England* will be the most directly relevant to this chapter, but you should also consult *Elizabeth I: Religion and Foreign Affairs* by Keith Randell. For information about the legacy of the Tudor period, you could dip into the early chapters of the Access Contexts book *An Introduction to Stuart Britain* by Angela Anderson.

Other books

A classic work on the period remains *The Government of Elizabethan England* by A. G. R. Smith (Arnold, 1967), but you will find digests of the main arguments in the same author's *The Emergence of a Nation State: The Commonwealth of England 1529–1660* (Longman, 1984). For a survey of the conflicts and co-operation between crown and Parliament, see *Elizabethan Parliaments, 1559–1601* by M. A. R. Graves (Longman, 1996). The impact of Mary Queen of Scots on Elizabethan politics can be traced using Jenny Wormald's biography of the queen (Tauris Parke, 2000). There are plenty of good modern evaluations of Elizabeth's personality and her achievements. A student textbook which would give you a good introduction to the issues is *Elizabeth I* by Neale Tonge (Longman, 2000). Beyond this, you could also consult *Elizabeth I* by Anne Somerset (Phoenix, 1997) which sets policies in the context of life at court, or *The Virgin Queen: Elizabeth I, Genius of the Golden Age* by Christopher Hibbert (Addison Wesley, 1992) which profiles the queen and other leading contemporaries to illustrate the idea of an Elizabethan 'golden age'. Finally, for a critical and provocative assessment of Elizabeth and her reign, it is essential to use *Elizabeth I* by Christopher Haigh (Longman, 2001).

7 RELIGION AND FOREIGN POLICY, 1558–1603

ISSUE:

How Protestant was Elizabeth?

1 The Elizabethan Settlement, 1558–63

a) Elizabeth's Religious Views

Working out precisely what Elizabeth's personal religious views were is a difficult task. As queen, she was conscious of the impression she made on others, especially at the beginning of her reign, so she was careful not to give too much support for just one point of view. Added to that is the problem that Elizabeth's priorities concerning the church were shaped much more by political considerations than by any religious ones. She wanted to establish a settlement of religion which would heal divisions between Catholics and Protestants and maximise her own control over the church, rather than creating something which necessarily reflected her personal theology. Like most people of the time, Elizabeth subscribed to the view that there could be no peace between different faiths, and that their mutual hostility would destroy national unity and lead to unrest and civil war.

None the less, there are clues that her preferences were for Protestant ideas. As the daughter of Anne Boleyn she had grown up connected to a family sympathetic to religious reform. Her education had been conducted by teachers such as Sir Roger Ascham who were knowledgeable about Lutheran ideas. Although Elizabeth was forced to live as a Catholic during her sister Mary's reign, incidents during her first years as queen have been used by historians to argue that she was a genuine Protestant. Within a month of becoming queen and before the national religious settlement was reached she forbade priests in the royal chapel to elevate the host (a point in the Catholic mass when the priest held up the communion bread and transformed it into Christ's body, as in Figure 21 on page 73). She was also apparently furious when the Dean of St Paul's Cathedral presented her with a copy of the Prayer Book containing illustrations of saints.

However, there were also signs that Elizabeth liked some traditional teachings. In particular, she enjoyed some of the comforting ornaments of the Catholic Church such as the crucifix, candles and church music. She also supported the traditional view that priests should devote their lives to God and not marry. One of the major disagreements she had with Matthew Parker, her first Archbishop of Canterbury, concerned an instruction she issued forbidding any clergyman to live with his wife on cathedral grounds or in a college. To hold such views whilst supporting more radical ideas about faith was not surprising. Religious change had been going on in England for all of Elizabeth's life so it was probable that, as an intelligent person, she should find some aspects of that change more acceptable than others.

b) Influences on the Religious Settlement

The Elizabethan settlement took shape in 1558–9, and its essential parts were in place within six months of the new queen's accession in November 1558. This does not mean, however, that the process of settlement was easy. The first attempt to introduce bills into Parliament early in 1559 was wrecked by the opposition of the **Marian bishops** and some noblemen in the House of Lords, who formed a solid Catholic voting block. They objected to the attempt in the legislation to bring back the Protestant Prayer Book of 1552 and to the prospect of the church being headed by a woman.

In political terms, Elizabeth had to proceed with care. England was still at war with France and unable to rely completely on the support of Spain. While the population of London had demonstrated massive support for a Protestant settlement, opinion elsewhere was less clearly in favour and the north of England remained deeply conservative. Beyond the northern counties lay Scotland, still firmly allied to the Catholic French, and whose young queen was wife of the

ISSUE:
What factors shaped the religious settlement of 1558–9?

MARIAN BISHOPS
During her five years in power Mary I had replaced the Protestant bishops appointed under Edward VI with more fiercely Catholic ones. These Marian bishops formed a solid block of opposition both within the church hierarchy and in the House of Lords to Elizabeth's proposed reforms.

THE SETTLEMENT OF THE CHURCH

1559 Acts of Supremacy and Uniformity passed; new Protestant bishops replaced those who resigned; Royal Injunctions issued; Revised Book of Common Prayer; Act of Exchange;

1563 Thirty-nine Articles issued by Convocation;

1566 Vestiarian Controversy; Archbishop Parker's *Advertisements* defined clerical garments;

1571 Thirty-nine Articles made law by Parliament.

ISSUE:
How did the settlement affect the organisation of the church?

heir to the French throne and next in line to that of England. Any alteration of religion in England, therefore, was bound to have an impact on England's relationship with France, Spain and Scotland.

Elizabeth was able to proceed with the settlement because of two events around Easter 1559. The first was the signing of the Peace of Câteau-Cambrésis between France and Spain. This drew the long-running wars between them to a close and ended English military action against France. The second was a government-sponsored debate between Protestant and Catholic clergy at which some of the Catholic bishops made the mistake of suggesting that they did not accept Elizabeth authority over them, allowing her to arrest and imprison two of them.

Once Parliament reassembled after Easter, it was a little easier to steer legislation through. Elizabeth made some concessions over her title and the wording of the Prayer Book and put considerable pressure on the noble members of the Lords to back her. This, plus the imprisonment of the two bishops in the Tower, gave her a majority of one vote.

c) The Nature of the Settlement

The issue of control over the church was settled by the Act of Supremacy in May 1559. It re-established the English monarch as head of the church, although Elizabeth chose to be titled 'Supreme Governor'. In effect, her status was the same as that which had been held by Henry VIII and Edward VI, but by choosing a less controversial title than 'Supreme Head' she was able to satisfy those people who still regarded the Pope as the rightful head of the church or who felt that it was wrong for a woman to hold the top position in the church.

The Act of Supremacy also required all churchmen to swear an oath of loyalty to their new Supreme Governor. To make sure that the change of leadership was truly being accepted at parish level, commissioners were sent out to investigate and a new court was established – the Court of High Commission – to prosecute those whose loyalty was suspect.

Beyond the change of leadership, little else was altered about the national organisation of the church. England would continue to have two archbishops – Canterbury and York – as it had done during Catholic times, and bishops would remain. This form of organisation did not appear in any of the Protestant churches in Europe, where much more emphasis was placed on each congregation organising itself.

The Act of Uniformity of May 1559 set out rules about the appearance of churches. Essentially, it said that any practices which had existed in 1549 when the first Prayer Book had been issued should still be followed. So, although the altar was replaced by the more Protestant communion table, Catholic artefacts such as crosses and candles could be placed on it. The Act also set out what priests should wear to conduct services, another nod towards Catholics since Protestants felt that what mattered were the words being spoken, not what the preacher looked like. By keeping a Catholic appearance to the church, those who drew up the settlement made probably their wisest move. They judged, correctly, that most people were not likely to be too bothered about theological disputes over precisely what went on during the communion service, so would accept the introduction of mildly Protestant ideas about worship; but they would find abrupt changes to the appearance of their church jarring.

> As for the manner of their service in church and their prayers, except that they say them in the English tongue, one can still recognise a great part of the Mass, which they have limited only in what concerns individual communion. They still keep the Epistle and the Gospel, the Gloria in Excelsis Deo and the Creed. They sing the psalms in English, and at certain hours of the day they use organs and music. The priests wear the hood and surplice. It seems, apart from the absence of images, that there is little difference between their ceremonies and those of the Church of Rome.

Source A From a report by the French ambassador de Maisse, written in 1597.

To make sure that there was uniformity of worship, attendance at church was made compulsory. Anyone failing to attend could be fined, and the money collected distributed to the poor. Attendance at mass, rather than the communion service of the Church of England, was treated as a serious offence, with a heavy fine. Anyone saying mass could face the death penalty.

It was impossible to set out all the regulations governing the reformed faith in a single Act of Parliament, so further instructions – the Royal Injunctions of July 1559 – were issued. There were 57 instructions, including rules that:

▼ preachers had to be licensed by a bishop before they could begin preaching
▼ preachers had to preach at least one service each month or lose their licence
▼ every church had to display a Bible written in English
▼ pilgrimages were to be outlawed
▼ no more altars were to be destroyed.

The form of worship to be followed was set out in the Act of Uniformity. As its name suggests, its purpose was to establish a single agreed set of doctrines throughout the country, ending the quarrels between Protestants and Catholics. To achieve this, a new Prayer

ISSUES:
How did the settlement affect religious beliefs?

What do you think the motives behind these rules might have been?

How did the settlement affect religious beliefs?

Book was issued which set out the way that services should be conducted. In fact, the Book of Common Prayer issued in 1559 was a fusion of the two Prayer Books issued in Edward VI's reign, and amalgamated the moderate language of the 1549 book with the more openly Protestant words in the 1552 book. This might sound confusing, but it worked brilliantly as a compromise between what Protestants and Catholics wanted to hear when they worshipped.

The Meaning of the Bread and Wine

Central to disagreements between Catholics and Protestants was the question of what happened to the bread and wine during the mass. For Catholics, the priest literally transformed the bread into Christ's body and the wine into Christ's blood so that anyone consuming them would be taking God's presence directly into themselves, allowing the cleansing of sin and spiritual renewal. Protestants adopted a different line. To a greater or lesser extent the different Protestant reformers believed that the bread and wine were important symbols of Christ's presence, but that their physical elements did not change. This meant that the bread and wine could be used to create a moment of great intensity for the celebrant, but nothing more.

In the English Reformation a careful course was eventually picked between these two interpretations, as these extracts from different Books of Common Prayer show.

The 1549 Book of Common Prayer instructed the priest to use the following form of words:

> '*The body of our Lord Jesus Christ* which was given for thee, preserve thy body and soul unto everlasting life.'

The more Protestant 1552 Book of Common Prayer changed the phrase to:

> 'Take and eat this *in remembrance* that Christ died for thee, and feed on him in thy heart by faith, with thanksgiving.'

And in 1559, the Elizabethan Book of Common Prayer struck a balance by requiring priests to say:

> '*The body of our Lord Jesus Christ* which was given for thee, preserve thy body and soul unto everlasting life, and take, and eat this, *in remembrance* that Christ died for thee, feed on him in thine heart by faith and thanksgiving.'

A single act of Parliament could not completely set out a new faith for the country, however. In the following years, the Convocation of the church set about the task of producing a definitive statement of what 'Anglicanism' meant. The result was the Thirty-nine Articles of faith, published in 1563 and made law in 1571, which still remains the essential statement of belief in the Church of England today. The Thirty-nine Articles, like the rest of the settlement, welded together parts from the different Protestant and Catholic traditions into a whole that could be accepted by everyone.

ACTIVITY

The striking aspect of the religious settlement of 1559–63 is its achievement of a **compromise between the rival viewpoints of Catholics and Protestants**. Before moving on to look at the effects of the settlement on these religious groups, check that you have understood this by listing the ways in which the new church tried to attract support from both sides, using the following headings:

▼ control of the church
▼ structure of the national church
▼ appearance of churches
▼ religious doctrine.

Finally, summarise your findings by considering the following question: Was the Church of England in 1559 more Protestant than Catholic, or more Catholic than Protestant?

---

2 Immediate Reactions to the Settlement

ISSUE:
How popular was the 1559 settlement?

a) The Reaction at Home

Elizabeth hoped that the settlement would calm the tensions that had been growing since Henry VIII's reign and allow England to avoid the sort of religious warfare that had been seen in the German states of the Holy Roman Empire during the 1550s and which could be seen in France at the start of the 1560s. She had good reason to be optimistic: reaction among most Catholics and Protestants to the changes was muted. It has been estimated that around 400 of the clergy lost or resigned their livings because they would not accept the settlement. Virtually all the Catholic bishops appointed by Mary refused and were dismissed, but this gave Elizabeth the opportunity to make new appointments which created a leadership within the church enthusiastic about her reforms. Compared to the 800 or so

Protestants who had fled abroad in Mary's reign, the scale of refusal between 1559 and 1563 was minimal.

However, localised opposition was evident from the start. Some ministers simply ignored the new Book of Common Prayer and stuck to the traditional Catholic form of worship, whilst a survey of Justices of the Peace in 1564 found that only about half of them could be relied on actively to support the settlement. Some of the strongest reaction in England was against the financial side of the settlement and the seemingly minor issue of what priests wore to conduct services.

i) The Act of Exchange, 1559

Like her father, Elizabeth viewed the church as a treasure box to be used by the monarch. The disastrous war against France under Mary, and problems with Scotland at the start of Elizabeth's reign, had created a dangerous shortage of money in the royal treasury. Elizabeth followed Henry VIII by taking taxes that were traditionally paid to Rome into her own coffers, but also adopted a more controversial policy. In the Act of Exchange, Elizabeth was allowed to take over property belonging to bishops and to force them only to rent land to her. In practice, the Act was often used more as a threat to keep bishops who were critical of the settlement in line than as a means of gaining more land and property, which might explain its unpopularity.

ii) The Vestiarian Controversy, 1566

Vestments were the special clothes worn by the clergy during services. As part of the drive towards uniformity, Archbishop Parker issued a Book of Advertisements in 1566 which insisted on the surplice and cope as standard costume. In London, 37 clergymen refused to follow this instruction and were suspended. Although the incident might seem trivial to modern eyes, it symbolised an important point at the time. The vestments chosen by Parker were very similar to Catholic clothing, so offended Protestant preachers who were forced to wear them. Their refusal raised the further question of how far the queen's authority as Supreme Governor of the church extended.

Q

Why was the Vestiarian Controversy an important issue?

b) Foreign Reaction

Elizabeth was also concerned about the reaction from abroad. Both France and Spain were Catholic powers and could pose a threat to the settlement. In the event, neither showed much inclination to be critical. France was becoming absorbed in civil war and Philip II of Spain was prepared to give Elizabeth the benefit of the doubt. Neither he nor the Pope saw the changes in England as permanent, and hoped that Elizabeth could be persuaded (perhaps by marrying Philip or another Catholic prince) to return the church to Rome. However, as the 1560s progressed, Elizabeth began to regard Spain as more of a threat. During this decade the international balance of power was destabilised by events which left English foreign policy reeling:

▼ in 1562 the French state collapsed into civil war between rival groups of nobles and their clients for control of the crown. Although this was good news for Elizabeth because it removed the immediate threat from France, it also tipped the balance of power decisively towards Catholic Spain

▼ the deliberations of the Council of Trent finally ended in 1563. The council was a meeting of Europe's leading Catholic clergy to discuss the future of the church. Ominously, the council produced a series of hard-line decrees ending the possibility of a peaceful compromise with Protestants. Elizabeth became concerned at the threat of either or both France and Spain attacking England

▼ in 1566–7 the northern provinces of the Netherlands rebelled against Spanish government. Within months of the rebellion beginning, 10,000 Spanish troops arrived in the Netherlands, dangerously close to England.

Elizabeth saw the signs of a dangerously powerful Catholic Spanish monarchy behind these events. Her response was to search for a way of containing the might of Spain without overextending her limited resources. In the end, she was forced by events to make war against Spain, but by that time she was facing a country with the image but not the substance of a superpower.

3 The Catholic Threat in England

ISSUES:
How did English Catholicism threaten Elizabeth? What was her response?

In the first decade of her reign Elizabeth clearly hoped to win over the English Catholics to her compromise church. Public celebration of the mass was forbidden, but little was done to limit private worship. **Recusancy** laws were passed to force attendance at church, but she hoped that, by keeping many traditional ceremonies, she could make the new Church of England an acceptable alternative for all but the most dedicated Papists.

However, between 1568 and 1572 Elizabeth found it increasingly difficult to sustain her tolerance. A number of events at home and abroad changed the image she had of English Catholics as a discontented group into a positive threat to her survival:

▼ in 1567 the Pope showed his hostility to the religious settlement by instructing English Catholics not to attend Anglican church services.

▼ in 1567 the Spanish Duke of Alba was sent to the Netherlands to put down rebellion that had broken out there. The presence of 10,000 Spanish troops just across the Channel from southern England raised fears that Spain might be intending to force England back to Catholicism.

▼ in 1568 Mary Queen of Scots arrived in England seeking sanctuary. As Catholic heir to Elizabeth's throne, she became the focus for those

> ### RECUSANT
> The term recusant applies to those who refused to attend their parish church on a regular basis. Attendance was made compulsory by Parliament and anyone who failed to go was fined, initially 1 shilling [5 pence] for each failure. This was a significant amount of money for anyone below the gentry, and may be one reason why Catholicism lasted longer within the gentry and nobility.

unhappy with the Protestant drift in the church.

▼ in 1568 a school for priests was founded by William Allen in Douai in the Netherlands to train missionaries to go to England to support Catholics.

Source B From a report in the Spanish state papers, dated 28 December 1579.

> The number of Catholics, thank God, is daily increasing here, owing to the College and seminary for Englishmen which your Majesty [Philip II] ordered to be supported in Douai, from where there has come in the last year (and from the College of Rome) a hundred Englishmen who have been ordained there, by which means a great number of people are being converted, generally persons who have never heard the truth preached before. These priests go about disguised as laymen, and although they are young men, their good life, fervency and zeal in their work are admirable.

▼ in 1569 leading Catholic northern nobles, led by the Earls of Northumberland and Westmorland, rebelled against Elizabeth (see page 181). They hoped to depose her and install Mary as queen.

▼ in 1570 the Pope finally excommunicated Elizabeth. In doing so, he declared that all Catholics were free of any oaths of loyalty to her.

Figure 49 A contemporary drawing of the Pope issuing the document excommunicating Elizabeth in 1570.

The Popes bull against the Queene.

▼ in 1571 the Ridolfi Plot was uncovered which planned to murder Elizabeth and replace her with Mary.

▼ in 1572 Catholics in France slaughtered Protestants during the St Bartholemew's Day celebrations and brought the religious wars there to a temporary close. Elizabeth feared that France would now turn its attention to heresy in England.

Despite this list of problems, Elizabeth was cautious about provoking an outright confrontation with English Catholics. A new Treason

Q Why do you think Elizabeth adopted a cautious policy towards English Catholics?

Somerviles haste to Kill the Queene.

Figure 50 An engraving of one of the attempts to assassinate the queen. This image should be read like a cartoon because it shows a number of events. In the left panel the would-be assassin is arrested. In the centre, the queen is shown safe on the throne. On the right, the remorseful assassin commits suicide before his trial by drinking poison.

Act was introduced in 1571 making the denial of Elizabeth's supremacy or the importation of the Pope's order of excommunication acts punishable by death, but, beyond that, she consistently blocked attempts by the more aggressively Protestant MPs to increase penalties for recusancy or attendance at mass.

In many ways the decline of Catholicism in England from the 1570s was brought about by the Catholics themselves rather than by Elizabeth's actions. By forbidding them to attend church the Pope exposed Catholics to fines for recusancy that few could afford and forced them to choose between their loyalty to Rome and loyalty to friends and neighbours, because in many ways the parish church lay at the centre of village life. Attacks by foreigners on Elizabeth, such as the excommunication order and the plotting by Ridolfi and others, were not popular with English Catholics, who could see a difference between Elizabeth as the illegitimate head of the church and Elizabeth as their rightful monarch. The plots also allowed the government to justify sterner measures such as the 1585 Act against Jesuits, seminary priests (i.e. those trained at the Douai school) and 'such other like disobedient persons', which allowed priests to be automatically assumed guilty of treason without specific evidence. The revolt by the northern earls was serious, but once defeated, allowed Elizabeth to reorder lands in the north to make sure that Catholic influence was weakened.

Divisions and quarrels among the Catholic authorities created further difficulty. From 1580 the efforts of the Douai priests to maintain Catholic worship in England were reinforced by the arrival of **Jesuits**. Some, like Edmund Campion, were courageous and charismatic, but others proved arrogant and disruptive. Robert Parsons was a Jesuit who set up an effective system for smuggling priests into England and

How was Catholicism undermined in the 1570s and 1580s?

JESUITS
Founded in 1534, the Society of Jesus, or the Jesuits as its members were more commonly known, was a religious order dedicated to serving the Pope. Jesuits underwent rigorous spiritual training to emerge as dedicated enemies of anti-Catholic beliefs and used their influence as educators to the rich and powerful in Europe to mount an effective counter-attack against Protestantism.

THE DECLINE OF ENGLISH CATHOLICISM

1567 Pope forbade Catholics to attend Anglican services;

1568 foundation of Catholic seminary at Douai to train priests for England; arrival of Mary Queen of Scots in England;

1569 Revolt of the Northern Earls;

1570 Excommunication of Elizabeth by the Pope – not well received by many English Catholics;

1571 Treason Act against bringing the letter of excommunication into England; Ridolfi Plot;

1580 arrival of Campion and Jesuit missionaries;

1581 execution of Campion;

1583 Throckmorton Plot against Elizabeth;

1585 Act against Jesuits and Seminary Priests assumed Catholic missionaries were automatically guilty of treason;

1586 Babington Plot against Elizabeth;

1587 execution of Mary Queen of Scots;

1588 English Catholics rejected call to support Spanish Armada;

1598 Pope's choice of Jesuit George Blackwell to lead missionary work in England caused the Archpriest Controversy;

1603 rough estimates place number of Catholic sympathisers at about 10 per cent of the population, but not all were recusants (probably only 2 per cent of the total population).

came to play a leading role in managing English Catholicism. In 1588, he called on English Catholics to fight alongside Spain (see pages 221–4). However, he was contradicted by one of the Douai priests who said that Spain was pursuing its own interests, not those of the church, so had no call on the loyalty of Catholics. This was one example of the friction between the Jesuits and the Douai priests which left ordinary Catholics bewildered about who to follow.

-Profile-

EDMUND CAMPION (1540–1581)

Edmund Campion was one of the first Jesuits to work as a Catholic missionary in England. He arrived in secret in 1580 and travelled to Lancashire, which had the greatest concentration of Catholics who would not accept the Anglican beliefs of Elizabeth's church. There, and later in London, he preached in the homes of important Catholic families, disguising his identity and using safe houses to avoid arrest. Although this afforded him some protection, the government was sufficiently concerned about the threat of the Jesuits to use spies to locate, arrest and execute him in 1581.

On Monday, being the twentieth of November, Edmund Campion, Ralph Sherwin, Lucas Kerbie, Edward Rishton, Thomas Coteham, Henry Orton, Robert Johnson and James Bosgrave were brought unto the high bar at Westminster where they were severally and together indicted upon high treason. When they convicted them of these matters (which with obstinacy they still denied), they came to the intent of their secret coming into this realm, which was the death of her Majesty and the overthrow of the kingdom. 'Yea,' saith Campion, 'never shall you prove this, that we came over either for this intent or purpose, but only for the saving of souls, which mere love and conscience compelled us to do, for that we did pity the miserable state of our country.'

Source C A report of the trial of Edmund Campion, from Raphael Holinshed's *Chronicals of England, Scotland and Ireland* (1577).

Tensions between English Catholics and the Jesuits came to a head in the Archpriest Controversy in 1598. When it was decided to appoint a head priest, or Archpriest, to supervise the Catholic Church in England, the post was give to a Jesuit despite the opposition of English priests. When the case was taken to Rome for adjudication, the English representatives were prevented from meeting the Pope and Jesuit power was upheld. This unsatisfactory treatment and outcome enraged English Catholics and revealed a deep split among them which prevented them from mounting a more united opposition to Elizabeth.

4 The Catholic Threat from Abroad

Clearly, Spain was implicated in some of the unsettling events in England. The arrival of Jesuit missionaries seems to have been partly inspired by Philip II's patronage of the training academy at Douai (see Source B on page 214) and the Spanish government was suspected of supporting the plots to overthrow Elizabeth in favour of Mary Queen of Scots:

> They have sent Northumberland's servant, who spoke to me before on this matter, to say that they will, by armed force, release Queen Mary and take possession of all the north country, restoring the Catholic religion. They only ask that, having released the Queen, they should be aided by your Majesty with a small number of harquebussiers [artillerymen].

Source D From a report by the Spanish ambassador to Philip II concerning the Revolt of the Northern Earls, 8 October 1569.

a) Tensions Between England and Spain, 1558–88

For these reasons, the deterioration of Anglo-Spanish relations is the key theme of Elizabethan foreign policy. Ironically, neither Elizabeth nor Philip II wanted this, but it became inevitable because of the situation in the Netherlands. Emperor Charles V had regarded the Netherlands as central to the Habsburg inheritance and had insisted that it should be passed to his son Philip in 1555. It was a poor decision: Spain and the Netherlands were not only hundreds of miles apart, but very different in other ways. Local nobles in the provinces which comprised the Netherlands were used to a degree of independence with which Philip II's overly bureaucratic style of government could not cope. Spain was Europe's foremost Catholic power and Philip one of the faith's staunchest defenders, but the Netherlands contained a growing number of Calvinist converts. After a decade of Spanish rule, tensions within the Netherlands broke into civil war in

ISSUES:
Why was the Netherlands so important in Elizabethan foreign policy?
How far were events in the Netherlands responsible for the breakdown of Anglo-Spanish relations by 1585?

1566. Philip adopted an uncompromising tone – 'Before suffering the slightest damage to religion and the service of God, I would rather lose all my states, and a hundred lives if I had them, because I do not propose to be the ruler of heretics', he told the Pope. He sent the Duke of Alba an 10,000 troops to restore order, which they did in a brutal manner.

Figure 51 The Massacre of the Innocents, by Peter Breughel. Paintings and propaganda such as this, which depicted the brutality of Alba's military government in the Netherlands, helped to create the 'Black Legend' of Spain among Protestant countries. This legend associated Spanish power and the Catholic Church with violent intolerance and strict royal control at the expense of people's liberties. It created a powerful fear of Spain and a determination within Protestant nations such as England to check the spread of Counter-Reformation values.

For England, the Netherlands had enormous economic and strategic importance:

▼ much of the export trade in English cloth was organised through ports in the Netherlands, such as Antwerp

▼ national security was believed to depend on ensuring that the coastline across the Channel was held by weak countries. During the Tudor period, this security was challenged by the defeat of Brittany by France in Henry VII's reign, the general revival of the French monarchy at the end of the fifteenth century, Philip II of Spain's inheritance of the Netherlands in 1555 and the loss of Calais in 1558.

As a result, it seemed to be of overwhelming importance to ensure that when the Netherlands rebellion broke out, Spain should not recover control. Elizabeth had little sympathy for the plight of the Dutch people – they were, after all, rebelling against a legitimate government – but she did recognise that England's interests were best served by encouraging the rebellion whilst not openly antagonising Spain. It was another difficult balancing act, and one which provoked the most argument among her councillors. Elizabeth was extremely cautious in maintaining her distance from the rebels (although she did nothing to discourage unofficial support, such as allowing rebel ships to stay in English ports or English pirates to disrupt supplies being transported to Alba's army). This policy was supported by the 'peace party' within the Privy Council, who felt that war against Spain was beyond England's capabilities. However, a second group of courtiers, led by the Earl of Leicester and Francis Walsingham, favoured military action. The debate between these opposing views dragged on for nearly 20 years until a true crisis was reached in 1584–5 and Elizabeth was forced to commit the country to war.

The collapse of Anglo-Spanish relations was gradual and not simply confined to their disagreements over the Netherlands, as Table 13 reveals.

Table 13 The deterioration of Anglo-Spanish relations, 1563–85.

Date	Event	Significance
1559	Philip II offered to marry Elizabeth	More a gesture than a genuine offer, designed to show support for Elizabeth
1562	Philip protested to Elizabeth about her support for Huguenot rebels against a Catholic government in France	Elizabeth responded to the complaint by keeping her troops from joining with the Huguenot army in northern France
1563	Philip's government in the Netherlands banned imports of English cloths	Officially, this was to protect the Netherlands against infection by plague from England, but the ban reflected annoyance that the balance of trade had turned in England's favour whilst Elizabeth turned a blind eye to piracy in the Channel and to the work of English merchants in spreading Protestant ideas in the Netherlands. Elizabeth responded by banning all imports from the Netherlands, but both sides backed down and normalised trade relations in 1564
1566–7	Outbreak of the Revolt of the Netherlands. Spanish Duke of Alba sent to the Netherlands to crush rioting by Calvinists and to restore firm government	Suddenly made the northern coast of the Channel insecure. Massive alarm in England that Alba's army might be turned against them once its work in the Netherlands was completed (possibly with aid of Guise faction in France if they won civil war)
1568	Spain expelled the English ambassador from Madrid and replaced its own ambassador in London with a more hard-line Catholic, De Spes	Added to tensions of the previous year, although the changes were for apparently innocent reasons. De Spes made contact with Mary Queen of Scots
	In the Caribbean, Spanish government ships attacked John Hawkins' fleet because it was trespassing on Spain's monopoly of the Atlantic slave trade	First signs of an issue that was to become a major source of Spanish grievances
	December: Elizabeth seized bullion being transported through the Channel for Alba's army	Alba's army was already owed pay and this action created a real crisis. Alba retaliated by confiscating all English ships docked at ports in the Netherlands and Elizabeth responded by banning all trade with the Netherlands and Spain. Trade was not fully restored until 1573
1569	De Spes negotiated with the Northern Earls, encouraging their rebellion to place Mary on the throne	

Table 13 (continued)

Date	Event	Significance
1570	Pope formally excommunicated Elizabeth and declared her deposed	Repression of English Catholics began to prevent them from carrying out the Pope's wishes
		Philip had not been involved in this decision and was genuinely angry that it had been taken – he refused to allow publication of the decision within his territories
	Elizabeth began to consider marriage to the Duke of Anjou, one of the brothers of King Charles IX of France, as a way of preventing France and Spain from acting together against her	
1571	Discovery of the Ridolfi Plot – uprising to overthrow Elizabeth in favour of Mary with Spanish military support – in which Philip and De Spes were implicated	De Spes expelled; repression of Catholics in England intensified
1572	Treaty of Blois – replaced idea of marriage to Duke of Anjou with a formal Anglo-French defensive alliance against Spain	A 'diplomatic revolution', but it quickly foundered because Elizabeth was not prepared to go to war in the Netherlands to support French ambitions. England continued to give unofficial support to the Huguenots
	Intensification of civil war in the Netherlands when rebels seized the port of Brill	Elizabeth was accused by Spain of encouraging the rebels by giving them safe harbour and allowing English volunteers to support the rebellion
1576	Unpaid Spanish soldiers mutinied in the Netherlands in the 'Spanish Fury', ransacking towns across the country	Elizabeth was urged by Leicester to send troops into the Netherlands, but she would only agree to financial help
1579	A new Spanish commander, the Duke of Parma, began to recover lands lost in the Netherlands to the rebels	
1580	Philip II inherited the Portuguese crown and its overseas empire in Africa and Asia	
1581	Elizabeth began to fund resistance to Parma	Philip was aware of what Elizabeth was doing and began to think seriously of an attack on England
1583–4	Spanish ambassador Mendoza expelled after being implicated in the Throckmorton Plot to overthrow Elizabeth and install Mary as queen	
1584	Treaty of Joinville signed between Spain and French Catholics	Death of Henry III's last brother and heir put the Huguenot Henry of Navarre next in line to the French throne. Catholics were alarmed enough at this to approach Spain for assistance. This treaty was important because it gave Philip the impression that if he attacked England, France would not react
1585	Elizabeth signed the Treaty of Nonsuch with the Dutch rebels	Parma's success in recovering territory finally convinced Elizabeth that action was needed. She agreed to send 7,000 troops under the Earl of Leicester to maintain the rebellion. UNOFFICIAL START OF THE ANGLO-SPANISH WAR

ACTIVITY

Use the information in the timeline (Table 13) to research answers to the following questions:

1. What issues drove England and Spain apart after 1563?
2. What evidence is there to suggest that Elizabeth's policies towards Spain were indecisive and ill-thought out?
3. When do you think war between England and Spain became inevitable? Justify your decision.

b) England at War, 1585–1604

English foreign policy shifted from maintaining independence from Spain to open warfare in 1584–5. The change occurred because at that point the possibility of a Spanish attack on England suddenly became a realistic prospect:

▼ in the Netherlands, the murder of William 'the Silent' deprived the revolt of its key leader at the same time that the Duke of Parma's efforts to recover control were gathering momentum
▼ in France, the death of the Duke of Alençon deprived Elizabeth of a useful ally who had been prepared to fight Spain in the Netherlands and pushed French Catholics into alliance with Spain because the line of succession now led to a Huguenot king.

These changes suggested to Elizabeth that the revolt in the Netherlands was nearing collapse. If it ended, Spain would be in control of the northern part of the cross-Channel frontier and would have a large unused army stationed there. She also recognised that the alliance of French Catholics with Spain might mean a joint attack on England, or at the very least undo her efforts to use France as a shield against Spain.

The solution was to step up support for the Dutch rebels. In the Treaty of Nonsuch (1585), Elizabeth made an open agreement with the rebel government of the northern provinces of the Netherlands to provide military support. By sending the Earl of Leicester and English troops into the Netherlands, Elizabeth was publicly defying Philip and inviting war with Spain.

The Anglo-Spanish War of 1585–1604 was a curious one. There were few occasions when English and Spanish troops actually met face to face. Elizabeth's strategy was to attack the vulnerable points of the Spanish Empire, using her naval forces rather than large land armies (which England neither possessed nor could afford).

How was the Anglo-Spanish War conducted?

Apart from the famous incident of the **Spanish Armada** (see box), most of the fighting took place in the Netherlands, northern France and on the high seas in the Caribbean.

The Spanish Armada

The most famous incident of the Anglo-Spanish War – and of Tudor foreign policy in general – was the defeat of the Spanish Armada in 1588. According to popular legend the invading Spanish fleet was put to flight by brilliant tactics of naval warfare and God's 'Protestant wind'. Whilst these stories contain essential truths, they do not reveal the full reasons for the defeat of the Armada. By looking beyond contemporary accounts, both the importance of the defeat and the extent of the English victory are diminished.

Plans for the Armada had been initiated in Spain before war was declared against England in 1585. Such a large campaign took careful planning and needed long-term preparation to bring together the fleet, supplies and men. It was also a risky venture: the plan was for the Armada to sail along the Atlantic coastline into the English Channel to rendezvous with Spanish troops waiting in the Netherlands. This army would then be transported to England for the invasion.

Problems with this strategy were obvious even to the Spanish commanders leading the expedition. First, it could not be a surprise attack. The distance that needed to be travelled and the fact that the fleet would have to pass the length of the south coast of England to reach the Netherlands prevented this. Secondly, the venture required close co-ordination between the fleet and the waiting troops in the Netherlands (after all, Spanish troops were in the Netherlands because they were trying to suppress a rebellion there) but once at sea, there was no way for either arm of the operation to communicate difficulties to the other. Thirdly, the fleet was under-provisioned and poorly led. Philip II placed his faith in God's support and left the Armada in the control of the Duke of Medina Sidonia who had the pedigree, but not the naval experience, to front the mission.

Figure 52 A nineteenth-century depiction of Sir Francis Drake's flagship *Revenge* capturing a Spanish galleon.

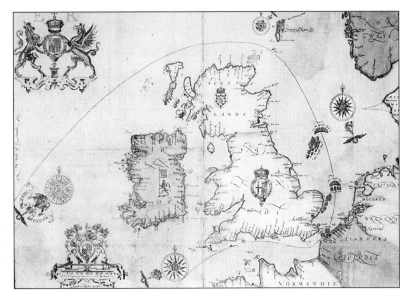

Figure 53 A chart commissioned to commemorate the English victory, showing the battle in the Channel and the Armada's flight around the British Isles.

Philip had also failed to plan what would happen once his troops in the Netherlands joined the Armada. Could they seriously hope to invade England? English Catholics had built hopes at the Spanish court that there would be popular rebellions against Elizabeth once the Armada appeared, but this was a grossly exaggerated interpretation of what might happen. Perhaps Philip hoped that the mere presence of the Armada would force Elizabeth to see reason over the Netherlands and her Protestantism.

Finally, geography rather than God was also against Spain. Philip's advisers ignored the fact that the fleet had to have deep hulls to navigate the Atlantic Ocean's currents but that all Dutch ports were in shallow water. It was simply not possible for the troops in the Netherlands to board the Armada unless they were prepared to swim out to it in full armour. The English also praised the 'Protestant wind' which scattered the Spanish fleet. In fact, the winds in the Channel blow from the south-west, making it relatively easy to sail into the Channel from the Atlantic but much more difficult to turn about and sail from the Netherlands to England.

All these factors meant that the Armada was essentially doomed from the start, but that should not lead us to ignore the role of the English completely. Brilliant naval tactics definitely played their part. Elizabeth's navy positioned itself to force the Armada to sail into the wind and used long-range guns to batter the fleet. When the Armada tried to find refuge along the French coast, English fireships burned and scattered its ships, driving the fleet away from the Netherlands and into a suicidal journey around the north coast of Scotland to find a route back to Spain.

The defeat of the Armada was hailed as a magnificent English victory against a larger and more powerful enemy. It seemed to indicate God's approval of Elizabeth's government and the Anglican Church it had created. Elizabeth was quick to see the propaganda value of the victory, as the 'Armada Portrait' on page 174 shows. However, the long-term effects of the defeat of the Armada were negligible. During the remainder of the Anglo-Spanish War Philip recovered his resources sufficiently to launch three more armadas against England.

ACTIVITY

Evaluating the Catholic Threat

By working through sections 3 and 4 you will have looked at the two sides of the 'Catholic threat': the continued existence of committed Catholics in England and the growing distrust between Elizabeth and Philip II.

In his *History of the Most Renowned and Victorious Princess Elizabeth*, William Camden reported some of the disagreements in the Privy Council about the government's priorities when dealing with the Catholic threat: 'In this troublesome season, some beat it many times into the Queen's head that the Spaniards abroad were not so much to be feared as the Papists at home, for the Spaniards abroad would not attempt any hostility against England but upon confidence of help from them.'

To evaluate the seriousness of the Catholic threat, research answers to the following questions. If you are able to work in a group, divide these tasks up – some of you take questions 1 and 2, the rest questions 3 and 4, then come together to discuss your thoughts about question 5.

1. What did English Catholics do during Elizabeth's reign that threatened national stability?
2. Did their actions ever seriously threaten either Elizabeth or national stability?
3. What did Spain do during Elizabeth's reign that threatened English national stability?
4. Did Spain's actions ever seriously threaten either Elizabeth or national stability?
5. Based on all these answers, do you think the assessment given in Camden's account is correct?

ISSUES:
Who were the Puritans? How did they threaten the stability of the Elizabethan settlement?

5 The Puritan Challenge

Just as the Elizabethan church settlement had offended hard-line Catholics, it also was rejected by some Protestants. Inevitably, by creating a church which drew on both traditions, the settlement included elements that *pure* Protestants found offensive. In particular, they opposed the survival of bishops within the new order, arguing that they were an invention of the Pope to maintain his power rather than a creation of the early Christian church. These Protestants also examined the Bible for other evidence that the shape of the English church was not that ordained by God and discovered that, amongst other things, making the sign of the cross during baptisms and the wearing of clerical vestments had no scriptural authority.

This sort of hard-line stand against Catholicism within the English church, together with a desire to create a simpler, more biblical form of worship, characterised the Puritan tendency. From the outset, we must be careful not to think of the Puritans as a 'group' because there was no real organisation amongst them and they held various shades of opinion about what they would and would not accept about the Elizabethan settlement and about how far they wanted further religious reform to go. However, all shared the belief that the English Reformation had not been completed in 1559 and, because of this, they threatened the stability of the Elizabethan settlement just as effectively as Catholic recusants.

In practice, there were three main strands of Puritan thought in Elizabeth's reign:

▼ the **Presbyterian** strand, which called for a thorough reform of the structure of the church and the simplifying of faith and ritual

▼ the **moderate Puritan** strand, which reluctantly accepted the structure of the church and pressed for reform of beliefs and religious practices along the lines of the European churches

▼ the **Separatist** strand, which broke away from the national church to pursue its own radical Protestant reformation, on a parish-by-parish basis.

a) The Early Stages of Puritanism in Elizabeth's Reign

Puritanism pre-dated the Elizabethan settlement. The educated élite of merchants, lawyers and craftsmen who had criticised the state of the Catholic Church during the 1520s (see Chapter 3, pages 74–8) had used arguments that would have been recognised by their grandchildren in the 1570s. So the Puritan element in society began to voice its concerns at the nature of the church settlement devised in 1559 before the ink was even dry on the Acts of Supremacy and Uniformity. Their complaints that the settlement was too Catholic came to a head during the discussions in Convocation about the Thirty-nine Articles of faith in 1563 (which were passed by only one vote) and in the Vestiarian Controversy of 1566 (see page 212).

However, it was a series of lectures by the Professor of Divinity at Cambridge University, Thomas Cartwright, in the spring of 1570 which brought the radical dimension of Puritanism to national, and royal, attention. In his lectures Cartwright argued for the abolition of bishops and called for a form of church government based on that developed by the reformer John Calvin in Geneva. Calvin had established a structure in which control was exercised by the minister of each

THE PURITAN CHALLENGE

1566 Vestiarian Controversy;
1570 Cartwright's lectures;
1571 Strickland's amendments caused the failure of the 'Alphabet Bills';
1575 appointment of Grindal as Archbishop of Canterbury;
1576 Elizabeth ordered Parliament not to discuss religious matters without permission; suppression of prophesyings and suspension of Grindal for defending them;
1580 Brownist congregation established in Norwich;
1583 appointment of Whitgift as Archbishop of Canterbury heralded renewed attacks on Puritanism;
1589 publication of Marprelate Tracts;
1590 Cartwright and others appeared before the Court of High Commission;
1593 Act against Seditious Sectaries.

ISSUE:
When and why did Puritanism emerge as a threat?

church, helped by respected elders of the community. This model, argued Cartwright, could be adapted to fit the parish system in England and could be given national cohesion through Calvin's other idea of having regional committees and a national assembly of the whole church. Such a system, known as a Presbyterian model of the church, was said to be closer to the form of organisation justified in the Bible.

Elizabeth's reaction to Cartwright's ideas was open horror. The Presbyterian system involved abolishing bishops and left very little room for a 'Supreme Governor'. If she had any doubts about the revolutionary implications of this sort of change, she had only to look to Scotland, where the introduction of Presbyterianism in the 1560s had been accompanied by the overthrow of Mary Queen of Scots. Elizabeth remained sufficiently worried about the Puritan threat to political stability to write to King James VI of Scotland about the matter in 1590:

Source E From a personal letter written by Elizabeth to James VI of Scotland, 6 July 1590. (James became King of England in 1603 so inherited this problem from her.)

> Let me warn you that there is risen, both in your Realm and mine, a sect of perilous consequence, such as would have no Kings but a presbytery, and take our place while they enjoy our privilege. I pray you, stop the mouths, or make shorter the tongues, of such ministers as dare presume to speak out for the persecuted in England for the Gospel. Suppose you, dear brother, that I can tolerate such scandals of my sincere government? I beseech you not to give more harbour-room to vagabond traitors and seditious inventors, but to return them to me, or banish them from your land. Your most assured and loving sister and cousin, Elizabeth.

b) The Development of Presbyterianism in England, 1570–83

ISSUES:
How did Puritans attempt to spread Presbyterian ideas? What was Elizabeth's reaction?

Cartwright's bold statement of the Presbyterian position encouraged others to add their voice to the campaign for further reform along these lines. Inside Parliament, the MP William Strickland tried to amend a series of bills (nicknamed the 'Alphabet Bills') along more Presbyterian lines. His attempts backfired, and angered some bishops enough for them to enforce existing rules about licensing preachers more carefully, to keep Presbyterians away from their parishes. The government also took action, imprisoning Strickland in 1571 and exiling Cartwright in 1573. From that point, each time Puritans attempted to use legislation to bring about religious change their bills were vetoed by the queen. Moreover, she gave explicit instructions in 1576 that MPs were not to debate religious matters without her permission, and imprisoned Peter Wentworth in the Tower when he challenged her about this:

Her Highness' pleasure is that from henceforth no bill concerning religion shall be received into this House of Commons, unless it has been first considered or liked by the clergy.

Source F A message from Elizabeth to the House of Commons regarding their privileges of debating legislation, 22 May 1572.

I have never seen in any Parliament but the last the liberty of free speech in so many ways infringed, with so many abuses offered to this honourable House. The Queen said that we should not deal in any matters of religion, except what we receive from the bishops. Surely this was a doleful message; for it meant, 'Sirs, ye shall not deal in God's causes, no, ye shall in no way advance His glory.' It is a dangerous thing in a prince unkindly to abuse his or her nobility and people, and it is a dangerous thing in a prince to oppose or bend herself against her nobility and people, yeas against most faithful and loving nobility and people.

Source G From Peter Wentworth's speech in the House of Commons, 8 February 1576.

Outside Parliament, the government became alarmed at the spread of 'prophesying'. Prophesyings were generally well-organised gatherings of clergymen at which young or unlicensed preachers could practise their art and receive advice from their more experienced colleagues. In doing so, the Puritan clergy was able to increase the number of competent preachers at its disposal and get around the tight licensing laws. In 1576 news reached Elizabeth of some unorthodox preaching at a prophesying in Southam, in Warwickshire. She ordered her new Archbishop of Canterbury, Edmund Grindal, to suppress prophesyings, but he consulted other bishops and came to the conclusion that the meetings were not dangerous. He therefore refused to accept the queen's instructions and, for good measure, lectured her about the importance of this sort of work in spreading the word of God and ensuring the well-being of souls:

I and others of your Bishops have found by experience that these profits come from these exercises [prophesyings]:
1. The ministers of the Church are more skilful and ready in the Scriptures, and apter to teach their flocks.
2. It withdraweth their flocks from idleness, wandering, gaming etc.
3. Some suspected of doctrinal error are brought to open confession of the truth.
4. Ignorant ministers are driven to study, if not for conscience then for shame and fear of discipline.
5. The opinion of laymen about the idleness of the clergy is removed.
6. Nothing beateth down Popery more than that ministers grow to such a good knowledge by means of these exercises.

Source H From a letter by Archbishop Grindal to Queen Elizabeth I, 1576.

Elizabeth did not respond well to this godly instruction. She had Grindal placed under virtual house arrest in his residence at Lambeth Palace, and for the remaining seven years of his life he was unable to function as leader of the church. Meanwhile, Elizabeth issued direct orders to her bishops that prophesyings were to stop.

It is clear, then, that the queen was deeply alarmed at the spread of Presbyterian ideas, but that she found ways to contain the problem both inside and outside Parliament (see Figure 54).

Figure 54 Summary of royal efforts to contain Presbyterianism in the 1570s and 1580s.

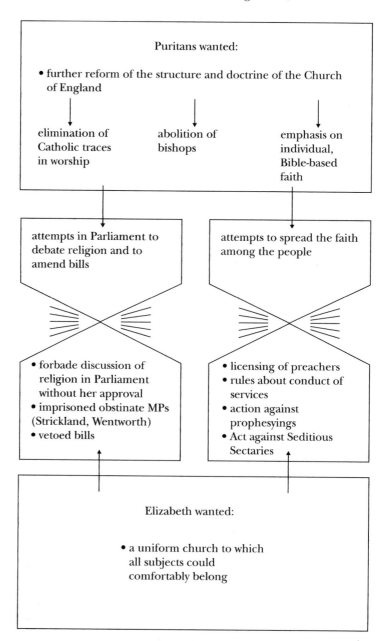

Puritans wanted:

• further reform of the structure and doctrine of the Church of England

elimination of Catholic traces in worship

abolition of bishops

emphasis on individual, Bible-based faith

attempts in Parliament to debate religion and to amend bills

attempts to spread the faith among the people

• forbade discussion of religion in Parliament without her approval
• imprisoned obstinate MPs (Strickland, Wentworth)
• vetoed bills

• licensing of preachers
• rules about conduct of services
• action against prophesyings
• Act against Seditious Sectaries

Elizabeth wanted:

• a uniform church to which all subjects could comfortably belong

c) Presbyterianism in the 1580s

The 1580s saw the purging from the national church of its Presbyterian elements. In 1583 Edmund Grindal died and Elizabeth appointed a devout Anglican, John Whitgift, to replace him. Whitgift, who was known affectionately by Elizabeth as 'my little black husband' because of his sombre clothing, shared many of Elizabeth's views and prejudices (he was unmarried, for example). He had no sympathy with the Puritans and was determined to enforce uniformity. He immediately issued Three Articles that would have forced all ministers to swear an absolute acceptance of bishops and of all that was contained in the Prayer Book and the Thirty-nine Articles. The result was uproar, and within weeks about 300 ministers had been suspended in the south of England alone. Letters of complaint from local gentry enabled many of these men to be reinstated, but the tone of the new church administration had been set. Over the next few years strict controls were enforced to end prophesyings and other forms of stealthy development of Presbyterian ideas.

> **ISSUE:**
> What factors helped to contain the spread of Presbyterianism?

d) The Separatist Movement

Because Protestantism insisted that the Bible was the only source of religious teaching and that it should be made available to all in their own language, the separate development of individual churches was always a possibility. In England, some congregations did follow that path, using isolated, voluntary gatherings to explore the Bible and to reach their own conclusions about the direction their faith should take them. Evidence of early Separatists is notoriously difficult to gather since their activities were illegal and therefore secret. The experience of persecution under Mary had certainly created some Separatist groups, but hope of real reformation under Elizabeth meant that the vast majority of Elizabethan Puritans were, and remained, members of the national church. By 1583, however, it was clear that they were not going to bring about reform by remaining within the Anglican Church, so small groups of Separatists began to emerge.

> **ISSUES:**
> What was Separatism? Why was it difficult to control?

i) Brownists
The Brownists are one of the best documented of the Separatist groups. In 1580 an impatient reformer named Robert Browne had established a Separatist congregation in Norwich. After a brief spell of imprisonment he left England and settled in Holland where he wrote *A Treatise of Reformation Without Tarrying For Any*. In it, Browne argued that the Church of England was corrupted by its Catholic traces and lack of moral discipline. He said that true Christians should leave it in favour of separate, voluntary gatherings of 'saints'

who would exercise proper discipline. In 1583 John Copping and Elias Thacker were hanged for distributing Brownist pamphlets.

ii) The Marprelate Tracts

The Separatist movement reappeared in 1589 in the form of the scurrilous Martin Marprelate Tracts, a bitter written attack on the church and the bishops that used foul language and abuse to make its case. Although Puritans like Cartwright were horrified by the tracts, and hurriedly disassociated themselves from them, the reaction of both the authorities and public opinion allowed the Privy Council to bring about the final destruction of organised Puritanism. Cartwright and his associates were hauled before the Court of High Commission and forced to reveal what they knew about the remnants of the prophesyings movement. Government propaganda linked Puritanism to Separatism, and Separatism to treason. In 1593 Parliament was persuaded to pass an Act Against Seditious Sectaries which allowed the authorities to execute those suspected of being Separatists. The emergence of Separatists and the publication of the Marprelate Tracts had provided the ammunition the government needed for an all-out attack on Puritanism. However, it was more difficult to eradicate it as a force in English religious thought.

> **Q**
>
> Why do you think Tudor authorities regarded the Separatists as 'treasonous'?

ACTIVITY

Evaluating the Puritan Threat

The Puritans could be regarded as a serious threat for a number of reasons:
▼ They undermined the Church of England from the inside
▼ They had support from important people, including members of the Anglican Church hierarchy
▼ Their use of prophesyings helped to create trained and committed preachers
▼ They offered people a simple and direct form of religion with a promise of salvation as one of the predestined elect (see the theology of John Calvin on pages 225–6)
▼ They received advice and support from Calvinist churches in Europe.

Do you think that these points suggest that the Puritans were a greater threat to Elizabeth than Roman Catholics? Look back at the answers you gave to the activities on page 224 to help you decide.

6 The Church of England by 1603

The material in this chapter suggests that the new Anglican Church was assaulted by both Protestants and Catholics during its first half century of life. Yet both of these attacks had failed to move the church from the direction set out in the 1559 settlement. Why?

▼ Elizabeth had a strong interest in maintaining the 1559 settlement because she saw it as the best way to create both religious and political stability. Her opposition to Puritans meant that they found it difficult to use parliamentary means to change elements of the settlement

▼ Elizabeth was aided, after 1583, by John Whitgift, her Archbishop of Canterbury. His uncompromising support for Anglicanism gave her a powerful ally against radical elements within the Church of England

▼ The establishment of the Court of High Commission gave the authorities a means to prosecute religious radicals, and laws such as the Treason Act acted as a deterrent to those thinking of reacting against Anglicanism

▼ Radicals, by definition, put forward extreme views. Most people accepted the middle-of-the-road approach of the Church of England, with its traditional Catholic appearance and its doctrines which put more stress on personal fulfilment through faith, and disliked the 'innovations' proposed by the Puritans. Because of this, radicalism was not as widespread as might be suggested by the events of the period

▼ Peer pressure was important. Attendance at Anglican services was made compulsory from 1559 and fines were introduced to enforce this. In small communities non-attendance was the subject of gossip and could lead to isolation from the rest of the village

▼ Catholicism in England was discredited by its association with rebellion against the legitimate monarch, and by its undertones of foreign (Spanish and papal) control

▼ Events in Europe during Elizabeth's reign – bitter divisions between Puritan minorities and their Catholic rulers in France and the Netherlands resulting in civil wars – reminded Englishmen of the dangers of encouraging religious disagreements

▼ By 1603, the Anglican Church had influenced the attitudes of two generations of English people. During this time the religious authorities had made the church's position more secure by discussing and defining its essential beliefs and by using a licensing system to monitor the quality of the clergy.

ISSUE:

How did the Church of England survive Catholic and Puritan attacks?

Q Why was the 1580s such a crucial decade in defeating challenges to the Church of England?

The Laws of Ecclesiastical Polity, 1593

Anglicanism survived because it had powerful support and because it offered an acceptable compromise between the extremes of Roman Catholicism and Puritanism. Its supporters gradually developed its theology and were able to establish a credible justification for it. The most effective case for the Anglican Church was made by Richard Hooker in *The Laws of Ecclesiastical Polity* in 1593.

Hooker accepted that the Church of England represented a compromise between the Catholic tradition and the ideas of continental reformers, but argued that this was far from being a mere convenience. Instead, the Anglican 'middle way' represented the true Christian faith, built on medieval tradition and enjoying continuity from the early church. He said that the unnecessary and superstitious additions made by the medieval papacy had been stripped away, to reveal the essentials of early Christianity required for salvation. These essentials were relatively few and simple – faith in Christ based upon reading the Bible, and commemoration of Christ's sacrifice on the cross. Other matters such as the nature and conduct of ceremonies and the extent and role of decoration were 'matters indifferent', which could safely be left to the discretion of the monarch and the bishops. Hooker viewed the bishops as not essential to the church, but accepted them as a convenient and effective way of organising it. For the sake of order and Christian unity the existing ceremonies should be accepted and enjoyed for the decency and order that they provided.

How far had Anglicanism been established by 1603?

The 1559 settlement had been shaped by political concerns, but time, practice and the authority of tradition had finally enabled it to establish a genuinely Anglican identity that many wished to defend. Catholicism had declined and the attachment that many people had to its ways had been transferred to the Anglican Church. Puritans had pushed too hard and too fast for radical change and had been defeated because of this. Nevertheless, the divisions that Elizabeth had inherited had not been healed entirely, and as Anglicanism became more firmly established in its own right those divisions became more obvious, not less.

In political terms, the establishment of Anglicanism had been a success. England had avoided the destructive civil wars over religious identity and choice that had affected France and the Netherlands. Elizabeth had emerged as a strong and independent monarch partly because she was not bound to the wishes of the Pope, and partly because governorship of the church gave her important powers of patronage as well as a new source of authority over her people.

In religious terms, the change to Anglicanism produced more mixed results. It did not necessarily answer the criticisms of the clergy that had helped to begin the demand for reformation in the 1520s. Set against the high standards that the Puritans demanded of their ministers, the Anglican Church seemed to contain the same moral laxity that had tainted Catholicism:

Mr Ocklei, parson of Much Bursead: a gamester.

Mr Durdent, vicar of Stebbing: a drunkard and a gamester and a very gross abuser of the Scriptures (witnesses: Mr Denham, Mr Rogers, etc.)

Mr Durden, parson of Mashbury: a careless man, a gamester, an alehouse haunter, a company keeper with drunkards and he himself sometimes drunk (witnesses: Richard Reynolds, John Argent, etc.)

Mr Cuckson, vicar of Linsell: unable to preach, he hath been a pilferer.

Source I From a Puritan *Survey of Ministers* conducted in Essex in 1586.

Small reformation has been made in Lancashire and Cheshire as can be seen by the emptiness of churches on Sundays and holidays. The people so swarm the streets and alehouses during service time that many churches have only the curate and his clerk present. The people lack instruction for the preachers are few, most of the parsons unlearned and no examination is made of schools and schoolmasters. The proclamation for the apprehension of Jesuits, seminaries and mass priests is not executed.

Source J From a report to the Royal Council concerning the state of religion in Lancashire and Cheshire in the early 1590s.

Q On what grounds might you be cautious about using these sources as evidence of the state of the Anglican Church and clergy during Elizabeth's reign?

Working on Religion and Foreign Policy, 1558–1603

Summary: Key Events and Developments in Religion and Foreign Policy

Year	The Puritan Threat	Developments in Anglicanism	The Catholic threat at home and from abroad
1559	Presbyterian Reformation in Scotland led by John Knox; attempts of English Puritans to introduce amendments to legislation establishing Anglicanism	Acts of Supremacy and Uniformity established structure of Anglican Church; revised Book of Common Prayer and 57 Royal Injunctions set out doctrine of Anglicanism	Opposition to Anglican Reformation reduced by resignation or removal of Marian bishops
1563		39 Articles of Faith defined Anglican beliefs for future generations	
1566	Vestiarian Controversy		
1567			Pope ordered English Catholics not to attend Anglican services; Spanish troops arrived in the Netherlands to crush rebellion there
1568			Mary Queen of Scots arrived in England; foundation of the Douai school for training Catholic missionaries to England
1569			Revolt of the Northern Earls
1570	Thomas Cartwright's lectures proposed a Presbyterian structure to the Church in England		Pope excommunicated Elizabeth
1571	Strickland imprisoned for trying to attach Puritan reforms to government bills in Parliament	39 Articles made law	Ridolfi Plot to assassinate Elizabeth and install Mary as queen
1573	Cartwright exiled		
1576	Elizabeth banned Parliament from having free debates on religious matters; attacks on prophesyings began	Bitter disagreement between Elizabeth and Archbishop of Canterbury (Edmund Grindal) over value of prophesyings	
1580	1580s – Emergence of Separatist congregations, especially 'Brownists'		First Jesuit priests arrived in England, led by Campion
1581			Arrest, trial and execution of Campion
1583		Death of Grindal, appointment of John Whitgift as Archbishop of Canterbury	
1585			Act against Jesuits and Seminary Priests; outbreak of war with Spain
1587			Execution of Mary Queen of Scots
1588			Spanish Armada
1589	Marprelate Tracts published		
1590	Cartwright and others examined by the Court of High Commission		
1593	Act against Seditious Sectaries	Hooker's *Laws of Ecclesiastical Polity* gave Anglicanism a philosophical justification	
1598			Archpriest Controversy split English Catholicism

How historians have approached the topic

As we saw in the comments made at the end of Chapter 6 (see pages 200–01), Elizabeth has been treated generously by historians. Sir John Hayward wrote one of the first accounts of the entire reign in 1612 and was overawed by Elizabeth's personality and achievements: 'Excellent Queen! What do my words but wrong thy worth? What do I but gild gold? What but show the sun a candle in attempting to praise thee whose honour doth fly over the whole world upon the wings of Magnanimity and Justice, whose perfection shall much dim the lustre of all other that shall be of thy sex?'. Protestant historians saw much to congratulate in the Elizabethan church settlement, although Catholic writers have been more critical. They have pointed out evidence of ruthlessness in the application of policies and have questioned the wisdom of the whole settlement given the divisions it caused. Foreign policy has received less attention, but writers in the last half century have skilfully unpicked the story of the Armada to show that the victory was a combination of poor planning by Philip II, English good fortune and naval strategy.

Key Skills

This study guide differs from the others in this book because we will not be focusing directly on how to answer the different sorts of extended writing and document tasks which you will come across in examinations. Instead, we will look at how to use the material on the reign of Elizabeth covered in Chapters 6 and 7 to generate Key Skills evidence. By working through the following tasks, you will create enough work to complete a portfolio for Communication at Level 3.

The tasks need to be read with the specification for Level 3 in mind and we strongly recommend that you have a copy of these. Part B of the specification is crucial in setting out what your portfolio must contain, and Part A will give you guidance about the standard expected.

In general, however, you should follow the tasks bearing in mind the following points:

▼ at Level 3 standard you, not your teachers, should be making the critical decisions about where to find information, what to use and how to organise and present it.

▼ don't just use the chapter in this book for information. Consult some of the books recommended in the further reading section at the end of this chapter, those in your school/college and local libraries, and other resources such as history magazines and websites.

▼ record-keeping is important. Pay attention to what evidence you will need to keep and how to assemble it into a clear portfolio.

▼ check the spelling, grammar and punctuation of your work carefully. Assessors will expect a high degree of accuracy.

Task One

Locate and gather material about the contemporary and historical image of Elizabeth I. As part of your research, select primary sources and pictures which you think reveal aspects of her character and the image of the queen that has been manufactured.

Key Skills advice:

▼ make sure that you use at least two extended texts (i.e. passages of at least three sides) in your research

▼ keep a note of the location of all the information that you find – if from books, note down the title, author, publisher and page references; if from websites, copy down the site address.

Task Two

Produce an illustrated report of your findings entitled 'The Image of a Queen – Contemporary and Historical Impressions of Elizabeth I'. Select a suitable format and style for your work which communicates your findings to an audience interested in the subject matter, but without much prior knowledge.

Key Skills advice:

▼ your report MUST be over three sides in length

▼ it MUST contain some of the sources and images that you have discovered. However, these should not be used merely to add decoration. You must analyse what they reveal about Elizabeth and include these points within the main body of the report

▼ think about the layout and presentation of your report, so that it communicates your findings effectively

▼ check spelling, grammar and punctuation carefully (use a spell-checker if you are word processing the report) to ensure that your meaning is clear.

Task Three

To the end of your report, add a further short document which lists all the sources that you have used to compile the report (a bibliography) and a brief summary of how you used each of these sources (e.g. whether it was for specific facts, arguments, or to provide the framework for all or part of your writing). Attach this to the back of the report when you hand it in for marking.

Task Four

Schools teach about the Spanish Armada during the Key Stage 3 topic 'The Making of the United Kingdom'. You have been invited to produce a package of materials that can be used in the classroom to teach children *why* the Armada was sent against England and the *outline of events*.

Produce relevant materials suitable for the age group (11–14). Once you have developed your ideas sufficiently, make a presentation of what you have produced to others and seek their feedback about the quality of your work.

Key Skills advice:

▼ think about the sorts of items which would make your target group interested in the subject matter

▼ when you make your presentation, have some of these materials ready to show to your audience (or even try out). Make the presentation interesting and appealing to your audience by asking them to do things, not just sit back and observe

▼ explain what you have produced and why you have chosen your particular style and format for the materials.

Task Five

Conduct some further research into the failure of the Armada. Working in a group of four, develop evidence in pairs for and against the view that:

'The defeat of the Armada in 1588 was a magnificent achievement by the English.'

When your research is finalised, hold a discussion between the four of you about this statement.

Key Skills advice:

▼ before you start the discussion, decide which side will go first

▼ be prepared to question and challenge what the other side has said

▼ if you are not tape recording the discussion, each person should write a summary of what was said at the end of it. Then, using a highlighter pen, go through the summary and identify the places where you made a point, asked a question or led the discussion.

Compiling this work into a portfolio

Once you have completed these tasks to the required standard, collect together all the documentation you have and assemble it logically. Number each of the pages and write on any that seem unclear what the material it contains relates to. Remember that the person verifying your work will not know what you have done, so help him or her to make an accurate judgement about your skill by explaining the relevance or purpose of anything that seems unclear.

Your tutor should give you a log sheet which you can use as a contents page to show clearly where all the evidence is. The information you will need for it will look something like this:

C3.1a Contribute to a group discussion
▼ What you did – a discussion about why the Spanish Armada was defeated in 1588
▼ Your evidence – perhaps a tape recording of the discussion or a summary of what was said and what part you played, together with a statement from your tutor

C3.1b Make a presentation
▼ What you did – a presentation to promote a pack of teaching materials for Key Stage 3 on the Spanish Armada
▼ Your evidence – examples of the teaching materials you made, notes / a script from your presentation, written comments about the presentation from members of the audience and your tutor

C3.2 Read and synthesise information
▼ What you did – research on the contemporary and historical image of Elizabeth I
▼ Your evidence – the additional sheet attached to your report with a bibliography and description of how you used information

C3.3 Two pieces of written work, one of which is extended and includes an image
▼ What you did – (1) a report on the contemporary and historical image of Elizabeth I
                  (2) teaching materials about the Spanish Armada for Key Stage 3
▼ Your evidence – the report and examples of the teaching materials.

Further Reading

Books in the *Access to History* series
Both of the themes in this chapter are given full coverage in Keith Randell's *Elizabeth I: Religion and Foreign Affairs*. You will also find it useful to consult the companion volume by John Warren: *Elizabeth I and the Government of England* for supplementary information, as well as *Disorder and Rebellion in Tudor England* by Nick Fellows for details of the Revolt of the Northern Earls and plots against the queen, and *The Sixteenth Century Reformation* by Geoffrey Woodward for material on the Anglican Reformation and its consequences. If you are interested in seeing how the war with Spain and Puritan resistance

to the church settlement worked themselves out after Elizabeth's death, *The Early Stuarts* volume in the Access Series will give you a clear analysis.

Other books

On foreign policy, one of the shorter and best guides is Susan Doran's *England and Europe 1485–1603* (Longman, 1986). A more detailed survey can be found in R. B. Wernham, *The Making of Elizabethan Foreign Policy* (University of California Press, 1980) and Wallace T. MacCaffrey's *Elizabeth I: War and Politics* (Princeton, 1994). For a controversial account of Elizabethan religious policy, try Christopher Haigh's *Elizabeth I* (Longman, 2001). The two opponents of the English Reformation can be traced in *English Catholicism, 1558–1642* by Alan Dures (Longman, 1983) and *English Puritanism* by Patrick Collinson (Historical Association, 1983). For documents relating to religious changes, see *History at Source: The English Reformation* by Peter Servini (Hodder and Stoughton).

GLOSSARY

Index